434649

D0230684

Brief Histories

General Editor: Jeremy Black

Modern Greece

Thomas W. Gallant

A member of the Hodder Headline Group
LONDON
Co-published in the United States of America by
Oxford University Press Inc., New York

First published in Great Britain in 2001 by
Arnold, a member of the Hodder Headline Group,
338 Euston Road, London NW1 3BH

http://www.arnoldpublishers.com

Co-published in the United States of America by
Oxford University Press Inc.,
198 Madison Avenue, New York, NY10016

British Library Cataloguing in Publication Data
A catalogue record for this book is available from the British Library

Library of Congress Cataloging-in-Publication Data
A catalogue record for this book is available from the Library of Congress

ISBN 0 340 76336 1 (hb)
ISBN 0 340 76337 X (pb)

1 2 3 4 5 6 7 8 9 10

Production Editor: James Rabson
Production Controller: Bryan Eccleshall
Cover Design: Terry Griffiths

Typeset in 10/13 pt Utopia by Phoenix Photosetting, Chatham, Kent
Printed and bound in Malta by Gutenberg Press Ltd

What do you think about this book? Or any other Arnold title?
Please send your comments to feedback.arnold@hodder.co.uk

To Rosie

Contents

Acknowledgements

I would like to thank a number of people who have contributed to the production of this book. Gerasimos Augustinos, Jeffrey Adler, and the anonymous reviewer for Arnold read and provided valuable comments on the text. The numerous undergraduates at the University of Florida who over the years have had to sit through the lectures on which this book is based also deserve some notice for the time they put in listening to me go on at length about Greece. I would like also to thank Christopher Wheeler for his patience and assistance. Yet again I owe a special debt of gratitude to my wife, Mary Gallant, for taking the time from her own research and writing to cast her usual critical eye over my attempts to write readable prose.

I should also add a word about the transliteration system used in this book. There is still no accepted standard for transliterating Greek words into English. With the exception of places and people's names which would look foolish if transcribed literally from Greek into English rather than appearing in their more customary Latin form, I have tried to employ a phonetic system that I hope faithfully replicates the form and pronunciation of the word in Greek. Though I am sure that fault will be found with the scheme I have employed, I hope at least to have been consistent in its application.

Preface

The burden of history lies heavily on Greek society. To take a contemporary example: in order to address the modern needs of mass transportation and to alleviate the modern ill of massive air pollution, Greece has built an underground subway network through the heart of Athens. With each shovel full of dirt, the rich legacy of the past is laid bare. The repositories of Greece's museums are now filled to overflowing with the material remains of the past: remnants of houses from the *Turkokratia* (the era of Ottoman rule), coins and shops from the period of the Byzantine Empire, pottery remains from the Greek workshops which flourished during the Roman Empire, and graves, shrines, and houses from the Classical period when Athens stood at the head of its own empire. It will take archaeologists and historians decades to study these material testimonies to Greek society's long and rich history.

It has recently been argued that Greece's 'problem' is that it has 'too much history.'[1] To a historian, of course, this sounds faintly silly. It is hard to accept that there is somewhere out there in the celestial order three figures akin to the ancient Fates, who spin, measure and cut the length of each nation's history. The problem is not that Greece has too much history but that there are two related but still distinct histories involved – one being the history of the Greek people which, depending upon how one defines the term 'Greek', extends back thousands of years and the other being the history of the Greek nation-state, which has a relatively short history. Greece, then, is a young state with an old culture. But even that seemingly simple assertion is far more complicated.

All societies deploy the past to explicate the present. Fundamental elements of any society are legacies of past developments. Just as importantly, however, history is also deployed as the tool to invent contemporary society's understanding of them. The first statement is a truism; the second is not. Greece has neither too much nor too little history. What is a defensible proposition, I would argue, is that because Greece possesses an old culture in a new state, history has become especially implicated in the process of constructing the nation-state over the last two centuries. The past stands as both a blessing and a curse to modern Greeks. On the one hand, the glories of ancient Greece

Figure 1. Contemporary Greece.

and the splendour of the Christian Byzantine Empire give them a proud and rich heritage. The resilience and durability of Greek culture and traditions through the turmoil of past invasions and foreign occupations imbues them with a sense of cultural destiny. These two legacies have led to what Richard Clogg has referred to as 'ancestoritis' (*progonoplexia* in Greek),[2] by which he refers to the excessive veneration of the past, and especially the ancient past. These elements place a heavy burden on Greeks of the present. On the one hand, this rich history provides a source of national pride, and on the other, it supplies the meat and marrow of an inferiority complex and a convenient scapegoat. Much of the history of Greek society in the modern age has witnessed a playing out of these contradictory forces.

No short book can tell the rich and varied history of Greece and the Greeks in the modern age satisfactorily. The present endeavour has far more modest aims. It intends only to supply the reader with a sufficiently detailed narrative to enable an understanding of how and why Greece as it is today came to be. *Modern Greece* traces the rich and varied history of Greece and the Greeks over the last two centuries. By addressing topics drawn from social history and anthropology such as urbanization, class formation, economic development, modernization, national identity, gender and culture change, this short book differs from most other studies currently available. Privileging the history of society does not mean that the study of the great events that shaped the nation is neglected. Of course they are discussed, but with a difference: the aim is to comprehend how those great events had an impact on the everyday lives of Greeks.

A number of themes run through the book. The first of these relates to Greeks' identity. Standing astride the crossroads of Asia, Africa and Europe, Greek society has always manifested complex features reflective of its almost unique geographical situation. We shall study the complicated and continuing process of identity formation within the context of state building.

Another focus of the book is the Greek diaspora and its relationship to the construction of the modern Greek state and society. For centuries, the 'Greek world' meant far more than just the southern tip of the Balkan peninsula. The experience of the diaspora has been a crucial element in the development of Greece and Greek society. And while I do not devote separate chapters to the diaspora, I have tried to include discussion of its impact.

Still yet another theme relates to the enduring interplay between Greece and the Great Powers of the past, and the issue of foreign dependency. During the modern age, relations with Europe and the United States have shaped the development of Greek society in integral ways. The social, cultural, and economic history of the Greek people, then, is bound up with forces and developments on a scale larger than just southeastern Europe. An understanding of Greece's history thus entails an examination of this complex interplay between indigenous development and foreign influences.

The last thread that gives coherence to my story focuses on the development, or modernization, of Greek society. I am aware that modernization is a loaded term and that in its most robust form modernization theory has come in for considerable criticism, much of which I accept. However, I would suggest that modernization theory may still provide us with a useful heuristic device for categorization or a yardstick against which we can measure developments in any specific culture. In other words, if we accept for the sake of argument that certain features of the developed western world may be labelled as 'modern,' then we can employ for the sake of argument the term 'modernization' as a form of shorthand abbreviation for a comparison of those specified features found in the developed world and elsewhere. I employ the term in this limited sense. And so using this notion, we shall examine the social world, in its widest sense, of Greek men and women over the last two centuries.

In the final analysis, however, my overarching aim is to tell the story of Greek society during the modern age. And if the reader comes away with an appreciation of how it developed over the recent past and how that development both bore resemblances and manifested marked differences from other areas of Europe, I shall feel well satisfied.

The Ottoman Legacy

All societies develop myths that they deploy to explain why key aspects of their culture developed the way that they did and why they appear the way that they do in the present. These myths provide the basis for the construction of stereotypes about 'national character' and 'national identity.' In the United States, for example, the myth of the 'frontier' is still presented as an explanation for both positive (American grit and rugged individualism) and negative (the persistently high rate of interpersonal violence) aspects that Americans believe to be key characteristics of their society. In England, the idea of the 'freeborn Englishman' has roots that go far back into time, and the notion has repeatedly been conjured up to explain the supposed distinctiveness of English history.

In the case of Modern Greece, the central trope often deployed to explicate the essential character of its society is the period of Ottoman rule, the 'four hundred years' as it is often referred to. Like a magnet, the era of the 'yoke of foreign domination' attracts the blame for almost every ill manifested in Greek society.[1] But like all nationalist myths, this one is largely an invented tradition. This is not, of course, to say that the Greek society that developed from the nineteenth century onward was not influenced in many ways by the experience of being incorporated into such a vast, multi-ethnic empire. It was. But, in this introduction rather than tracing the history of the Greek people from 1453 until 1821, my aim is merely to sketch out those key elements of the Ottoman legacy that most deeply shaped Greek society on the eve of the revolution of 1821.

I focus on the Ottoman legacy as it related to Greek identity, the role of the Orthodox Church, the nature of the class system, administration and local society, the economy of the region, and the development of the Greek diaspora.

GREEK IDENTITY AND THE ROLE OF THE ORTHODOX CHURCH

The Ottoman state was a theocracy based on strict notions of hierarchy and order. At the pinnacle of society was the Sultan, a divine-right absolute ruler. As the one selected by God to lead the chosen people, his authority was unquestionable and so he was owed total obedience. In return, the Sultan safe-guarded the religious and civil laws upon which social justice was founded. The peoples of the empire were divided by religion into two main groups: the *darülislâm*, the domain of the faithful, i.e. Moslems, and the *darülharb*, the domain of war, the non-Moslems. A person's duties, obligations, and rights were integrally bound up with their position as a member of one of these two groups. A conversion to Islam was possible, but the conquering Ottomans did not demand it. Instead further subdivisions, based once again on religion, were used to divide the subject populations into smaller and more easily governed groups.

The non-Moslem members of the darülharb were subdivided into groups or *millets* on the basis of religious confession rather than ethnic origin. In addition to the Moslem millet, there were four others: the Jewish millet, the Gregorian Armenian millet, the Catholic millet, and the largest and most important of the non-Moslem groups, the Orthodox, or Millet-i Rum (literally the 'Roman' millet). The millet system developed over a long period of time and did not achieve its final form until the nineteenth century; nonetheless from early on in its development, Ottoman law accorded the millets a fair amount of autonomy. At the head of each millet was a *Millet-bashi*, a religious leader who was responsible for the care of the millet's members and for ensuring his flock's continued obedience to the Sultan. The head of the Orthodox millet was the Ecumenical Patriarch of Constantinople. He was also the *ethnarch*, or leader of the nation, and this gave him wide-ranging powers in secular as well as spiritual matters.

The Orthodox Church as an institution played a vital role in Greek society in matters both religious and secular. The Church, however, was in an ambiguous and paradoxical situation. On the one hand, it helped to keep the Greek language alive and as the predominant educational institution it did the most to pass on the traditions of the past. By so doing, it helped foster a sense of Greek cultural identity. The so-called secret schools at which this instruction supposedly took place remain firmly rooted in Greek popular historical memory. For example, a recent reassessment of the secret schools has suggested that they were far less prominent than scholars have previously believed.[2] Ottoman tolerance toward the Christian faiths meant that religious instruction did not have to take place under a clandestine cover. On the other hand, because of its relationship to the Ottoman Empire, the Church was duty bound to maintain order. This made it a very conservative institution. Greeks were cut off from the great intellectual currents of the west, the Reformation and the Enlightenment, by the inherent conservatism of the Church. When secularization began, it was in the Greek communities of the diaspora.

Regarding identity, we have to be very careful to not equate membership in the Millet-i Rum with being 'Greek'. The millet,

> embracing as it did all Orthodox Christian subjects of the sultan, reflected in microcosm the ethnic heterogeneity of empire itself. It contained Serbs, Rumanians, Bulgarians, Vlachs, Orthodox Albanians, and Arabs, while the strictly 'Greek' element itself, although firmly in control of the *millet* through its stranglehold over the Ecumenical Patriarchate, the Holy Synod, and the higher reaches of the Orthodox ecclesiastical hierarchy, was by no means homogeneous.[3]

What, then, did it mean to be 'Greek' (or Serb or Albanian) in the Ottoman Empire? Clearly membership in the Millet-i Rum was part of it, but it was not enough. Just as speaking Greek was part of it; but, since Greek was the language of the Church and all members of the Millet-i Rum were by definition its members, knowledge of the Greek language was widespread, even if it was a second or third language, and so language alone was thus insufficient as the primary boundary marker of ethnic identity.

We have to accept that the national or ethnic identities of Balkan nationalities as we think of them today are relatively recent creations and that they emerged only during the heyday of nationalism during the nineteenth century. During the eighteenth century, Greek identity was rooted in a variety of elements – religion, language, customs, etc – but also in class and occupational status. It was very common for society at the time to label shepherds as 'Vlachs', peasant farmers as 'Serbs', and merchants as 'Greeks' regardless of what their internalized image of their identity was. It seems to me that for most of the population of the Ottoman Empire, after religion, their identity was rooted in a variety of local contexts that had little or nothing to do with ethnicity. Identity flows from a conscious perception of oneself vis-à-vis others, and, as we shall see in the next chapter, a specifically Greek national consciousness did begin to develop during the eighteenth and early nineteenth century, but even then the process was complex and the identification of who was a Greek was contested and complicated.[4]

Two important Ottoman legacies, then, were the insinuation of the Orthodox Church as a major force in Greek society and as a central institution in defining Greek identity, and the creation of cultural identities that were intricately multi-stranded and resistant to simple delineation.

ADMINISTRATION AND LOCAL SOCIETY

As in any pre-modern empire, because of the difficulties of communication, Ottoman rule tended to be decentralized. Though the Sultan technically was the absolute ruler and thus could exercise complete control over his empire, he could not effectively rule his domain alone. Instead a complex administrative hierarchy developed. Initially, sultans used conditional grants of land as a means of raising an army and of administering conquered areas. *Sipahis*, or cavalrymen, were given a *zimat* or parcel of land. In exchange for control of the land and all those on it, the sipah pledged to provide the Sultan with troops. These grant-holders tended to live on their estates or in nearby towns and thus assumed many of the responsibilities of local rule. Over time, this system broke down and the estates became hereditary and stopped serving their intended function. The policy, however, left a legacy of massive Ottoman-controlled land holdings worked by dependent Greek peasants. As the sipahi system broke down, a form of provincial administration took its place.

The Empire was divided into *pashaliks* that were governed by *Pashas*, who in turn subdivided their realms into smaller units overseen by *Beys*. In terms of local government among the Orthodox population, there was a dual administration. On the one side there were the Ottoman officials and religious judges, the *kadi*, who adjudicated civil and criminal cases involving Moslems and non-Moslems. On the other, there were the Orthodox priests and Christian primates (the *Kokabadjis*) who collected taxes, settled disputes, and effectively governed at the local level. At times the two systems competed and at times they operated in coordination. The end result was complexity, and this created much room for abuse. It bred also cynicism as to the 'rule of law'. In response to this systemic confusion, people sought protection through the formation of interpersonal bonds of patronage.

Another legacy of Ottoman rule was the creation of local communities that developed a very deep sense of local autonomy, inhabited by people who looked on outside institutions with deep distrust. This distrust stemmed from the treatment that the subject Christian population received from those Ottoman institutions that did intrude into their lives.

The non-Moslem population was discriminated against. There were special levies imposed only upon them, including a head tax and a minimum 10 per cent tithe on agricultural produce. They were subject to corvée labour as well. There were proscriptions on the type of attire they might wear, they could not bear arms, and they were prohibited from riding horses. In court, testimony of a Moslem would always be accepted over that of a non-Moslem. Marriages between Moslems and non-Moslems were illegal. Most hated of all was the forced conscription of non-Moslem male children for service in the military or in the civil service. This practice had ended by the eighteenth century.

The burden placed on the subject population was heavy, and it became increasingly more so during the eighteenth century as the Ottoman Empire suffered setbacks in conflicts against the Empire of the Russias. Compounding this was the capriciousness with which the law was enforced upon non-Moslems.

Some parts of Greece were able to escape the clutches of direct Ottoman rule. Areas like the inaccessible mountains of central Greece simply proved too remote to be controlled; thus, this area was called the *Agrapha*, the 'Unwritten', because no census or tax records were made of it. Other areas, like the Dervenochoria of Megara or the Zagorochoria of Epiros, were granted special status because they filled particular needs of the Empire. The Phanariot Greeks of Constantinople were able to achieve notable success and gain power because of the services they rendered to the Sultan as diplomats and interpreters, or serving as the *hospodar*, or prince, of Moldavia and Wallachia.

Maintaining order and control over such a vast domain required vast resources of manpower. Once the feudal system broke down, other means had to be found. A standing army would have been impossibly expensive to keep up. The solution arrived at was the appointment of non-Moslem men of violence as the guardians of specified areas. These *armatoliks* were to be self-sustaining, as the armed guards would be paid through the collection of local taxes and transit duties. This was a system susceptible to flagrant abuse. Bandits, or *klefts*, flourished in many of the remote areas of the Empire. Some were Christians who had committed crimes against state officials and so had to flee. Others were adventurers out to make money. Gangs of armed men formed and, depending on whether in the pay of the state or not, they could be considered brigands or armatoles. For most of the peasant population, the difference was not too important; they suffered abuses from both groups. Later myth-making would turn the klefts into proto-revolutionaries, but to contemporaries they were a force to be feared.

The nature of the Ottoman administration provided a space for another group of Greeks to rise in stature and power. During the eighteenth century, as the Ottoman Empire found its internal situation becoming threatened, a group of families known as the *Phanariots* rose to positions of considerable power within the Ottoman administration. Most Phanariots were Greek by birth. They were very well educated, multilingual and wealthy. They began to fill key positions in the Ottoman administration, or the Porte as it was often referred to. As chief interpreters to the Porte they shared with the Ottoman foreign minister responsibility for the conduct of foreign policy. As interpreters to the commander of the Ottoman fleet, they obtained considerable influence over the Greek islands of the eastern Mediterranean. In the role of hospodars, or princes, of the Danubian principalities of Moldavia and Wallachia, they became powerful rulers in their own right, recreating in their courts in Jassy and Bucharest luxurious imitations of the imperial court in Istanbul. The Phanariots became notorious for their corruption and intriguing. Some, however, did take the lead in promoting legal changes and land reform, and in promoting Greek education and culture. The Greek Phanariots became a powerful and wealthy group, and they played an important role in the movement for Greek liberation.

THE ECONOMY OF THE REGION

The years of Ottoman rule also left a lasting imprint on the economy of the Greek lands and on the economic situation of the Greek world on the eve of independence. One aspect of that legacy focused on agriculture and the rural economy. We have already seen that a form of feudal regime existed in the Greek countryside from the onset of Ottoman rule. By the end of the eighteenth century, that form of land tenure had been replaced by the *çiftlik* system. This was a type of plantation-style agriculture in which wealthy landowners, both Christian and Moslem, created large estates that were cultivated by peasants, usually under some form of sharecropping or tenant agreement. The cultivators had no rights of ownership over the land they tilled and very limited input over which crops they cultivated. Increasingly çiftliks aimed at producing cash or commercial crops earmarked for the export market: currant grapes in the northern Peloponnesos, wheat and other cereals in Thessaly, tobacco and cotton in Macedonia and Asia Minor.[5] The peasants attached to such estates lived a very precarious existence and were among the poorest groups in the region.

There also developed another type of agrarian system. This one focused on the villages of peasant families who cultivated their own land. Over time some villages had obtained certain rights and privileges from the Sultan that made them exempt from the legal strictures of the usual land ownership law and that accorded them certain tax exemptions. The families in the *kefalochoria* practiced another form of agriculture, one more geared to ensuring that the subsistence needs of the family were met rather than in producing goods for the market. Many of these villages were located in upland areas where arable land was scarce and the climate inhospitable. So these families had to devise various strategies to make ends meet. Some of these included herding livestock, learning a craft and producing goods, like linens, to market, or seasonally migrating. In these mountain and upland villages, peasants implemented subsistence strategies that called on a variety of skills and talents. They also developed strong traditions of local autonomy.[6]

Greeks or Hellenized members drawn from other groups carved out a very important and lucrative niche for themselves as merchants. By the end of the eighteenth century Greeks controlled much of the terrestrial and maritime commerce of the Ottoman Empire. The Greek merchant families established warehouses and shipping facilities in every major city and market town in the Balkan peninsula. From this network of facilities, they controlled the overland trade in foodstuffs, textiles, industrial crops, and finished products.[7] By 1800, Greek merchants from Chios, Smyrna, and Istanbul, among others, had established a near-monopoly over the maritime commerce between the Levant, the Balkans, the Black Sea, and western Europe.[8] Related to the emerging Greek economic dominance of the maritime carriage trade, the export commodity production sector, and the brokerage trade, was the establishment by Greek merchants of commercial houses abroad.

THE GREEK DIASPORA

During the years of Ottoman domination, Greek speakers moved and settled widely both inside and outside of the Empire. As merchants and artisans, Greeks settled in large numbers in Rumania, the Black Sea littoral, and in all the major cities of the Empire. Greeks increasingly monopolized commercial dealings between the Empire and the outside world; as it was said at the time: 'To be a peddler is to be a Greek'. Over 80,000 Greek families, for example, resided in the Austro-Hungarian Empire. Thousands more settled in the cities of Venice, Leghorn, and the major commercial centres of the Russian Empire. Important merchant colonies were founded in Trieste, Naples, and Marseilles. Amsterdam, Antwerp, London, Liverpool and Paris all boasted of sizeable Greek populations.

The diaspora communities played a vital role in the development of Greek culture during the era of Ottoman rule. First, Greek identity formation was enhanced when Greeks found themselves as a distinct enclave resident in an alien culture. Second, the diasporic Greeks were exposed to intellectual currents and ideas; as we shall see shortly, it was in the diaspora that the ideology of revolution developed. Third, many Greeks became wealthy in the diaspora and they helped to support the communities in Greece through the foundation of schools and other such institutions.

THE LEGACY – A SUMMARY

The legacy of the Ottoman Empire was indelibly imprinted on the society that emerged in Greece after the bloody and lengthy revolutionary war. That legacy would continue to be part of Greek society for a long time to come. It is historically inaccurate to reconstruct a past where everything that came out of the lengthy period when Greeks were part of the Ottoman Empire was negative. Rather than render some value judgement, it seems to me preferable to summarize the salient features of Greek society on the eve of the revolution of 1821, which were, of course, the result of developments during the period of Ottoman rule.

First, the Orthodox Church stood both as a primary element in the definition of Greek identity and as the dominant institution in society. This had both advantages and disadvantages, as we shall see. Second, Greek society was highly stratified and marked by profound differences in wealth and power. Greeks were among the poorest members of the Millet-i Rum and they certainly constituted its higher echelons. Third, the structure of the economic systems that existed in 1821 possessed both severe faults and major positive aspects that persisted in influencing the material development of the new state for decades. Finally, by the end of the eighteenth century, if not well before, Greek culture was an international, if not global, society. The Greek diaspora had spread to much of Europe, the Far East, Africa, and even had extended across to the New World. The story of modern Greek society, therefore, will be not just the story of the little kingdom that came into being in 1832 at the southern tip of the Balkan peninsula, rather its scope will at some point or another reach almost everywhere around the world. But every story must have a beginning, and ours begins with a group of intellectuals who in the late eighteenth century started to think about a revolution.

The Birth of the Modern Greek State

The modern state of Greece came into existence as a result of a protracted, bloody war against the Ottoman Empire between the years 1821 and 1832. The significance of the Greek War of Independence transcends the bounds of Greece and Greek history. It was the first major successful war of independence by a subject population against an imperial power since the American Revolution of 1776. It was the first successful nationalist revolution and it provided a model for later nationalist struggles. Lastly, the conflict was the first real test of the conservative Concert of Europe that emerged out of the Great Power Congress of Vienna in 1815.

Revolutionary movements, whether successful or not, inevitably lend themselves to myth-making.[1] Revolutions make men and women either into heroes of the glorious struggle or martyrs to the lost cause. Following the lead of the sources, it is easy, therefore, to romanticize revolutions and revolutionaries, and to see the result of the national struggle as in some way inevitable. Certainly this is the case with Greece. When participants in the struggle later penned their memoirs, as they did in large numbers, they actively wove the fabric of the myth of revolution, which still shapes interpretations of the war to this day. We must, however, avoid the pitfall of *post hoc* interpretations, which impute motives and plans that only became evident after the fact.

Like any historical event, the Greek War of Independence was the end result of a wide range of factors and influences, and its successful outcome was far from preordained or inevitable. Much of what occurred was contingent on past events and on contemporary developments in the Europe of the 1810s and 1820s. The Greek war for liberation must be seen in the context of Europe during the heyday of the conservative counter-revolution that dominated the great power politics after the defeat of Napoleon.

THE PRE-REVOLUTIONARY CONTEXT

The first of these contexts focuses on ideology and the formation of a Greek nationalism. The origin of a specifically 'Greek' national consciousness cannot be pinned down to a precise moment in the past, but instead must be seen as part of an ongoing process. As we saw in the last chapter, discerning specifically ethnic or national identities among the subject populations of the Ottoman Empire is not easy, and care must be exercised in projecting nineteenth century national identities on to the past. Nonetheless, it is evident that the development of national consciousnesses amongst the subject populations of the Balkans took on greater coherence and developed more rapidly in the latter part of the eighteenth century and first part of the nineteenth century, especially after the French Revolution of 1789.[2] Diasporic Greeks had grown in affluence and prominence during the eighteenth century, and because of the greater freedoms accorded them and their exposure to intellectual currents in western Europe, it is not surprising that the intellectual basis of Greek nationalism was most coherently formed among this group.

The voluminous writings of these men constituted a Greek extension of the ideas and philosophies of the Enlightenment. Moreover, 'the Greek Enlightenment has left an indelible mark upon the full extent of Greece's *development* – upon both Greece's actual historical development and *the history of the discourse* on Greece's development'.[3] This intellectual movement had, then, a lasting impact on Greece. Among the contributors to the Greek Enlightenment, two men in particular stand out: Adamantios Korais (1748–1833) and Rigas Velestinlis (ca. 1757–1798).

Adamantios Korais was born in Smyrna to a Chiote father and a Smyrniote mother.[4] After receiving an eclectic and unconventional education, Korais was sent to Amsterdam to oversee his father's silk trading interests there. He was to remain abroad thereafter. From his home in Paris, Korais played a leading role in formulating the intellectual foundation of Greek nationalism. Repulsed by the violence he witnessed during the French Revolution but steeped in hatred for the Ottoman Empire, he was thus torn by his firm beliefs that Greece must be freed from the 'yoke of tyranny', but that it must not be by violent revolutionary means. Instead, he preached a middle way of emancipation through education.

Through his work in Classical philology, Korais aimed at inculcating in Greeks a sense of their ancient heritage. His emphasis on the need to resurrect Greece's ancient glory stemmed in large part from his intense hatred of the Orthodox higher clergy – 'monkish barbarians' as he once called them – whom he blamed for the degraded state of the populace. For Korais, then, the model for a new Greece should be ancient Athens rather than medieval Byzantium. It was, thus, through his efforts as a linguist and in particular his development of *Katharevousa* (a purely literary language that combined elements of ancient Greek with the popular spoken language called demotic

Greek) that he intended to give Greeks a means to invigorate that heritage. Though he had much to say about the 'moral' regeneration of the Greeks, he was strangely mute about the type of polity he foresaw rising from the ashes of the Ottoman Empire. Of course it was to be liberal, but beyond that he never addressed issues such as its size, composition, and governmental system. He lived to see the creation of an independent Greek state, though he played no major active role in its creation and, in fact, worried when hostilities broke out that the rebellion was premature.

Rigas Velestinlis more than anyone else was the father of the revolution.[5] A Hellenized Vlach, Velestinlis had a chequered career; his most notable post was that of secretary to Alexander Ipsilantis, the *dragoman* of the Porte, in Constantinople. Rigas spent much time in Wallachia in the service of Phanariote *hospodars*. Highly educated and a gifted linguist, he was well suited to act as the conduit for the transmission of revolutionary ideas and ideals from the west to the east. Based in Vienna and imbued with the revolutionary fever emanating from France, he actively sought to spread the contagious creed of liberation to the Balkans.

In a series of works, Rigas both spread the gospel of revolution and sketched out a vision for the new Balkan republic that would emerge from the ashes of the Ottoman Empire. In his *The Rights of Man*, he transferred some of the key aspects of the French *Declaration of the Rights of Man and the Citizen* into a Balkan context. In Article Three on the equality of all men before the law, for example, he explicitly stated that this included both Christians and Moslems. Other articles as well emphasized that these fundamental, natural rights appertained to all groups and all religious denominations. He also called for the abolition of slavery and for the use of Greek as the common tongue of the new motherland.

In the *New Political Constitution of the Inhabitants of Rumeli, Asia Minor, the Archipelago, Moldavia and Wallachia*, he provided a more detailed blueprint for the new state's constitution. The new polity was to be a secular, democratic republic. He referred to it as a 'Greek Republic' but, as he clearly noted, Greek in this context meant citizen, not ethnicity: 'The Greek People [consists of all] those living in the Empire, without distinction of religion or language ...' (Article Two). He was even more explicit in Article Seven: 'The sovereign people consists of all inhabitants of this Empire, without distinction of religion and speech, Greeks, Bulgarians, Albanians, Vlachs, Armenians, Turks and every other kind of race'. In sum, Rigas wanted a secular, multi-ethnic, liberal democratic state that geographically resembled the Byzantine Empire. This was a noble vision that was not to be. Finally, he recognized that the rabble needed more than political ideals to be roused to action, and so he penned a revolutionary anthem: the *Thourios*. This stirring poem became the Greek *Marseillaise*, and it was widely disseminated and sung. It ends with the following call for action.

> Let us slay the wolves who impose the yoke,
> Who cruelly oppress both Christians and Turks;
> Let the Cross shine over land and sea;
> Let the foe kneel down in the face of justice;
> Let men be purged of all this sickness;
> And let us live on earth, as brothers, free! (lines 121–6)

While attempting to spread the gospel of national revolution, Rigas was captured in Austrian-controlled Italy. He was transported to Vienna where he was imprisoned. After intense lobbying by the Porte, he and seven other Greek radicals were extradited to the Empire. On the night of 24 June 1798, Rigas was executed by strangulation in a Belgrade prison. With the following words, Rigas became the first martyr to Greek independence: 'This is how brave men die. I have sown; soon the hour will come when my nation will gather the ripe fruit'.[6]

Rigas's was not the only vision of what a liberated Greek state should look like, nor was his the only voice calling for rebellion. The anonymous author of the *Greek Rule of Law, or A Word About Freedom (Elliniki Nomarheia, iti Logos peri Eleftherias)* published in 1806, for example, framed his call for revolution with a detailed catalogue of the horrors suffered by the subject Christian population of the Empire.[7] But unlike many others, he viciously attacked fellow Greeks for their roles in perpetuating the suffering of their people. He saved his most savage diatribe for the clergy. For this writer, the war of liberation meant not only throwing off the yoke of Ottoman rule, but also the tyranny of the Orthodox Church and heavy-handed domination of the 'Turkified' Greeks of the ruling class. Conversely, another widely held view was that it was the Church that held the key to liberation.

Proponents of this idea argued that Orthodoxy was the only force capable of mobilizing the mass of people to rise up against the infidels. They looked back to the past to chart the future for their new Greece. What they foresaw was a new Byzantine Empire: Greek, theocratic, and monarchical. The idea of Byzantine Hellenism resonated most loudly with the Phanariotes of Constantinople. That there was not a single revolutionary vision is not surprising. What is significant is that all shared in the belief that the time was ripe for some form of relief from the worst aspects of Ottoman rule.

The uprising of 1821, thus, has to be seen in the context of previous attempts to confront Ottoman rule. While the millet system allowed some autonomy and provided a means for accommodation within the ruling structure of the Empire, there were some efforts to confront the Sultan's rule directly. Such episodes provide the prehistory to the War of Independence. The most important of these events was the Orlov Rebellion of 1769–1770. In the belief that Russia, which was at the time embroiled in a war with the Porte, was committed to liberating the Christians of the Ottoman Empire, an uprising took place in the Peloponnesos beginning in February of 1769. Under the ostensible leadership of the Orlov brothers, the venture quickly fell apart because there was neither an organized base of support nor a coherent ideology to guide the rebels. The uprising rapidly degenerated into a melée of looting and pillaging by both sides. Within a few months, the rebellion was over. Its significance lay in the precedent it set for open, violent resistance to Ottoman rule and for the oppressive measures that the Porte instituted in its aftermath, which only served to broaden and deepen the feelings of resentment against the Empire.

If a revolution is to be successful, three conditions must be met: there must be an ideological framework which gives aims and a direction to the movement; there must be an organizational structure which can coordinate and lead the movement; and finally there must be adverse material conditions among the populace which make mass support for action possible. In the Balkans in 1821 all three of these conditions were met.

During the decade from 1810 there was a confluence of developments that contributed to the perception that the time was ripe for rebellion. Rigas, Korais, and other intellectuals had provided the language and ideas necessary for a nationalist struggle. Those ideas had filtered down the social ladder to the lower orders of society in songs, speeches, and pronouncements from the pulpits. Folk beliefs and millenarian prophecies lent credence to the belief that the time for national regeneration had arrived. Episodes like the Orlov Rebellion provided a collective memory of violent resistance. Moreover, the partial success of the Serbian uprising of 1808 encouraged the belief that the Empire was weakening and that rebellion could succeed.[8]

Fuelling further the belief that independence was possible was the creation in 1815 of the first independent Greek state since 1453: the United States of the Ionian Islands. The seven islands of Kerkira, Paxos, Lefkada, Kefallenia, Ithaki, Zakinthos, and Kythera had for centuries been part of Venice's Levantine empire. After the demise of the Serenissma Republic in 1797, the islands were passed back and forth between the various Great Powers – France, Russia, and Great Britain. With the defeat of Bonaparte, their status was in limbo. Each of the Great Powers wanted them, but none would let the others have them.

The solution struck upon was to declare them a sovereign state under the protection of Great Britain. This landmark event had two immediate consequences: first, the islands stood as an example that independence could be achieved, and second, the way that the Ionians had gained their independence raised hopes and expectations that the western powers would intervene in Greek affairs on the Greek side.

During the 1810s, three other major developments helped bring matters to a head. The first was the global economic crisis that followed the cessation of the Napoleonic Wars. Napoleon's continental blockade of Britain had provided a great opportunity for those willing to risk violating French reprisals. Numerous Greek merchants and captains seized the moment and made huge profits. The boom in Greek shipping came to an abrupt end. First, immediately after the war, all of Europe, and Britain in particular, was plunged into a depression as industries tried to cope with the greatly reduced demands of a peacetime economy.

Second, compounding this crisis of the manufacturing sector, severe weather conditions, in part due to a series of volcanic eruptions in the south Pacific, greatly reduced the yields of most major food crops. 'The last great subsistence crisis of the Western world', as one historian has described it, struck.[9] The Balkans were not spared these traumas.

Third, when conditions began to ameliorate, the mercantile fleets of England, Holland and the others, who had suffered under the French blockade, regained their former prominence. Greek merchant shipping between 1815 and 1820, for example, fell by almost 40 per cent on average. Prices for subsistence grains soared as supplies declined. Across much of the Balkan peninsula near-famine conditions obtained.[10] The general economic crisis and the singular inability of government at any level to address the widespread distress exacerbated the existing feelings of resentment among the rural populace. Indeed, rather than taking active measures to alleviate the suffering, the Porte raised taxes. As the experience of France during the 1780s had shown, hungry bellies and revolutionary discontent went hand-in-hand. Only one final element, that of organizational leadership, was needed before the situation in the Balkans would be truly ripe for revolution, and that also developed during the 1810s.

The *Filiki Etairia*, or 'Friendly Society', was the most important of the many clandestine revolutionary groups that had sprung up since the 1770s.[11] Emmanouil Xanthos, Nicholaos Skoufas and Athanasios Tsakalov, three merchants from different regions of the Ottoman Empire, founded the Filiki Etairia in 1814 in Odessa on the Black Sea. Xanthos was initially the driving force behind the organization. Though based in Odessa, he travelled widely in the Balkans because of his olive oil business. One of his trips took him to the island of Lefkada, one of the Ionian Islands. The ideas of the French Revolution had taken root there during the period of French rule. Not only did Xanthos become stirred by the notions of liberty and freedom while staying on the island, but he was also introduced to the murky world of secret societies when he was enrolled in the island's Masonic lodge. Like many members of the diaspora communities, Xanthos believed that liberation for the Greeks would be achieved through the actions of the major western European powers. The Concert of Europe crafted by Klemens von Metternich at the Congress of Vienna dashed any such hopes. The conservative crowned heads of Europe combined to maintain the status quo, and that policy extended even to relations with the Ottoman Empire. The Filiki Etairia was established when it became clear that if freedom was to be attained, the Greeks and the other Christians in the Balkans would have to do it themselves.

If the Filiki Etairia was to have any chance of success it would have to appeal to a wide spectrum of Balkan Christians and would have to recruit as members as many prominent men as possible. Accordingly, the central committee appointed 12 men, the Apostles, and assigned them the task of recruiting as many leaders as possible in their assigned region. After this move, the organization's membership expanded rapidly both in size and in geographical scope. Influential men both inside and outside of the Ottoman Empire joined.

Organizationally, the membership was divided into four hierarchically ordered civil ranks and two military ranks. The ranks were based on wealth and responsibilities. In order to maintain secrecy, only members from the highest ranks knew the identities of members from outside of their immediate cell. This compartmentalization meant that, unlike other such groups, the Filiki Etairia was able both to attract a substantial membership and to elude detection and suppression. It brought together men from many levels of society – merchants, professionals, large landowners (*proesti*), members of the clergy, *klefts* (bandits) and *kapoi* (warlords), and even some prominent Phanariotes, like the former Russian general Alexander Ipsilantis, who eventually emerged as the group's paramount leader. It was not a real mass movement in the truest sense of the term; according to the membership lists that have survived very few peasants, shepherds, or workers were members. This should not, however, be interpreted as a sign that they did not support the goals of the organization, but only that the leadership was reluctant to include them in the membership.

The Filiki Etairia grew to be the largest secret society, and it provided an organizational base for the dissemination of revolutionary ideas and for coordinated action. But there was a very significant downside to its large size. Along with size came diversity of aims, ambitions, and viewpoints. Ideologically, except for the goal of liberation from the Porte, little else connected the membership. Some prominent leaders envisioned a new Byzantine Empire, based on a Greek theocratic monarchy; others fervently wanted to create a multi-ethnic secular republic founded upon the principles of the French Revolution. These fissures would only emerge after the actual onset of hostilities. Initially at least, because of its size and the number of important leaders whom it counted as members, the Filiki Etairia had emerged as a Balkan-wide revolutionary organization. By 1820, all of the pieces were in place for a Christian uprising in the Balkans. Only a spark was required to set ablaze the conflagration of war.

THE GREEK WAR OF INDEPENDENCE, 1821–1828

The precipitating factor in the Greek War of Independence was the revolt of Ali Pasha of Ioannina against his master, Sultan Mahmud II. In a cultural landscape littered with colourful characters, Ali Pasha stands out as larger than life – though his story has until recently been curiously neglected by historians.[12] An enormous man with enormous appetites, the so-called 'Lion of Ioannina' left a lasting imprint on the history of Greece and the Balkans. Ali was born at Tepelni in 1744 into a very powerful Albanian Moslem family. His father was Pasha of a small pashalik,[13] but he was killed when Ali was seven or eight. Influenced by his domineering mother, he began his career as a sheep-rustler and brigand at the tender age of 14. The experience made him a hard man and he soon rose to lead his own gang. As often happened in the Ottoman Empire, his reputation as a man of violence led to his being appointed as a keeper of the peace. He rapidly climbed the ladder of politics and in 1786 he was appointed Pasha of Trikala. Soon thereafter, Epiros was added on. He moved his base of power to Ioannina, leaving his son Veli in Thessaly.[14]

Ali had created a mini-kingdom stretching from central Albania, through Epiros and Thessaly into central and even southern Greece. He was in total control, having either co-opted or driven out all of the armed armatoles, or border guards, and klefts, or outlaws (though in reality they were often the same men).[15] He had also surrounded himself with an excellent staff, including many well educated Greeks and Christian Albanians: Alexandros Noutsos, Ioannis Kolettis and Manthos Oikonomou and his brother Christos for example. During the period from 1800 to 1815 Ali skillfully played the game of power politics, putting down all opposition to his rule, consolidating his hold over continental Greece, playing the Great Powers, especially France and Great Britain, off against one another. Eventually, Ali began to rival the Sultan in his power. He then began to flex his muscles against the Sultan's appointees to the north, but by so doing he went too far.

In 1820 Mahmud II gave his Balkan rival 40 days to appear before him in Istanbul or else face the consequences. The Lion smelled a rat, and demurred. The Sultan duly ordered one of his underlings, Ismail Paso Bey, to attack Ali. The civil war so initiated provided the opportunity for the Filiki Etaireia and its leader Alexander Ipsilantis to launch the Greek uprising.[16]

Ali Pasha had known of the existence of the Filiki Etairia for some time. Indeed, some of his key advisors were high-ranking members of it. Recognizing the need to forge alliances against the coming storm, Ali negotiated pacts with warrior groups like the Souliotes and various Albanian bandit gangs, and he made overtures to the leadership of the Etairia. Each side saw an opportunity to achieve its objectives by cooperating with the other. There was also deep mutual distrust. The winter of 1820–1 was a busy time. Ismail Paso Bey was gathering arms and mobilizing his forces. Ali was bracing himself for the onslaught, promising much to his erstwhile allies hoping thereby to buy their loyalty. The leadership of the Etairia was endeavouring as best it could to coordinate the activities of agents and Apostles scattered across all of south-eastern Europe in an attempt to initiate a Balkan-wide, pan-Christian uprising. Everything came together in the spring of 1821.

The onset of the war of liberation appears far more coherent than it really was. Though the various groups of revolutionaries and secret societies were in contact with one another, there was little coordination: mutual distrust and the difficulties of communication saw to that. As the war clouds gathered, the aims of the major participants seemed to have been these. Ali Pasha wanted to withstand the initial assault against him by Ismail Paso Bey. Then, depending on the outcome of the fighting, he could open negotiations with the Sultan either as a submissive supplicant begging for forgiveness or as a powerful leader who could restore peace in the Balkans on his terms. The etairist leadership sought to ride the coattails of Ali's war. Assuming that the bulk of the Ottoman forces would be arrayed against Ioannina, the plans were to foment rebellions by Christians in three regions – the Danubian Principalities of Moldavia and Wallachia, Constantinople, and the Peloponnesos. Each strategy had its own rationale and its own set of problems.

An uprising in the Peloponnesos was crucial. Its remoteness from the centre of the Empire, the very high ratio of Christian to Moslem inhabitants, the number of powerful Greek landowners resident there, and the considerable number of Christian and Moslem Albanian armed bands operating in the region whose allegiance was up in the air elevated the chances that a rebellion would be successful. It could then, the argument went, provide the rump of a Greek-Christian state or, at worst, provide a base of operation for further attacks against the Porte. Riots were planned which would spill blood on the streets of Constantinople – thus bringing the rebellion right to the Sultan's doorstep, and this development would force the hand of the Orthodox Patriarch to support the movement. Finally, the Danubian Principalities were key.

Alexander Ipsilantis was headquartered with his forces in southern Russia. Given that the Principalities already enjoyed a special, quasi-autonomous status within the Ottoman Empire and that Russia had a special interest in their affairs, the idea was that Ipsilantis would invade Moldavia. At the same time, forces under the command of local leaders, like Tudor Vladimirescu, Ali Farmakis, Georgakis Olimpios, and perhaps even the Serb leader Milosh Obrenovich, would join them in what would amount to a rebellion of the Millet-i Rum. With the entire region up in flames, Tsar Alexander I would have no choice but to bring the might of Russia into play on their behalf.

Among the etairist leadership, then, there clearly was a plan and some crude assumptions about how the revolt should proceed, but these masked a multiplicity of aims, intentions, and interests among the various groups throughout the region. Moreover, there were formidable logistical obstacles that had to be faced, the most important of which was that the vast majority of the subject Christian population did not possess firearms, and so initially at least, the bulk of the fighting would have to be done by small groups of trained troops and by much larger numbers of former klefts and armatoles. If, and at the time it was a big if, the masses of peasants joined the insurrection, then arms, powder, and supplies had to be found for them. In addition, the costs of financing an uprising would be huge, and no secure source of money had been found. Victory would only come if initial success was quickly followed by Russian intervention.

From its inception, little about the uprising went according to plan. First, the Lion of Ioannina proved to be a paper tiger. His forces melted away like spring snow before the Ottoman army and by the middle of February, he was defeated. Locked in an island fortress, he awaited his inevitable execution that finally came the following year. The bulk of the forces under the command of Khursid Pasha, who had replaced Ismail Paso Bey, were thus free to be deployed elsewhere in the empire. Second, the proposed riots in Constantinople never materialized. Third, the pillars of power, on which the insurgents pinned their hopes, denounced them. Tsar Alexander announced in no uncertain terms that he would not support the rebels and Patriarch Grigorios

V excommunicated them. As a consequence of these developments, the campaign in the north was a debacle.

On 5 March 1821, Ipsilantis and his army of 4,500 men crossed the river Pruth and raised the banner of rebellion. Few flocked to it. The local non-Greek Christian peasantry had little sympathy for the Greek cause and indeed saw the Greek elite of the Principalities as their oppressors.[17] In addition, Grigorios's action in excommunicating anyone who joined the rebellion put paid to the idea that the uprising was to be a pan-Christian rebellion, and this also eroded support among the non-Greek Christian population. In the absence of the Tsar's support, Vladimirescu switched sides. Thus, isolated in hostile territory, the rebels stood no chance. Though they gamely fought on, they stood little chance of winning and were finally wiped out at the battle of the Dragatsani River on 2 June 1821. With the rapid defeat of Ipsilantis by the middle of the summer, all eyes turned toward the south where the war would be fought henceforth.

On 25 March 1821, as legend would have it, Bishop Germanos, the Metropolitan of Patras, raised the flag of revolution at the Monastery of Agia Lavra near Kalavrita, and the second theatre of hostilities was opened. In large part, Germanos's act only solemnized actions that were already underway. The clouds of war had been gathering over the Peloponnesos since midwinter. Gangs of armed predators had robbed Moslem tax collectors and attacked farms and villages. By late March Petrobey Mavromichalis, leader of the powerful Maniate clans, was marching with his forces against the important town of Kalamata in Messenia. The noted kleftic chieftain, Theodoros Kolokotronis, had assembled his warriors and was closing in on Tripolis, the capital city of the region. Germanos's proclamation, coming as it did at a meeting of the leading wealthy landowners and officials, gave a stamp of approval to these actions and symbolically served as a signal to begin in earnest the assaults on the Moslem-controlled towns and fortresses.

The initial phase of the war in the south resembled a civil war, character-ized by the awful bloodletting that such internecine conflicts cause. In 1821, approximately 40,000 Moslems inhabited the Peloponnesos, as opposed to about 350,000 Greeks. Most of the Moslems were civilian families who had lived in the region for a long time. As hostility toward them increased, many sought refuge in the walled towns and fortresses at Patras, Tripolis, Kalamata, Korinth, and Nafplion. Stationed there to protect them were relatively modest numbers of troops, mainly Albanian mercenaries, that Khursid Bey had left behind when he marched north to face Ali Pasha. The combination of irregular bands of former brigands thirsting for booty and oppressed Christian peasants hungry for revenge against their overlords was a lethal one. When the

Turkish-held fortresses capitulated, bloodbaths ensued: as much as one-third to one-half of the Moslem population fell to the insurgents' bullets and blades.

To be sure, each side could tell its tales of butchery and slaughter. The Greeks recoiled in horror when news of the pogroms in Constantinople, Smyrna, and Thessaloniki and the massacre on the island of Chios reached them.[18] The ignominious death inflicted on Patriarch Grigorios V was so awful that it blinded many to the fact that he had not supported their revolt. On the Ottoman side, the news of the massacre of thousands of men, women and children at Kalamata, Nafplion, and Tripolis, in some cases even after the Greek leaders had promised them safe passage, fuelled the cries for a *Jihad* against the Grecian infidels. In the period from March 1821 to December 1823, it is estimated that the combined casualties were of the order of 50,000, mostly unarmed non-combatants. Each round of massacres only served to make finding a political solution to war even more difficult.[19]

Militarily, phase one of the rebellion saw the insurgency meet with success. During this period, the Greek forces were able to capture many of the major strongholds of the Peloponnesos and establish a strong presence in central Greece as well. Indeed, by December of 1823, they had conquered and controlled all of the major garrisons and towns in central and southern Greece. The Souliotes and others from western Greece had joined the movement, as had the great chieftain of central Greece, Odysseus Androutsos. Many of the Greek islands also threw their lot in with the insurrection and so the war took on a naval dimension as well. Victories on land were coupled with successes at sea: most notably Admiral Kanaris's sinking of the Ottoman flagship off the island of Tenedos on 10 November 1822. Just as importantly, Greek control of the seas made it impossible for the Porte to relieve its besieged garrisons or to launch a counter-attack anywhere but overland from the north. But the crucial question remained open: could the Greeks translate their military success into a political victory?

Divisions regarding the political goals of the war existed among the Greek rebel leadership from the start, and the rifts only became deeper and more diverse as Greeks from the diaspora, from the disbanded court of Ali Pasha, and from the Phanariot community of Constantinople arrived in the Peloponnesos. As Douglas Dakin has noted,

> The [indigenous] Greek upper classes wanted Ottoman
> society without the Turks, the military classes [*kapoi* and
> *armatoli*] wanted to carve out for themselves so many
> independent satrapies and become miniature Ali Pashas,
> while the lower orders simply desired to improve their lot,

escape taxation, to own and increase the size of their plots
and to move up the social scale.[20]

In addition, there were the Greeks of the diaspora who flocked to the
'motherland' with heads filled with republican ideologies and dreams of a
resurrected democratic past. Keeping these competing and disparate interests
together proved one of the greatest challenges of the war.

All parties agreed on a few issues. That political victory, in the form of independence, required Great Power intervention was one. Another was that they
had yet to face the full might of the Ottoman Empire, and that they had to take
advantage of the Porte's indecisiveness. A third was that they needed money
and arms desperately and quickly. As we have seen, a cold wind blew from St
Petersburg. And in the midst of the ongoing political unrest in Portugal, Spain,
Piedmont, Naples, and Belgium, the other Great Powers were equally
unsympathetic to the Greek cause. In order to garner the support of the
western powers, the Greek leadership had to declare unilaterally their
independence and to promulgate a constitution creating a government, which
could then open negotiations with the Great Powers. All the while they had to
cast their cause not as a national struggle based on liberal principles, which
would have won them few supporters in post-Napoleonic Europe, but as a
religious conflict of an oppressed Christian population against their Islamic
oppressors.

Three days after Germanos raised the banner of revolt, Petrobey
Mavromihalis issued a proclamation that served as the Greek declaration of
independence:

> The insupportable yoke of Ottoman tyranny has weighed
> down for over a century the unhappy Greeks of the Pelo-
> ponnesos. So excessive had its rigors become, that its
> fainting victims had scarcely strength enough to utter
> groans. In this state, deprived of all our rights, we have
> unanimously resolved to take up arms against our
> tyrants .... Our mouths are opened; heretofore silent, or
> employed only in addressing useless supplications to our
> tormentors, they now celebrate a deliverance which we
> have sworn to accomplish, or else to perish. We invoke
> therefore the aid of all civilized nations of Europe, that we
> may the more promptly attain to the goal of a just and
> sacred enterprise, reconquer our rights, and regenerate our
> unfortunate people. Greece, our mother, was the lamp that

> illuminated you; on this ground she reckons on your
> philanthropy, Arms, money, and counsel, are what she
> expects from you. We promise you her lively gratitude,
> which she will prove by deeds in more prosperous times.[21]

Six weeks later, the Maniate chieftain convened a congress in Kalamata to draft a constitution and establish a government. Representing almost exclusively the Peloponnesian ruling elite, the congress created a Senate and elected Petrobey as President. Neither enjoyed much legitimacy anywhere else in Greece. The bandit chieftains and the other warriors bearing the brunt of the fighting, for example, felt that they had been cheated out of power. Dimitris Ipsilantis, brother of Alexander, claimed that he spoke for the Filiki Etairia and, since it was the body representing the interests of the rebels, on its behalf he refused to accept the writ of the new government. Finally, as other areas of Greece became liberated the leaders in each formed their own ruling councils, until there were no less than three regional assemblies. All, of course, claimed to represent the interests of liberated Greece.

To deal with the situation, a National Congress at which all parties would be represented was convened in Epidavros in December 1821. After weeks of intense debate, the delegates passed a new national constitution, modelled on the French constitution of 1795. The new Greece was to be a democratic republic founded on the principles of civil liberties and equality for all. Alexandros Mavrokordatos, a learned Phanariot and the chief drafter of the constitution, emerged as the first President. The new government's main goals were to mobilize the peasantry and prosecute the war, press the Greeks' appeal for assistance from the west, and end the factional squabbling. It succeeded somewhat with the first but failed utterly with the others.

A second National Congress was called in April 1823 to modify the constitution and to elect a new government. The Peloponnesians, and especially the military captains, dominated this session. Petrobey emerged as the new President and Kolokotronis as his Vice-president. The virtual exclusion of leaders from western and central Greece and of western-orientated diaspora Greeks, who with the exception of Mavrogordatos were actually forbidden to hold high offices, doomed this national government as well. Unity was absent even within the administration. Shortly after his election, Petrobey turned to his reluctant second-in-command and cryptically asked him, 'So, are you going to dance, Kolokotronis?' To which the warlord menacingly responded, 'As long as you are singing, I shall dance. Stop the song and I stop the dance.'[22] The song and dance did not last for long.

Frustrated by the actions of executive council members who were not military men, Kolokotronis seized and imprisoned them. Open conflict between factions in the government erupted soon thereafter. This lack of political unity, at times lapsing into actual civil war, was to prove very costly.

A pivotal point in the war occurred in 1824. Militarily, the gains of the previous three years soon began to slip away and were finally lost. The masses of peasants who had initially joined in the fighting lost their enthusiasm as the war dragged on. They had not signed on to serve garrison duty besieging walled towns, especially not while land was lying free for the taking back home. Many returned to their farms and villages to reap the immediate benefits of the departure of Ottoman landlords. Only very reluctantly, and often by threat or coercion, did they rejoin the fighting.[23]

This left the fighting to be done by the bands of irregulars, former bandits and border guards. While they could be an effective guerrilla fighting force, they were ill-suited for sustained, disciplined military campaigns; they owed their allegiance to their captain; and they were largely interested in pay and booty.[24] From such material military machines were seldom built. Politically, civil war erupted between the various factions. Some warlords even switched sides and joined with the invading Ottoman forces, further jeopardizing the future of the revolution.[25] Internationally, however, for a variety of reasons, the Greek cause became far more visible and took on a new importance in the diplomatic deliberations of the Great Powers. One of the great ironies of the war was that success was achieved at a time when the Greeks were in fact losing on almost all fronts.

On 5 January 1824, Lord Byron arrived in liberated Greece. He had been on the scene for some time, residing on the British-controlled Ionian Islands. But his actual arrival on Greek soil was rife with both practical and symbolic importance. The Greek War of Independence touched a chord in western Europe. Imbued with a feeling of romanticism and a burgeoning sense of neo-classicism, men, such as Lord Byron, found a 'noble cause' in the Greek struggle against the Ottoman Empire. Philhellenes, as these men and women came to be called, played a critical role in the war.[26] Military men left without a war since the demise of Napoleon, romantic youths seeking their classical roots, liberal reformers who saw in the Greek struggle a chance to strike a blow for liberty, religious zealots who likened the struggle against the 'infidel' to the Crusades, and other assorted freebooters and misfits rallied to the Greek cause as fundraisers or donors, soldiers and sailors, lobbyists and advocates. The Philhellenes were responsible for raising monies to support the insurgents, bringing the conflict to the attention of the wider world, and for keeping it there until the Great Powers could be cajoled into intervening.

The military gains made in the first phase, however, were soon lost. A new strategy came to dominate the Sultan's approach to the Greek rebellion. Mahmud II remained as wedded as ever to the plan to destroy the Greek rebellion by 'fire and sword', but it had become painfully obvious to him and his advisors that the old style military, based on janissaries, mercenaries, and irregulars, was obsolete and ineffective. A complete overhaul of the war machine was required, but this would take time and money and he was running short of both.

During the winter of 1824, Mahmud II struck a bargain with Mahomet Ali of Egypt. Though nominally his vassal, Mahomet Ali was to all intents and purposes a ruler in his own right. The bargain they arranged was that in exchange for control of Crete and the appointment of his son, Ibrahim Pasha, as governor of the Peloponnesos, Ali would deploy his French-trained western-style army and navy against the Greeks. Shortly after agreement had been reached, Mahmud abolished the janissary army and created a new one manned by troops trained in the European manner. This allowed him to launch a two-pronged attack. The Sultan's forces, totalling almost 20,000 men, marched from the north, one branch down the Ioannina–Arta corridor in the west, the other through Boiotia toward Attika and the Isthmus along the east. Meanwhile, the army of Mahomet Ali under the able leadership of his son Ibrahim Pasha had already successfully established a beachhead and was in fact a permanent army of occupation in control of much of the Peloponnesos. Soon, Ibrahim advanced from the south with the aim of catching the remaining Greek forces in a vice.

The strategy worked. The fall of the fortress at Mesolonghi in the spring of 1826 gave the Ottoman forces control of western Greece and of the Gulf of Patras; Athens fell later that summer and that restored all of central Greece to Ottoman control. Even the sectors of the Greek forces that had been trained as a western-style army were unable to stem the tide. Outgunned, outmanned, and running desperately short of supplies because of the horrendous devastation wrought in the countryside by Ibrahim's army of occupation, the situation was becoming grim for the Greeks. The Balkan conflagration was quickly being reduced to a series of brushfires. Had the Great Powers not intervened, the rebellion would have been crushed during the summer of 1827.

Great Power interest in the Greek rebellion can only be understood in the context of the conservative counter-revolution exemplified by Metternich's Concert of Europe. Stability and maintenance of the status quo were the order of the day, but eventually the disruption to the economic interests of each of the powers, as well as their mutual distrust, led them to intervene in the eastern Mediterranean. Over time Great Britain came to play the leading role in the search for a solution.[27] Even though the British government had been unsupportive of the rebellion at the start, many prominent political figures personally were sympathetic to the cause. Also, the widespread Philhellenic sentiment of the British people created a climate supportive of British intervention.

In the summer of 1825, the Greek government passed an 'Act of Submission.' In this petition, the Greeks agreed to place themselves under the protection of His Majesty's government and they accorded Britain the right to select a ruler for the Greek state. Even though Foreign Minister George Canning rejected the petition, the door was now open for more direct Great Power involvement. It swung open wide with the death of Tsar Alexander I in December and his replacement by the much more ambitious Nicholas I early in 1826.

The new Tsar's more aggressive stance toward the Ottoman Empire and his more open sympathy to the Greeks increased the risk of a Russo–Turkish war and of much greater Russian dominance in the region. To prevent these things from happening, Canning sent the Duke Of Wellington to Russia to open negotiations. The result of these talks was the Anglo–Russian Protocol of 4 April 1826, in which the British proposed that Greece become an autonomous state within the Empire, that it pay a tribute to the Porte, and that its ruler be designated by the Sultan. In return, the Sultan was to withdraw his troops.

A number of developments made the negotiations more difficult and more protracted. First, the war was going so well militarily that Mahmud II hoped to make the negotiations moot by reconquering Greece before he would have to face an ultimatum. Second, Canning was in failing health. In the summer of 1827 he informed King George IV that he was withdrawing from active politics, and his successor, the Duke of Wellington, had the Eastern Question much lower on his foreign policy agenda. On the plus side for the Greeks, however, was the election of Ioannis Kapodistrias as the new President of Greece by the tumultuous Third National Assembly on 11 April 1827.[28] Because he enjoyed much greater credibility with the western powers and in fact resided in Paris, he was a more effective advocate for the Greek position. In addition Nicholas I was becoming ever more impatient with the lack of action and the reactionary Charles X began to push for greater French involvement in the region.

The result of these developments was the Treaty of London signed by Great Britain, the Russian Empire and France in July 1827. This agreement reiterated many of the key aspects of the April Protocol, but it also called for an immediate armistice, set a time limit for compliance, promised Great Power protection during the armistice and authorized the dispatching of a joint fleet to guarantee the peace.

The signing of the Treaty of London set up the likelihood of direct military intervention by the Great Powers in the face of the Porte's intransigence. In the end, it was the combined might of the British and French fleets which decided the issue. Sent to the region to ensure that the stipulations of the agreement were enforced, Admiral Lord Codrington and his French counterpart de Rigny deployed their forces along western Greece. Ibrahim, fearful that unless an agreement was reached soon his entire force of 40,000 men might be lost, called on his father to lobby the Porte on his behalf. But matters dragged. Finally in autumn of 1827, Codrington had run out of patience. Together with the French and Russian forces, he entered the bay of Navarino in southwestern Greece and then issued an ultimatum to Ibrahim: quit the Peloponnesos or face the consequences.

The Battle of Navarino on 20 October 1827 witnessed the destruction of the Ottoman fleet with the loss of 60 out of 89 ships and a casualty roster of over 10,000 men. With Navarino the die was cast. There would be an independent Greek state; foreign intervention had seen to that. The exact boundaries, nature, and disposition of the new polity remained to be determined, but nonetheless by the spring of 1828 a free Greece had been established.

THE PRESIDENCY OF IOANNIS KAPODISTRIAS

Ioannis Kapodistrias was elected President of the fledgling state and took up the post in January 1828. Kapodistrias had enjoyed a long and fruitful career in the foreign service of the Russian Empire, at one point holding the rank of Privy Councillor to Tsar Alexander. Greek nationalists, including the Filiki Etaireia, had long wooed Kapodistrias, a native of the island of Kerkira; he did not join them, though both of his brothers did. When Ipsilanti launched his invasion and started the rebellion, Kapodistrias spoke out against him, expressing his belief that the time for action was not right. Consequently, though he supported the idea of Greek independence, he remained above the fray throughout the wars.

For a variety of reasons, then, he seemed an ideal choice for President at that crucial moment in 1827 when the Great Powers were equivocating on what action to take and still deliberating on the fate of Greece. First, he was not associated with any of the existing factions and so was not caught up in the highly charged political vendettas that the civil war had created and which continued to hamstring every effort at creating a united government. Second, he was an accomplished diplomat and so had credibility with the foreign offices of the Great Powers. In the end, his tenure proved to be as short as it was turbulent.

The problems facing Kapodistrias were tremendous. First, the Ottoman Empire had still not given up hopes of carrying the day. Indeed even after Russia declared war and invaded the Danubian Principalities, Mahmud II continued to press the hard line even though some of his advisors were now telling him that the best course of action would be to seek 'peace at any price in the name of saving the remaining part of the Empire'.[29] With the continued ascendancy of the war party within the inner circle of the Porte, hostilities continued. Inside Greece, various factions, each revolving around a cluster of 'big men' or patrons, continued to control what amounted to private armies. Much of Greece lay in ruins, the war still dragged on, and the coffers of the state were empty.

In addition, the Constitution that Alexandros Mavrodgordatos had drafted at the Third National Assembly was deliberately intended to circumscribe the powers of the presidency. It required, for example, that all presidential orders had to be countersigned by one of the cabinet ministers. It gave the Legislative Assembly broad powers of impeachment, denied the president the power of the veto, and forbade presidential access to legislative sessions. So, the newly elected president could not use his powers of persuasion to present his agenda to the lawmakers; he could not stop them from passing new laws, which he might oppose; and finally, his own position could be easily challenged. Kapodistrias was able to introduce modifications to the Constitution that shifted the balance slightly toward the executive, but nonetheless, the difficulties of governing an already fractious group were only compounded by the power sharing scheme established by the Constitution.[30]

In spite of these formidable obstacles, he introduced many reforms aimed at solving some Greece's most pressing problems. He pushed through legislation for land distribution, awarding grants of land to some, providing loans for the purchase of state lands, and awarding legal recognition to lands usurped during the first days of the war. New taxes were imposed. He facilitated the development of the regular army, and allowed French troops and officers to form the backbone of the new army.[31] Local administration was radically reformed, shifting the balance of power from the local community to the central state. In short, within a relatively short span of time and during an ongoing war, Kapodistrias tried to mould revolutionary Greece into a 'modern' western polity.

He failed. By temperament, Kapodistrias was ill suited to play the role of mediator and conciliator; tired of having to barter with indigenous Greek powerbrokers, he opted instead to rule through enlightened despotism even though this entailed his eventually abrogating the constitution on the basis of which he had been elected. Exasperated by the incessant opposition to his efforts to establish a western-style, centralized, bureaucratic administration, Kapodistrias finally concluded that 'Greece is now in the hands of God, and the Great Powers'. His own fate lay in the hands of assassins who claimed his life in October 1831.[32] That of Greece was more than ever in the paternalistic care of Great Britain, France and Russia.

Three agreements, the Treaty of Adrianople (September 1829), the London Convention (May 1832), and the Treaty of Constantinople (July 1832), vouchsafed once and for all the existence of an independent Greek state by placing it under the protection of the Great Powers, defined its boundaries, established its systems of government, and determined its first ruler – Otto, son of Ludwig of Bavaria. In 1832, then, Greece came into existence. A pale comparison to the lofty 'new Byzantium' dreamed of by men like Rigas, it was a tiny, foreign-ruled, and utterly dependent polity. Nonetheless, for the first time in history there was a state for the Greek nation.

6 February 1833 ... formed an era in the history of Greece, nor is it without some importance in the records of European civilization. A new Christian kingdom was incorporated in the international system of the West, at a critical period for the maintenance of the balance of power in the East. The scene itself formed a splendid picture. Anarchy and order shook hands. Greeks and Albanians, mountaineers and islanders, soldiers, sailors, and peasants, in their varied and picturesque dresses, hailed the young monarch as their deliverer from a state of society as intolerable as Turkish tyranny. Families in bright attire glided in boats over the calm sea amidst the gaily decorated frigates of the Allied squadrons. The music of many bands in the ships and on shore enlivened the scene, and the roar of artillery in every direction gave an imposing pomp to the ceremony. The uniforms of many armies and navies, and the sounds of many languages, testified that most civilized nations had sent deputies to inaugurate the festival of the regeneration of Greece.[1]

This was the spectacle when the newly anointed monarch of an independent Greece arrived at Nafplion. Jubilation and optimism characterized popular feelings on that august winter's day. Neither, unfortunately, would last for long. The second son of the Philhellene ruler of Bavaria, Otto of Wittgenstein was a mere 17 years old when asked to ascend the throne of the newly formed Kingdom of Greece. His reign lasted 32 years and, because of developments we shall discuss shortly, it falls neatly into two periods: the first from 1833 until 1844 and the second from 1844 until Otto's forced abdication in 1862. Otto had many faults – he was vainglorious, stubborn, and frivolous – but he grew to love his adoptive kingdom and saw the state through some very difficult times. After Otto's overthrow, a new dynasty was established. Members of the Danish Glucksberg family would rule Greece off and on for almost a century. In this chapter, then, we examine the political development of the newly established Greek state up until 1897.

Fig. 3.1 'King Otto'. This depiction of King Otto shortly after his arrival on Greece
    captures his youthfulness and his arrogance. Dressed in traditional Greek
    garb, the young German monarch tried to strike a regal pose. Despite all of his
    attempts to become 'Greek', Otto never fully became accepted by the people,
    with whom he had a love and hate affair for over thirty years. (Illustrated
    London News, 15 May 1843.)

REGENCY AND ABSOLUTISM: THE POLITICAL SETTLEMENT OF LIBERATED GREECE

The second son of King Ludwig I of Bavaria, Otto emerged from the Great Power negotiations as an attractive possibility to become ruler of Greece. Among the advantages of Otto's candidacy were, first, that his father was not firmly aligned to any of the major powers, second that the youthful prince was an ardent Philhellene, third that his political views were moderately conservative, and fourth that he was young and malleable. The Powers, however, initially passed him by in favour of Leopold, Duke of Saxe-Coburg, because of two drawbacks to his candidacy – his inexperience and his Catholicism. When Leopold removed himself from consideration and a bevy of other possible candidates demurred, the Powers turned once again to the Bavarian monarch to inquire about his son. After a series of lengthy negotiations, Ludwig signed a treaty with Russia, France and Great Britain (notably absent of course were the Greeks) that installed Otto as the first King of Greece. The most important terms of his selection were these. Otto, or Otho as he came to be called in Greece, became absolute monarch and his crown was to be passed on through hereditary succession based on the customary aristocratic practice of primogeniture (whereby the crown is passed on to the male heirs in order of age from eldest to youngest). Concerned about his son's safety because of the ongoing conflict and in order to guarantee as well as possible his future security, Ludwig insisted that the treaty mandate that a force of 3,500 Bavarian troops accompany the new King and that Bavarian officers be appointed to supervise and train the regular Greek army. Lastly, the three powers guaranteed the sovereignty of the new state and pledged loans totalling 60,000,000 francs; the money was to be distributed in three payments, only the first of which was actually scheduled in the treaty. Thus secure in its borders, protected by the shield of the west, and bankrolled by western loans, liberated Greece greeted its youthful ruler and the Regents who would rule in his name. It would not be too long thereafter that they would all be 'sucked into the vortex of [Greek] party politics'.[2]

Since Otto was a minor, the treaty gave Ludwig the authority to appoint a three-man Regency to rule until his son came of age on 1 June 1835. To carry out this challenging task, he selected Count Joseph von Armansperg, Law Professor Ludwig von Maurer and General Karl Wilhelm von Heideck. This troika exercised almost complete control over the Greek government. Von Armansperg exercised executive control; von Maurer was charged with devising the system of local and central government, promulgating codes of law and designing a system of civil and criminal justice, and overseeing the daily operation of the government; Heideck, of course, had the daunting task of administering the military affairs of state. Though an absolute ruler, Otto's role in the government was rather minor – this was to be on the job training for him – and instead it was his father who acted as adviser to the Regents.

Greek leaders played only subsidiary roles in the governance of their own state. Westerners were appointed to almost every major position of importance. This 'Bavarokratia' (the term by which Greek critics referred to the period of the Regency)[3] became a source of much friction among Greek politicians. Compounding the Greek dependency on the Bavarian protectorate was the considerable influence exerted by the representatives of the Great Powers. The factionalism that had developed during the war continued, and each party looked to one of either the French, English or Russian delegations as their protector.

The so-called Russian Party had at its core men who had been important supporters of Ioannis Kapodistrias. Prominent among them were the old warrior Theodoros Kolokotronis, the Ionian Islands magnate Andreas Metaxas and military men such as Konstantinos Tsavellas and Dimitrios Kallergis. What united this group and its followers was the belief that because of their shared religion Russia was the Great Power most likely to further Greek interests. The movement was socially conservative, anti-liberal, and economically they sought to further the interests of small landowners.

Ioannis Kolettis led the French Party. He had been an advisor to Ali Pasha and in that role he had had numerous dealings with French representatives during the Bonaparte years. A curious combination of military warlords from Central Greece, Peloponnesian kokabadjis, and island ship owners constituted the core of the party. Kolettis brought them together by promising to address the demands of each group: land and estates for the Moreotes; open commerce and restitution of wartime losses for the islanders, and military commissions and back pay to the warlords. The link to the French delegation was through Kolettis himself.

The English Party was the movement of the western-orientated progressives. Led by Alexander Mavrogordatos it brought together those who favoured liberalism and westernization. It found its strongest followings in the towns and cities (Athens, Nafplion, Hermoupolis, and Patras) and among bureaucrats, intellectuals, and the 'commercial class'.[4]

Each of these parties was constantly in contact with, and some were used by, the foreign delegation of the country they looked to for support. In many ways, then, the war for 'liberation' from a foreign yoke had resulted merely in a change of masters. Finally, further exacerbating the political turmoil was the persistent power struggle between the Regents, which led eventually to two of them being recalled.

During the brief period of the Regency Armansperg emerged as the dominant leader. When Otto became monarch in his own right on 1 June 1835, Armansperg stayed on for a brief period as Arch-Chancellor and was then replaced by another German, Count von Ruduck. Whether it was under Armansperg or Otto, the government of Greece was autocratic and its administration dominated by Germans and other westerners. To be sure, there was some participation by Greeks as members of a cabinet of advisors to the crown, but as was made evident on numerous occasions when important actions were taken and key decisions made without even a nod in their direction, the Greeks' role in practical governance was largely irrelevant.

A good example of the cavalier attitude that the Bavarians evinced toward the Greeks and their traditions in regard to crafting the institutions of the new state was the legal system. Rather than taking into account the customs, traditions and laws that had shaped the process of dispute resolution and jurisprudence in the past, the Bavarians cobbled together a hybrid system that drew its structure and trappings from the French system, and its philosophical basis from German thought.[5] Though the legal reforms supposedly created a national system of civil and criminal courts, including a system of justices of peace who were to adjudicate minor disputes, the system never effectively functioned outside of Athens, Syros, and a few other major towns.

The political scene in postwar Greece was turbulent to say the least. A convoluted triangle of factions and power groupings developed that made for some very strange bedfellows. Factions developed within the Bavarian administration and each of them forged alliances of convenience with one of the Greek parties and with one of the foreign delegations. The Greek factions likewise sought the support of one of the big three, France, Britain, or Russia, which were themselves intensely active in promoting their country's vested interests in the eastern Mediterranean. Any endeavours to reconstruct war ravaged Greece, then, had to negotiate these turbulent political waters.

REBUILDING A BROKEN LAND

Notwithstanding the complicated political situation, the problems facing Otto and his advisers from 1832 to 1843 were formidable. Economically, the country was in ruins. Politically, the Bavarian regime faced a serious crisis of legitimacy. Westernized Greeks who had fought for the ideals of the American and French Revolutions were profoundly disappointed to find themselves saddled with a foreign absolute monarchy. Phanariotes and indigenous kokabadjis who saw it as their right to succeed the Ottomans as rulers of the land were furious at being frozen out of power. Granted that the more thoughtful of the Greek leaders recognized that only a foreign leader not tied to any of the entrenched factions could possibly salvage the situation, many still resented the Bavarians. In addition, the wounds from the civil war of 1832 were still fresh, and with thousands of armed warriors still roaming the land, the cauldron of internecine conflict could easily boil over again.

Bread and butter issues topped the Bavarian agenda. During the course of the war of liberation and the subsequent civil war of 1832, over 662 villages had been devastated. In spite of the significant strides made during the presidency of Kapodistrias, there were still thousands of refugees who needed food and shelter. In towns such as Patras, Kalamata, Tripolis and Athens, few houses stood above their foundation. Visitors to these ruined settlements paint stark pictures of the devastation and of Greeks living like beasts in makeshift hovels and shacks. 'Homeless men roamed the land looking for work, while orphans and widows sought some kind of protection and sustenance'.[6] Thus, destitute and displaced, the rural populace looked to their new King for relief.

The agricultural infrastructure on which the economy was based lay in ruins. Over two-thirds of the olive trees and three-quarters of the vineyards had been destroyed. Three-quarters of the olive and flour mills had been reduced to rubble. Of the estimated prewar flocks of over 100,000 goats and sheep only approximately 10,000 remained. Vast sums of money were needed to rebuild the infrastructure of the agrarian economy. But above all, economic reconstruction depended completely on the redistribution of land. The peasants, then, looked to the young King for bread, land, and peace.

Other groups felt that they were owed much because of their roles during the war. The primates who had led and paid for the war wanted land, power, and pay for their men. The ship owners who had been the backbone of the fleet and who had spent a great deal of cash on the war wanted indemnity payments. The men at arms who had fought the war wanted regular pay as soldiers, or land, or both. Satisfying all of these claimants, even with the monies available through the foreign loans, was impossible.

Throughout his reign Otto faced fiscal crises. Dwelling within his kingdom's bounds were only 750,000 Greeks compared to over two million still under Ottoman rule. Most importantly in respect to the economic future of the kingdom, the fertile plains of Thessaly and lacustrine basins of Macedonia lay outside the kingdom. The major Greek cities and entrepôts of Thessaloniki and Smyrna and the island of Crete remained in the Ottoman Empire. In spite of the expertise and connections that the Greeks of the diaspora brought with them as they migrated to the new kingdom, manufacturing and trade remained underdeveloped. The economic conditions in Greece presented the government with a major challenge: how to stimulate growth, satisfy the immediate needs of the population, and pay the war indemnity owed to the Porte. The only feasible internal source of revenue entailed taxing the very thing that needed to expand – agriculture. Even before that could become an issue the government had to deal with a complicated but crucial issue of land redistribution.

The land situation in Greece was chaotic. As we have seen, during the period of Ottoman rule, 65 per cent to 75 per cent of the cultivated land in Greece was in Moslem hands, either through private ownership or in one of the conditional tenures bestowed by the Sultan. By the war's end, the vast majority of the Moslem population had either fled or been killed. The land of the deceased was up for grabs, and while some of those who fled the carnage managed to dispose of their land, many others had not. The revolutionary governments nationalized all such property and used the newly confiscated lands as collateral for international loans. At the war's end, some Greeks possessed land that they had legally purchased before the war. Others held legal title to estates they had purchased from Moslems during the war. And still others were in possession of land they had usurped as war booty or had been given by Greek warlords in lieu of payment for their services. When Kapodistrias came to power one of his top priorities was to commission a survey to determine who legally owned which lands and thus to determine the location and extent of the national lands, and to calculate the amount owed as compensation to the previous owners. Kapodistrias's programme met with stiff resistance and had not progressed very far at the time of his assassination. The land issue was of such crucial importance, however, that it quickly became a priority for the new Bavarian regime.

On 7 June 1835, less than one week after he had become sole ruler, Otto issued the 'Law for the Dotation of Greek Families.' The culmination of many years' labours, this legislation was to be the capstone of the Bavarian economic and social policy of reconstruction. While thoughtfully crafted in theory, the law paid scant attention to the realities on the ground in the Greek countryside, and so it produced results very different from those intended by the lawmakers.

The law stipulated that all native-born and foreign-born Greeks, and all non-Greeks who had fought in the war and continued to reside in Greece, were eligible to receive a 2,000-drachma government credit certificate with which to purchase national land. Each head of a household, and this included war widows, could bid on parcels of land varying in size and quality up to the limit of their certificate. No one could obtain more than four hectares of national land. Once purchased the land became private property to be held in perpetuity. In return the owner incurred a mortgage that mandated a payment of six per cent of the purchase price annually for 36 years. Two successive defaults in payment and the land was returned to the state for reallocation. The crown claimed an additional three per cent of the purchase price in taxes that was to be paid in cash and not in kind. This then was the scheme that the government hoped would create a stable landholding peasantry and that would set the state on the road to fiscal responsibility.

The programme, however, was fraught with difficulties. First, the four-hectare maximum was too low. Even under the best of conditions, this amount of land would barely provide basic subsistence to the average family, let alone cover the mortgage and taxes.[7] Moreover, the 2,000-drachma allocation was predicated on the average price for a hectare of cultivable land being 500 drachmas. This proved to be unrealistic. Prices at the land auctions varied on average from 1,350 drachmas per hectare for basic arable to 2,600 for land with vines to over 5,000 drachmas per hectare for irrigated gardens.[8]

As a result those peasants who had to rely solely on the government certificate were able to acquire farms of only between one and three hectares, and usually the land they purchased was of the lowest quality. Even in the best of years, such minifundia would not have fed the average family. But Greece possessed a very high-risk agricultural environment in which even a six-hectare farm would have failed to provide subsistence one-sixth of the time.[9] Peasants either had somehow to acquire non-national lands – almost an impossibility – or they had find other sources of income, of which there were precious few in postwar Greece. In addition, as mentioned above, since landholders had to pay in cash a three per cent tax based on the purchase price, many proprietors were compelled to find non-agricultural sources of cash income or borrow the money to pay their taxes.

The family farms created by the dotation scheme were born into dependency and debt, and that soon translated into poverty. At the same time, the auction system was very susceptible to manipulation and corruption. A few wealthy men were able to exploit the loopholes in the system to acquire sizeable estates with the best land. In short, the rich got richer and the poor poorer. The novelist Pavlos Kalligas aptly captured the peasants' verdict on the dotation law:

> What else are the laws and the state today but an exitless
> labyrinth of rules deliberately multiplied to satisfy a swarm
> of insatiable intriguers who are nourished by the sweat of

the people whom they render each day more impoverished
and drive to brigandage.[10]

Land, debt and poverty remained persistent features of the Greek
countryside throughout the modern era.

Otto's government then found itself in a difficult situation, on the one hand
passing land reform laws in order to distribute land to the peasants and of
providing low interest loans to enable families to cultivate that land, while on
the other having to claim back these resources in the form of taxes. In addition
to the taxes on the national lands, a tithe of ten per cent was levied on
privately held land. The collection system combined the older mechanism of
tax-farming with one operated by government civil servants. Both were open
to manipulation and corruption. Evasion by tax payers became rampant and
peculation by tax collectors rife. The result was a very insecure income to the
state. Since internal sources of revenue were inadequate, borrowing from
Greeks abroad, foreign banks, and European states was repeatedly resorted to.
Indebtedness was the result in both cases. Debt remained a serious problem
for Greece throughout the modern epoch.

In spite of the obstacles the reconstruction of Greece from the devastation
of 11 years of war did occur. The merchant marine recovered from the wartime
losses and once again much of the sea-borne freight of the Mediterranean was
in Greek hands. According to one estimate, the value of mercantile trade
handled by Greek ships rose by 194 per cent between 1833 and 1840, and by
1840 the value of that trade was in the order of 80 million drachmas. Not
surprisingly given the low level of agricultural production and very modest
industrial output of the kingdom of Greece, most of the trade handled by
Greek ships was transit trade between the Ottoman and Russian Empires and
western Europe.[11] Because of the development of mercantile trade, islands
such as Syros and port cities like Patras began to flourish once again.

Syros in the Aegean literally became the crossroads of the Mediterranean.
By 1837 the majority of trade between east and west passed through the island.
Its capital city of Hermoupolis grew in size, from a population of 150 in 1821
to over 12,000 in 1840, and in wealth.[12] Patras on the northwestern tip of the
Peloponnesos also witnessed a remarkable recovery during the age of Otto.[13]
The first decade of Otto's rule, then, witnessed an economic recovery of sorts,
but the nature of that recovery, based on mercantile trade rather than a solid
base of production, was to have a lasting impact on the Greek economy.

After the economy, the paramount issue facing the royal government was
security. The war of liberation had been fought by a combination of a very
small army made up of western-trained regular troops and much larger bands

of former bandits, ex-paramilitary police and armed peasants. Military warlords held sway over their band as their own personal army. The Bavarians, as had Kapodistrias before them, recognized that no national government was secure so long as warlords commanded personal armed bands. They faced roughly the same options as the ill-fated first president: either incorporate or eradicate the rootless gangs of irregulars. If anything, the situation facing them was even more acute than it had been for Kapodistrias. The civil war of 1832 had elevated the level of militarization of the countryside and its outcome left stranded large numbers of disgruntled tough men who wanted their back pay, land and a livelihood. They looked to the boy king to give these things to them.

Otto and his Regents had other ideas. They believed that a modern army, trained in the western style and loyal only to the monarchy could ensure the government's security. The 3,500 Bavarian troops that accompanied the King were soon augmented to 5,000, all German volunteers. They were to form the core of the new regular army. On 2 March 1833, the Regency issued a decree disbanding the irregulars; another law that banned the possession of firearms without a government licence quickly followed it. Enforcement of these laws, however, could easily have plunged the nation into civil war yet again.

So the Regents offered some inducements for compliance. Older warriors would be enrolled into an honorary battalion and be provided with retirement benefits. They could send their sons free of charge to the newly established military school on Aigina. More generally, the disbanded irregulars could join the new regular army. The idea was that Greek troops, trained and commanded by German officers, would complement the Bavarian mercenaries in the new modern army. Still others were offered the opportunity of enlisting in the new gendarmerie that had been established to police the countryside.

Few Greeks responded favourably to these measures. Warlords were loath to relinquish the stick that gave them leverage in their struggles to gain political power locally. Uniforms, strict discipline, hard training and low pay were anathema to the proud and independent mountain warrior/brigands who made up the rank and file of the irregulars. For the old warhorses of the revolution 'it was obviously better to sleep on the mountains in a goatskin cloak as a Kleft than to wear the hated Bavarian uniform'.[14] Thus, few answered the government's appeals favourably. Only a handful of able-bodied men enlisted in the regular army. More became gendarmes because this gave them complete discretion to exploit the local peasant villages in ways that they already had been doing.

One old warhorse at least saw as a sham the government's other schemes to disarm them by offering medals and honours, characterizing them as 'a bone to lick until their teeth finally fell [out]'.[15] Most reverted to the old ways, and became brigands and gunmen for hire. Some bands crossed over into Ottoman-controlled northern Greece and plied their craft there, using the border as means to play the Porte and government in Athens off against one another. Others formed bandit gangs that roamed the countryside of Attika and the Peloponnesos. Armed conflict between them and the forces of the state was inevitable.

Between 1834 and 1840 numerous armed uprisings occurred. Some, like those in the Mani in 1834 and in Akarnania in 1836, involved hundreds of men and required a sustained campaign by government forces before peace was restored. Just as significant was the endemic banditry that flourished throughout the peninsula. Otto made a number of concessions, like dismissing the Bavarian troops and replacing them with Greeks, that helped to alleviate the situation somewhat. But brigandage and unrest would continue to plague his government and insecurity was a perennial problem.[16]

Political stability proved elusive in the first phase of Otto's rule. He and his advisors showed little sensitivity to indigenous traditions in politics, law, and education as they attempted to impose western models. Increasingly the Greek elite split between *heterochthons*, Greeks from the diaspora who had migrated to Greece, and *autochthons*, the descendants of the old elite families or *tzakia*. Old cleavages from the war years remained and new ones developed connected to the struggle for power in local administration and for influence with the King. But, as Edmond About noted in his commentary on Greek life and politics, 'the future is for the black coats [i.e., the westernized Greeks]'.[17]

The old-timers, however, would not go down without a fight; and the political system established in 1834 made such partisan conflicts inevitable. The kingdom was divided administratively into 10 *nomarchies* (prefectures), 59 *eparchies* (sub-prefectures) and 468 *demes* (counties). Nomarchs and eparchs were nominated directly by the king; demarchs were appointed by him from a list of three elected by a small number of the wealthiest men in each deme. The absolute power invested in Otto rankled with the men who had fought the war in the name of republicanism. The extreme centralism at the heart of the new administration trampled on the long and storied tradition of local rule. And it challenged, in theory at least, the power of the local elites.

Adding further fuel to the political fire was the religious question. A decree by the Bavarian Regency in 1833 established an autocephalous Orthodox Church of the Kingdom of Greece with Otto at its head and this led to a rupture with the Patriarchate that would only be healed in 1850. The young monarch, however, remained a Roman Catholic and showed no inclination to alter that fact. After his marriage to the Catholic Amalia in 1839 and his failure to sire a child, the issue of the religion of his heir became a controversial one.

Greeks wanted an orthodox ruler, and Otto persisted in showing disdain for that widely felt sentiment. This stance infuriated in particular those of the 'Russian' party who believed in the vision of a greater Orthodox Greek state. Fiscal chaos, failed land reform, increasingly violent factionalism, and resentment at unfulfilled agendas all spelt trouble for the young monarch. Tensions came to a head in 1843.

CONSTITUTIONAL MONARCHY

The second period of Otto's rule officially began on 7 March 1844, the day on which the new constitution was promulgated. The age of absolutism in Greece was officially over. Since he had returned from Germany with his new bride in 1839, Otto had become ever more the absolute ruler. He dismissed many of his top-ranking German advisers; he showed disdain bordering on contempt for the Greek cabinet. He strove to concentrate sole power in his own hands. Otto was neither ruthless enough to be feared, nor compassionate enough to be loved, nor competent enough to be respected. He thus commanded the loyalty of no sector of society. Lacking any support among the general populace, at odds with the leaders of the major political parties, and estranged from the representatives of the great powers, the King found himself increasingly isolated; a condition only exaggerated by his dismissal of all of his most independent minded advisers. As discontent rose to open rebellion against his reign, Otto had no one to turn to and so had to compromise.

Colonel Dimitrios Kallergis, the cavalry commander of the garrison of Athens, led the coup that toppled the absolute monarchy, in what was to be the first, but by no means the last, time that the military would intervene in civilian affairs. Plots against Otto had been hatching for some time and their existence was well known, even as far away as London.[18] When Otto's attempt to have the ringleaders arrested failed, Kallergis called out the troops and marched on the palace. The square in front of it soon filled with people. Shouts of 'long live the constitution' and 'death to the Bavarians' rang out from the crowd. After consultations with Kallergis and other military leaders, meetings with heads of the major parties and audiences with great power delegations, Otto saw that his position was untenable. Without a drop of blood being shed, the Bavarian absolute monarchy came to an end.

In the wake of a military coup, Otto reluctantly agreed to convene a national assembly to draft a constitution. When the assembly finished its work that spring, a new system of government was established. Otto would rule as a constitutional monarch. There would be a bicameral legislature. One chamber, the *Vouli* or Lower House of Parliament, consisted of deputies elected on the basis of mass enfranchisement (any male property holder over 25 years of age could vote), and the other, the *Gerousia* Upper House or Senate, had members appointed by the King. Greece became in theory one of the most democratic states in Europe.

Intense debates ensued, however, over the question of who actually was a 'Greek.' The division between autochthonous Greeks (those who had been born in the territory of the new state) and heterochthonous Greeks (those who had moved to the kingdom from outside) led to rancorous debates when it was proposed that essentially there would be two categories of citizenship based on one's origins. In the end, the distinction based on place of origin was dropped. Otto, however, retained the power to appoint or dismiss unilaterally government ministers, to dissolve Parliament, and to veto legislation. With the counter-signature of a Minister, he could issue executive decrees as law, and with the agreement of the Prime Minister, he could appoint for life members of the Gerousia. He agreed in turn that his successor to the throne would be Greek Orthodox.[19]

Political parties did not arise in the wake of parliamentary democracy. Instead factionalism took a new form. Hierarchical pyramids of power centering on a single prominent man developed and were held together by patronage, or *rousfeti*. No one played the new power politics better than Ioannis Kolettis and he left his imprimatur on mid-century Greek politics. He was able to form working alliances with both the western modernizers and the traditional power brokers while becoming closely tied to neither. Politics by personalities as exemplified in the career of Kolettis set the pattern for the political culture of Greece until the 1870s.

This crafty veteran of the political intrigue was appointed Prime Minister of Greece under the new system in 1844 because he enjoyed the support of the King. His faction occupied only 22 of the 127 seats in the Lower House. Through lavish use of gifts and bribes, cajoling and intimidation, Kolettis managed the new Parliament. His faction grew in size and he personally monopolized power, holding the portfolios, at one point or another during his three-year term, of Foreign Affairs, Justice, Interior, Culture and Public Instruction, and Finance as well as Prime Minister. Coupled with his autocratic inclinations were his populist tendencies: he knew the value of popular support in a democratic system. As a contemporary, George Finley noted about Kolettis: 'He could hear the first whispers of public opinion, and he knew to avail himself of its support as soon as it made its voice heard'.[20]

During his administration, some important steps were taken to develop the economy and the nation's infrastructure, but financing such moves put the country further into debt.[21] Kolettis is best remembered as the man who first gave a coherent focus to the widely held belief amongst Greeks that the Greeks still residing in the Ottoman Empire had to be redeemed; this vision became known as the *Megali Idea*, or Great Idea. Kolettis had been able to manipulate the various parties and the King so as to strike a 'balance of forces'.[22] No one faction was able to gain ascendancy because the wily old veteran of the politics of patronage was able to play each side against the others. When he died in September 1847, the political situation changed for the worse. A series of episodes over the next few years served to expose the weaknesses of the system and began the slide in Otto's popularity that would end in his overthrow.

In 1848, the year of European liberal revolutions, even Greece could not escape the infectious spirit of rebellion. However, with the exception of a demonstration on 25 March 1848 during which university students gathered before the palace and shouted 'Long live the republic!', the uprisings in Greece did not challenge the institution of royal rule as the revolutions elsewhere on the continent did. There were nonetheless a number of rebellions; some, like the peasant revolt in central Greece, involved very large numbers of men. All of the uprisings had their origins in local causes. Disgruntled politicians who had lost their positions in the uncertain days after the death of Kolettis led some of the revolts. Many more were uprisings of peasants in protest over high taxes, skyrocketing debt and foreclosure, and the increasing immiseration of the countryside (see the discussion of the rural economy in Chapter 5 for the reasons behind these developments). So, even though the rebellions did not directly threaten the government and the monarchy, as happened elsewhere in Europe, they clearly highlighted the growing disaffection with them among the people.[23] Developments over the next few years only made matters worse.

On 15 January 1850, a British naval squadron under the command of Vice-Admiral William Parker laid anchor just off the port of Piraeus and an ultimatum was issued to Otto and his government. Three years earlier the house of a man named David Pacifico, a Portuguese merchant who had been born in Gibraltar and so was a British subject, was attacked by an anti-semitic mob in Athens. With the ardent support of Sir Edmund Lyons, the British Minister in Greece, Pacifico sought compensation from the Greek government for damages to his property and effects and for the suffering endured by his wife and children. After months of fruitless dialogue, Lord Palmerston had tired of negotiations and was now demanding that the Greek administration make good on the monies owed to Pacifico and a few others, or else the fleet would blockade Piraeus, Syros, Patras, and Nafplion. The blockade lasted for three months until at last, under the threat of an actual bombardment of Athens, Otto gave in.[24] The episode led to widespread anti-British feelings and generated, in the short term, support for Otto; in the long run, however, it also showed how weak and dependent the kingdom was. The debacle of 1854 exposed that situation even further.

The outbreak of the Crimean War seemingly presented Greece with an opportunity to gain major territorial concessions from the Sultan. In anticipation of an Ottoman defeat at the hands of Russia, Otto declared that as the only Christian King in the near east, he had a sacred duty [to protect the Christians of the Balkans] and exhorted further that God in His greatness would never abandon the 'Christian cause.' With these words he signalled his wholehearted support of the Megali Idea and his approval of Greece's participation in the conflict. Greek irregulars streamed over the frontier into Thessaly and Epiros with the blessing of the Monarch, the Parliament and the Greek people.

When Great Britain and France intervened in the war on the side of the Porte, everything changed. Greece was now embroiled in a conflict that pitted two of their protecting powers against the third one. Yet again the western powers issued an ultimatum to Greece: stand down or face the consequences. After a humiliating occupation of Piraeus by French and British forces in May 1854, Otto had to ignominiously give up the 'Christian cause' and had an administration selected by the foreign legations imposed on him.

> The fact [that] the ministry was imposed on Otho [vis. Otto]
> by the two representatives was not only humiliating for the
> king but was also seen by the majority of the Greek people
> as an open intervention in the internal affairs of the
> country.[25]

On the anniversary of this twenty-fifth year on the throne in 1858, Otto's popularity with the Greek populace was at its zenith. Yet, within a matter of a few years, he would be driven out of the country. A number of factors contributed to his demise. First, Otto had by and large reduced constitutional government to a sham, effectively ruling as an autocrat at the head of a royalist faction of sycophantic politicians. Opposition to the way the political system was being manipulated grew, especially among younger and university educated politicians whose political sympathies were more liberal and democratic. Second, Otto's initial response to the emergence of the Italian unification struggle, the *Risorgimento*, in 1859 eroded his popularity with the general public and provided his opponents with fodder to fuel the fire of discontent.

The public at large supported the Italian cause, seeing in it a reflection of their own irredentist dreams; Otto, on the other hand, openly favoured Austria in its attempts to put down the Italian uprising. Third, many Greeks looked at the support Great Britain and France were giving the Italian insurgents and speculated that Otto was the reason that the western Great Powers continued to look on the Greek nationalist cause with disfavour. Fourth, the issue of succession continued to plague Otto. The royal couple remained childless, and so in the event of Otto's death the throne would be passed on to one of Otto's brothers; all of whom refused to convert to Orthodoxy and so openly stated that they would decline the throne. Otto continued to refuse to reveal whom he would nominate to be his successor and the succession issue remained a source of unpopularity with the Greek people and with the Russian government, which was worried that the lack of an Orthodox heir would have a serious impact on their position in the region.

In a vain attempt to stem the tide of opposition to his rule, Otto attempted to foment a military venture against the Ottoman Empire. He inaugurated talks with Serbia and Montenegro, and even with Garibaldi in Italy, regarding a concerted campaign against the Sultan. But these efforts failed, plunging public assessment of his rule even lower and, further, incurring the displeasure of France and Great Britain. Symptomatic of rising opposition to the Bavarian monarchy were the attempt by radical university students to assassinate Queen Amalia in 1861 (which nearly succeeded) and the military revolt centred in Nafplion in early 1862 which was only marginally suppressed. Finally, in another bloodless coup later that year, Otto was forced to abdicate from the throne of the land he had grown to love.

THE AGE OF REFORM, 1864–1909

The overthrow of Otto created both constitutional and successional crises. The former focused on the relative balance of power between sovereign and Parliament; the latter touched directly on the question of sovereignty and autonomy. A constituent assembly was called in 1863 to address both issues, but it soon became evident that the Protecting Powers had no intention of relinquishing their prerogative to appoint the new King. Therefore, the assembly spent its energies debating the constitutional question.

While in theory the Constitution of 1844 shared power between King and Parliament, in reality it had given the monarchy sufficient powers to control the government. A National Assembly was convened on 22 December 1862 to draft a new constitution, which was eventually promulgated in 1864 and which was far more democratic than its predecessor. For a start, sovereignty was invested in the Greek people, not the monarchy. This was to be a *vasilevoméni dimokratía*, a democracy with a monarch or a 'crowned democracy'. Second, rather than being open ended, as they were in the 1844 charter, in the new constitution, the monarch's powers were restricted to those specifically adumbrated in the document. Structurally, there was to be a single-chambered Parliament vested with full legislative powers and elected by direct, secret ballot of all Greek men over the age of 21 who owned some property or who followed a trade or occupation. As the debates in the constituent assembly made clear, the King's powers, however, were still going to be considerable. He would have the power to appoint and dismiss ministers, dissolve Parliament, disburse funds, declare war, and contract treaties. Because the new King would thus wield considerable power, the question of who would sit on the throne of Greece was an extremely important one.

The people of Greece made clear whom they preferred as their new leader. In a plebiscite in December 1862, 241,202 votes were cast; 95 per cent for them were for Queen Victoria's second son, Prince Alfred. But having a member of the British royal family on the throne of Greece was completely unacceptable to the other protecting powers, and so the search for a suitable King continued. It had to be someone from a prominent, yet not too partisan royal house. Chosen eventually was Prince Christian William Ferdinand Adolphus George of Holstein–Sonderberg–Glücksbrug, the son of the future King of Denmark. He would reign as George I, King of the Hellenes until his death at the hands of an assassin in 1913.

George was 18 years old when he ascended to the throne. Determined to learn from the mistakes of his predecessor, he did not bring with him a large entourage of foreign administrators, he did not fall prey to the factionalism that so beset Greek politics, and he made it explicitly clear from the start that, though he intended to adhere to the Protestant faith, his children would be Orthodox. Finally, he was a firm believer in constitutionalism, and so he readily accepted in principle the idea that while he reigned as monarch, he did not rule the state. At times his impatience with Greek politicians gave him pause, but he never really challenged the separation of powers. He enhanced his position with the Greek people further by taking an Orthodox, albeit Russian, bride and then solidified it by siring an Orthodox son and heir, and by auspiciously naming him after the last emperor of Byzantium – Konstantine.[26]

In spite of the arrival of a new ruling dynasty and a new constitution, little seemed to change in the rough and tumble practice of Greek politics. Powerful personalities continued to hold sway through their networks of clients held together by bonds of patronage, in Greek referred to as *rousfeti*.[27] New cleavages did appear, however, based on broad differences regarding economic development and liberalism. One group, called the 'montaigne', tended to be more liberal supporting economic growth through industrialization and urging greater government intervention in both the social and economic spheres; this group drew its support primarily from younger, educated men who had a more western outlook and the growing urban middle class and entrepreneurs. The other group, referred to as the 'plaine', was conservative in orientation 'preferring security through stagnation rather than progress through friction'; its base of support tended to be among the old *tzakia* families and large landowners.[28]

More important in defining Greek political culture in the second half of the nineteenth century than these loose, volatile groups were the political clubs, which sprang up in increasing numbers.[29] Clubs like the 'Korais', the 'Athanasios Diakos', and the 'Rigas' united like-thinking men and enabled more coherent political discourse to develop; they also linked Members of Parliament with the local power brokers in their constituencies.

A good example is the club 'Athanasios Diakos' based in Lamia, Phthiotis. In 1875, this club had 59 members: 25 lawyers, 30 large landowners, and four physicians. The group was 'plaine' in orientation and so their leader Konstantinos Diovouniotis, whom they got elected in three successive elections, was a follower of Dimitrios Voulgaris. Diovouniotis was client to Voulgaris, seeking from him perks and privileges; Diovouniotis in turn answered to the members of his club by looking out for their interests; the members of the club shared their leader's ideology and promised their support by mobilizing votes.

The large landowner, Nikolaos Papaleksis, for example, in 1885 guaranteed at least 350 votes for his patron; how he could make such a boast was simple: that was the number of agricultural labourers employed on his large currant plantation near Olympia.[30] The implication was clear. Those of his workers who did not vote as he instructed them would soon be looking for other employment. Intimidation, extortion, and other strong-arm tactics made up what was referred to as the 'system' through which powerful men created their factions.[31]

In urban areas, artisans' associations and merchants' guilds, like the Athens-based Guild of Green Grocers, also provided vehicles for political acculturation and acted as vehicles for mobilizing electoral support. Out of this patchwork of clubs and guilds, political factions were formed and parliamentary democracy practiced under the 1864 Constitution.

In spite of the changes, the political system was deeply flawed. An examination of the period 1865–1875 shows these defects clearly. During that decade there were seven general elections, and more importantly, 18 different administrations: the longest lasted 20 months and the shortest a mere 14 days! The difficulty was that King George had the power to appoint or dismiss ministers, and so he could create or collapse administrations at will. If a key piece of legislation became blocked or if the budget failed to pass, the monarch dissolved the government. Political leaders constantly juggled a variety of demands in order to keep their fragile ruling coalitions together.

Most importantly, since the King could appoint as Prime Minister whomsoever he desired, men with only a handful of MPs supporting them were asked to form governments, and conversely, the leader of the largest group of members might find himself denied the leadership of the chamber. This was a recipe for political gridlock as well as a mockery of the democratic process.

In 1874, a 37 year old politician addressed the problem of gridlock and set himself on the path to becoming one of the most important leaders in the history of modern Greece. Harilaos Trikoupis was born in the same year that the nation was formed, 1832. He was, then, a 'new man', born into the first generation after the War of Independence. Trikoupis came from a prominent family and he spent the first 13 years of his life in England. Fluent in English (throughout his life his Greek was heavily accented) and western educated, he firmly believed that, in order to modernize, Greece had to emulate the countries of western Europe.

Trikoupis rose politically as a follower of Alexander Koumoundouros, the leader of the liberal 'montaigne', and he was appointed foreign minister by his patron in 1866. He entered the political fray on his own with the publication in 1874 of his anonymous article 'Who Is To Blame?' in the newspaper *Kairoi*, in which he examined the causes of Greece's political turmoil. The response to his rhetorical question was manifestly evident to him: it was the King who was to blame by not appointing only majority governments. In the firestorm that followed the article's publication and Trikoupis's subsequent arrest for treason when his identity as the author became known, King George eventually relented and recognized the principle of *dedilomeni*. By so doing the King agreed that in future he would ask only the leader of the declared majority of Members of Parliament to form a government. If no one could obtain the pledged support of a plurality, then the King would dissolve Parliament and call for a general election.[32]

The ramifications of the new policy were far-reaching. In the last 25 years of the nineteenth century, there were only seven general elections and much greater stability of administrations. Greater continuity of governance was the result. Two figures, Trikoupis and his conservative rival Theodoros Deliyiannis,

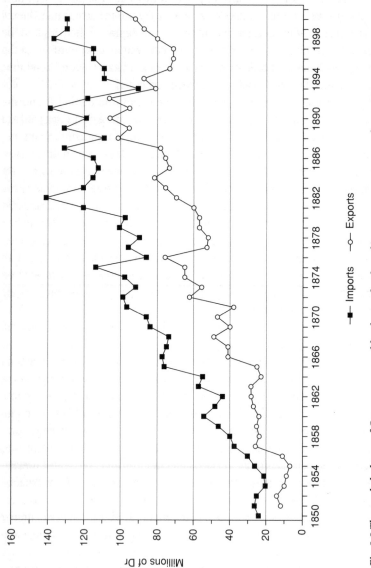

Fig. 3.2 The trade balance of Greece measured by the total value of imports versus exports from 1850 to 1900.

—■— Imports   —○— Exports

dominated Greek political life in last few decades of the nineteenth century. But it was Trikoupis more than any other who shaped the age and made it into an era of reform.

Trikoupis was utterly convinced that in order for Greece to become a 'modern' state it needed to develop economically and to become more liberal socially. For reasons discussed in the next chapter, it had also to be strengthened militarily. During his nearly continuous term of office in the 1880s, he set about the task of reforming and modernizing Greece. His reforms can be divided into two groups, economic and social.[33]

The Greek economy perennially operated with a trade deficit and the economy fluctuated widely in its performance, due in large part to its linkage to the more advanced economic systems of Europe, especially Britain and France.[34] Figure 3.2 depicts the balance of trade between 1850 and 1900. Even during the decade of the 1880s when Trikoupis enacted his reforms and we can see a marked growth in the export sector, imports still ran far in excess of exports. Greece imported both manufactured products and basic foodstuffs, in particular food grains. The major Greek export commodities were currant grapes and olive products, making the agricultural sector the backbone of the economy. Through the nineteenth century Greece remained a nation of agriculturalists. Roughly 75 per cent of the adult male population was involved in agriculture, fishing or forestry in 1870; the figure fell slowly but steadily through to the end of the century to the figure of 62 per cent in 1907. There were two countervailing forces at work in the Greek agricultural sector, and both inhibited economic development.

Since the War of Independence there had been a constant clamour among the peasantry for land redistribution. At issue was the disposition of the formerly Ottoman-held land and monastic properties. Otto had attempted a variety of land reform schemes over the years. Between 1835 and 1857, under the land dotation programme of 1835, individual household heads had purchased nearly 20,000 hectares. Two additional laws in 1871 attempted to rectify the deficiencies of the previous programmes and accelerated the distribution of national lands.[35] All of the land allotment schemes had drawbacks, and land redistribution remained a major issue into the twentieth century.

One result of the land allotment schemes was to establish a large number of small family farmers whose productive aims were focused on self-sufficiency rather than marketability. As studies of the Greek peasantry have shown and as I shall discuss in more detail in Chapter 5, subsistence security rather than profits made them risk averse. Consequently, one very large sector of the rural economy participated only marginally in the market as either buyers or sellers, and so offered little prospect of economic growth. The other result of the land dotation schemes was the formation of large agricultural estates or plantations. These were formed through manipulation of the land allotment laws and through foreclosures and expropriation of peasant families. In the western Peloponnesos, the Ionian Islands, and Thessaly (after 1882), large estates producing export commodities, especially currants, were worked by tenants and/or hired labour. This was the only sector that offered any hope of sustained growth, but as we shall see reliance on monocropped export items was to prove a very precarious base.[36]

Trikoupis focused his economic reforms on facilitating the growth of the export sector. He hoped to reduce overhead costs by expanding the transportation network. New roads, railroads, and harbour works were to allow for the more rapid movement of goods from the countryside to the cities and the ports. In addition the cultivable area of Greece was to be expanded through the drainage of waterlogged areas like the Kopais Basin. The Korinth Canal, begun under the Roman Emperor Nero, was at last to be completed, speeding up greatly travel time from the Aegean to the Adriatic. The transition from sail to steam allowed for larger cargoes delivered at cheaper prices. Between 1875 and 1895, steamship tonnage under Greek ownership rose from 8241 tons to 144 975.[37] Industrialization also developed under the paternal eye of the Trikoupis government. Between 1875 and 1900, the average number of workers per manufacturing establishment went from 45 to 71, and steam horsepower increased by over 250 per cent. Much of this growth centred in the textile trade.[38] Trikoupis's reforms facilitated economic development, but at a cost.

Echoing back to Korais, Trikoupis believed in advancement through education and under his tutelage public education was greatly expanded: the number of university students between 1860 and 1900 rose from 1,100 to 3,300, boys attending high school went from 6,000 to 24,000; boys enrolled in primary schools increased from 44,000 to 178,000 and girls from a mere 8,000 to over 82,000.[39] In addition to direct legislation, Trikoupis helped to foster a new cultural climate. During the latter part of the nineteenth century a bourgeois culture developed, self-consciously drawing on western trends in dress, architecture, art and manners. Part of becoming western was to look the part. It was indeed a time of change.[40]

The single greatest challenge facing Trikoupis and his administrations was how to finance their programmes of reform.[41] Like his predecessors he had to chart a treacherous course between the need to raise revenues and the danger of strangling economic growth in the process. Foreign debt was the engine that drove his reform programme. Between 1879 and 1890 six major foreign loans were arranged totalling 630,000,000 drachmas; by 1887, 40 per cent of total government expenditure went to servicing the national debt. Internally, sources of revenue that did not have a direct deleterious impact on one sector of society or another were simply not available. In the end Trikoupis had to tax the Greek populace heavily in order to pay the bills. He levied taxes on wine, tobacco, sheep, goats, oxen, and donkeys; the tithe on all agricultural produce was increased, as was the tax on land holdings. He established state monopolies on salt and matches, and the prices of both soared. High import tariffs raised revenues and prices but failed to abate the people's appetite for foreign goods. Export duties consequently had to be raised on precisely those commodities that formed the economy's lifeblood. The impact of Trikoupis's fiscal policies on the average Greek citizen was profoundly negative. And still the debt grew. Figure 3.3 presents a diachronic view of the government revenue surpluses and deficits between 1850 and 1900. The sustained deficits evident through the 1880s caused the collapse of the 1890s.[42]

The Greek economy had been buoyed up for some time by the rapid expansion of the international market in currants following the phylloxera epidemic that had destroyed many of the vineyards of France, Spain, and Italy. Through the 1870s and especially during the 1880s Greek exports of currants soared as prices on the international market rose. Cultivation expanded as demand grew. So long as these conditions lasted the precarious position of the public exchequer could be maintained, but in 1893 the bottom fell out of the Greek economy. Currant prices plummeted and debt mounted.[43] Trikoupis retired from public life and his successors, both from the right and from the left of his own party, opted for polices which only aggravated the situation to the point that in 1893 Greece was bankrupt.

The worst, however, was yet to come. With his old rival driven off the political stage, Theodoros Deliyiannis had the spotlight all to himself. Like many a politician before and after him, when faced with a restive populace and hard economic times, Deliyiannis played the nationalist card. Tensions were rising in both Crete and Macedonia and huge street rallies were held to demonstrate the public's support for the liberation movements there. I discuss the background to the Cretan revolution of 1896 in detail in the next chapter. What needs to be appreciated here is that the elevation in nationalist senti-ments gave Deliyiannis an opportunity to deflect criticism of his administra-tion for its economic policies. When fighting broke out on Crete, the *National Association*, a secret society dedicated to the Megali Idea, sent arms, men and supplies. Sultan Abdul Hamid II demanded that Greece cease and desist its activities in both areas. Unadvisedly, with dreams of territorial gains both to the north and the south, Greece mobilized for war. The ill-fated war began on 17 April 1897 and lasted for only 30 days. The Greek army under the leadership of Crown-Prince Konstantine was routed as the Turkish forces took Thessaly

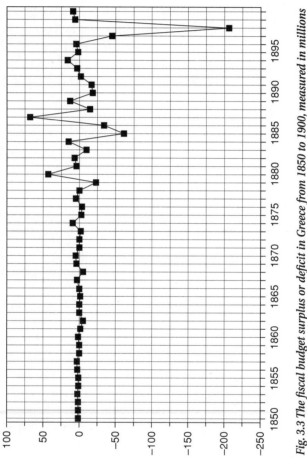

Fig. 3.3 The fiscal budget surplus or deficit in Greece from 1850 to 1900, measured in millions of drachmas.

and stood poised to march unopposed on Athens. Timely and forceful intervention by England and France prevented a total collapse, and even managed to salvage Greece from complete disaster. In the end, Greece lost little territory but had to pay a large war indemnity, which only compounded the kingdom's already terrible financial situation. This was not, however, just a defeat. This was a humiliation. With the debacle of 1897, the age of reform had come to an end. In spite of all the beneficial changes enacted during the previous 25 years, changes that left an indelible mark on the development of Greece, at the turn of the century Greece stood on the verge of collapse.

4 Constructing the Modern Nation

Irredentism, nationalism and identity in nineteenth-century Greece

> The Greek kingdom is not the whole of Greece, but only a part, the smallest and poorest part. Autochthon [indigenous] then is not only someone who lives within this Kingdom, but also one who lives in Ioannina, in Thessaly, in Serrres, in Adrianople, in Constantinople, in Terbizond, in Crete, in Samos ... in general every inhabitant of land which is Hellenic historically and ethnically .... The struggle did not begin in 1821; it began the day after the fall of Constantinople; [freedom] fighters were not simply those of 1821; fighters were and are always those continuing the struggle against the crescent for 400 years.[1]

No account of the development of Greece during the nineteenth century can be complete without an examination of foreign policy and the role of the *Megali Idea* in shaping it. In spite of all the factionalism and the multitude of regional differences and identities that continued to characterize the new kingdom, one thing that increasingly united the vast majority of its inhabitants was the ideology of irredentism. The War of Independence had been fought on the ideal of liberation of all Greeks in the Ottoman Empire and their inclusion in a Greek nation-state. As we saw, in the end only a fraction of ethnic Greeks dwelling in a small part of the eastern Mediterranean were constituted as the new state (Fig. 4.1). Even before the prominent politician Ioannis Kolettis gave coherence and vision to the irredentist ideal, moves had been made to continue the struggle to redeem the remaining 'Greek' lands. All foreign relations during the nineteenth century were in one way or another viewed through the lens of the irredentist dream called the *Megali Idea*.[2] Moreover, the very identity of the nation and the development of the state both became bound up in the ideology. Identity, nationalism, and irredentism,

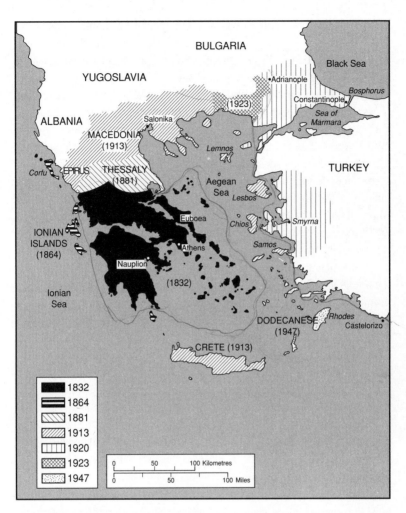

Fig. 4.1 The expansion of Greece from 1821 to the present.

then, formed an essential core that influenced almost every aspect of the development of Greece during the nineteenth century.

THE MEGALI IDEA AND THE STRUGGLE FOR TERRITORIAL EXPANSION

The so-called Arta-Lamia line that formed the northern border of the kingdom was an artificial demarcation that delineated no meaningful boundaries. Geographically, it did not follow along any topographical features that would have created a readily visible division between north and south; rather, it cut across some important ones. Nor did it conform to any significant cultural boundaries; instead, it divided groups, like the Vlachs and the Sarakatsanoi, some of them residing on the Ottoman side and others on the Greek side of the border. Not surprisingly the frontier region became a zone of contention.

As we saw earlier, the cessation of official hostilities left many warlords and their men in great difficulties. Some found themselves on the Greek side of the border where they confronted a hostile government that was refusing to recompense them for their efforts during the war and that was now making them unemployed. Many returned to their brigand ways. Others who had fought on the Hellenic side but whose homelands remained part of the Ottoman Empire had to submit to their Moslem lords, or face the executioner, or take flight as outlaws. Banditry flourished on both sides of the border, but was especially troublesome on the Greek side. Turkish officials also turned to a past practice and employed some of the bandit gangs to be the police and the border guards. The Greek government followed suit and frequently hired prominent bandit chiefs and their followers to be the national guards.[3]

In addition to the movements of brigands through the fluid frontier zones, there were the transhumant shepherds whose annual movements from mountain pastures to lowland fields constantly compelled them to violate the border – or else to pay hefty duties to the border guards for legal passage. Caravanners and merchants also preferred to smuggle their goods across the frontier, and to ensure their safety they often hired armed guards. The result of these developments was the paramilitarization of the frontier zone. Given that most Greeks believed that the border artificially separated them from their Hellenic brethren to the north, the area became a flashpoint for further nationalist conflicts in pursuit of the irredentist dream.[4]

As early as the late 1830s, Greek nationalist secret societies were actively hatching plots to foment rebellion in Thessaly, Epiros and southern Macedonia, taking advantage of conditions along the frontier. An opportunity presented itself in 1840. The Porte was facing an internal crisis with Mohamet Ali of Egypt. His imminent invasion of Syria occupied all of the Sultan's attention. With the tacit backing of Athens and the direct support of some key political figures, Captain Ioannis Valentzas, a well-known bandit/border guard, led a force of men across the border into Thessaly. The hope was that the oppressed Christian population would rise up and join them. At the same time, a group of monks were to lead a rebellion on Mount Athos and a Greek bandit chieftain named Karatasos led an attack on Thessaloniki.

Since some of the leaders of the insurgents were closely tied to the palace in Athens and to the Greek political elite, it was impossible for the government to deny plausibly that there was no official support for their activities. When the Great Powers demanded that the rebel activities cease or the much-needed loans that had been promised to Greece would vanish, Otto, though a supporter of irredentism, found himself in a difficult position.[5] The young Bavarian had no choice but to relent and thus his popularity with the people began to suffer. This episode helped contribute to the constitutional revolution of 1843. It also demonstrated how vulnerable the Greek irredentist cause was to the dictates of the Great Powers.[6]

The Russio–Turkish War of 1853 and the Crimean War, which grew out of it, presented Greece with its first real opportunity to gain territory from the Ottoman Empire. The early stages of the war saw successive Russian victories, and as discussed previously, Otto seized the chance to join the fray verbally and to turn a blind eye once again to the activities of the outlaws and the national guard; to the end, he remained reluctant to commit contingents from the regular army. The nation firmly believed that the year 1853, marking as it did the 400th anniversary of the fall of Constantinople, was a propitious one for the restoration of a 'Greater Greece'. And so they girded for war.

Between 4,000 and 5,000 armed warriors had already infiltrated well into Thessaly, Epiros and Macedonia, and they were able to generate sufficient popular support to lay siege to the town of Arta and even to threaten the walls of Ioannina. The intervention of France and Britain on the side of the Porte led to Otto's humiliating need to recall all of the forces and break off the struggle. Yet again, the cause of Greek irredentism was sacrificed on the altar of Great Power political expediency.[7] Moreover, this proved to be the case even when the Megali Idea met with success.

Greece's first major territorial gains on the continent came in 1881 with the acquisition of Thessaly and Arta. The irony was that these additions came about inadvertently rather than through the aggressive action of Greek governments. The change of dynasties and the adjustments to the political system had had little or no impact on popular nationalism. As we shall see shortly, the middle decades of the century witnessed the crystallization and dissemination of a more uniform Hellenic identity. An even more radically expansive view of the Hellenic ecumene accompanied it.[8]

At the same time, during the 1870s Greek attention was increasingly focused on developments in the Balkans to the north. In the wake of the Cretan revolution (see below) and the expansion of more militant nationalist movements among various groups in the Balkans, the Porte attempted to play the game of divide and rule. A major initiative along this line was the creation in 1870 of an autocephalous Bulgarian Orthodox Church lead by an Exarch. The establishment of a Bulgarian Exarchate accelerated the process of

Bulgarian nationalism. It also created tensions and competing interests between Serbia and Greece, and between them and the Bulgarian nationalists. Greece was also compelled to reassess its relationship with Russia because Pan-Orthodoxy, the idea which had previously been the rationale of Russian interest in the region, came to be replaced by Pan-Slavism: the former included Greece, the latter did not.

Greece, then, was not overly enthusiastic about joining with Serbs and Montenegrans in the summer of 1876 when they declared war on the Porte. Russian intervention in the face of Serbian defeat led to a change in Greek policy. Fearful of being left out of the settlement if the Russians were victorious and cognizant of the growth of anti-Turk sentiment in Britain over the 'Bulgarian Horrors', Athens had to adopt a more aggressive policy. This was a case as well of a government following the lead of their people. Greek popular opinion was overwhelmingly in favour of direct action.

Revolutionary societies, the most important of which was the National Defence, funded by domestic and diasporic merchants, artisans and labourers, channelled money and materials to the frontier. Irregulars under the command of recently decommissioned regular army officers streamed into Thessaly, Epiros and Macedonia. The following passage from a field correspondent for the *London Times* vividly captures the nature of the guerrilla tactics of the Greek forces:

> The mode of warfare adopted by the insurgents is the only one suited to the circumstances. It is necessary to them to economise men and to avoid the disheartening effect of a decided defeat. The object kept in view is not so much the defeat of the Turkish army as the expulsion from the land of the machinery of the Ottoman Government and the affording an opportunity to the inhabitants to express their true sentiments. They should, and generally do, strike no blow without a fair chance of gaining some tangible strategical or political advantage. The Greeks, with few exceptions, have no idea of fighting in the open. They are too intelligent to stand up and be shot at; and this, with the political considerations already mentioned, determines the nature of the tactics which they have recourse to. They keep to mountains, descending into the plain only to capture Turkish convoys of provisions – an operation which they effect with great success, even under the castle. Posted on the heights, behind rocks and breastworks of loose

stones, they fire with deliberate aim at the advancing battalions, and retire with scarcely any loss before they can be surrounded. However strong a village may be, they never occupy it, but take up positions on the surrounding heights, to avoid, as they express it, being taken as rats in their holes. In this way the defence is sometimes successful, sometimes not; but it is never disastrous. The Turkish troops shut up in a few towns are massed from time to time for the attack of some position held by the insurgents. The strategical disposition is often good, and they advance in overwhelming numbers; but the only result is that their losses are in overwhelming proportion to those of the enemy. That which is technically a victory becomes practically a defeat; and the work of suppression has to be begun over and over again.[9]

In Thessaly and Epiros, guerrilla tactics proved remarkably successful in tying down considerable numbers of Turkish troops and they effectively laid siege to the larger garrison towns by completely dominating the countryside. Moreover, unlike during earlier incursions, the masses of Greek and other Christian peasants rose up and joined in the fray. Wherever the Greek forces drove the Ottoman troops, they immediately set up free local governments. As the nineteenth century observer Lewis Sergeant noted, this practice more than anything else influenced the Great Powers into making territorial concessions:

The thing [restoration of the liberated zones to the Ottoman authorities] was physically, as well as morally, impossible. The Turkish system was destroyed throughout the provinces affected by the wars of 1876–8. The valis, the mutessarifs, the caimakans, the mudirs, had fled, or had been driven away; the whole civil administration of the vilayets, the whole military organization and the police of the country, so far as Turkish authority is concerned, were at an end. Not a pasha, not a bey, not a zaptieh, could return to his post and resume the power which he was wont to exercise.[10]

The uprisings in Macedonia, however, were not faring as well. Not only were the Greek forces up against better-trained Ottoman troops, but the complexity of the situation among the local Christian population complicated matters significantly. In February 1878, following in the wake of the successes of the irregulars in Thessaly and the uncertainty of the situation in Macedonia, King George gave Prime Minister Alexandros Koumoundouros the go-ahead to launch an invasion of Thessaly by the regular army. Unfortunately, the pace of events elsewhere had overtaken them. Shortly after the Greek mobilization, an armistice was declared between Russia and Turkey. If official Greek troops had occupied the liberated territories, then Greece would have been in a stronger position at the bargaining table. As it was, Greece nearly came away from the war with nothing.[11]

The subsequent Treaty of San Stefano left Greece out of the picture when a 'Greater Bulgaria', which included Macedonia and Thrake, was formed. Greeks and Serbs felt betrayed by Russia. Fortunately, the other Great Powers, in particular Great Britain and Austria, were also most displeased with the settlement. Diplomatic machinations continued until three months later a new conference was called by Otto von Bismarck and a new treaty negotiated. Greek diplomats and the King lobbied strenuously for Greek interests, while sabre-rattling in Athens continued in the background. Turkish intransigence to the Berlin Treaty led to greater pressure being placed on the Porte by the Great Powers.

Finally, in 1881, a bilateral agreement between the Sultan and Greece was reached. The territories where the Greek forces had been most successful and where they had liberated territories, Thessaly and southern Epiros (the area around the city Arta), were ceded to the Hellenic Kingdom. A major step toward realization of the *Megali Idea* had been taken with the addition of approximately 213,000 square kilometres of territory and 294,000 people. The diplomatic victory was marred in the public's view because the section of Epiros given to Greece did not include the capital city of Ioannina, no sections of Macedonia were included, and the great Greek island of Crete remained outside of the national fold. For the remainder of the century the irredentist struggle focused on these unredeemed regions.

THE CRETAN AND MACEDONIAN QUESTIONS

The story of the struggle for the liberation and incorporation of Crete into the nation-state of Greece began during the 1821 rebellion. Cretan Christians had joined their fellow members of the Millet-i Rum across the sea in the uprising and had been largely successful in the fighting against the Ottoman forces on the island. The tide turned, however, when Ibrahim Pasha invaded the island as part of his plan for the invasion of the Peloponnesos. The Porte was adamant that Crete not should be included in the new Greek kingdom, and the Great Powers agreed. The Sultan then granted the island to Mohamet Ali of Egypt as a reward for his efforts during the war.

Egypt ruled the Christian population harshly and intercommunal relations on the island remained very tense. Taking advantage of Mohamet Ali's uprising against the Sultan in 1839 and his consequent fall from grace, a delegation of Cretan leaders petitioned the Great Powers for *enosis*, or union, with Greece. Their plea fell on ears deafened by the dictates of nineteenth-century super-power politics. The Ottoman authorities instituted a number of reforms aimed at addressing some of the most pressing demands of the Christian population, but nothing they could do dampened the unionist movement.[12]

On 3 August 1866, the general assembly of Cretan leaders met at the village of Apokorona. A force of 14,000 Turkish and Egyptian troops confronted them and demanded capitulation. Shots were fired from the Turkish ranks. Seeing no other choice, the Cretans returned fire. In this manner, the first of three Cretan revolutions was begun. Crete is the second largest island in the Mediterranean and since antiquity it has been eagerly sought by any power with pretensions to control the region. Consequently, as the Eastern Question took on increased prominence in Great Power international relations during the second half of the nineteenth century, so did the status of Crete become more problematic. The island was simply too important strategically for it to fall into the hands of any of the Great Powers, though the British in particular sought to be the island's 'protector' on numerous occasions. Ceding the island to Greece would, it was argued, have brought war to the region. The solution repeatedly opted for was to leave it in the hands of the Sultan, but to ensure that the lot of the Orthodox population was improved.

In the 1860s matters came to a head for a number of reasons. First, the successful 'Risorgimento' of Italy, and the Great Power acquiescence in it, raised hopes that a similar unification of Greece would also find favour. Second, in 1864, Great Britain had ceded the Ionian Islands to the Kingdom of Greece after having occupied them for almost 50 years; if they could be united with the motherland, why not Crete, many argued. Third, the Orthodox population had been steadily growing as the Moslem population declined so that by 1866 the former outnumbered the latter by 200,000 to 62,000. More-over, nationalist sentiments among this group were also rising. Fifth, the government of Dimitrios Voulgaris in Athens was whispering to the leaders on Crete that assistance was assured, and as tensions mounted even King George let it be known that he was prepared to lend moral and material support. For all of these reasons, the time seemed ripe for rebellion.

The rebellion on Crete took on the contours of a guerrilla war. From their mountain strongholds, the Cretan rebels and their Greek supporters pledged 'to fatten the eagles of the White Mountains [of central Crete] on the bodies of Turkish Pashas and Beys ...'.[13] Unchecked they roamed the wilder regions of the island with impunity while Ottoman forces focused their attentions on the towns and villages. In many ways, this conflict resembled the one in Thessaly we discussed earlier. Volunteer brigades formed in Greece and street demonstrations drew thousands of Athenians from their homes. Men, material, and money were collected and sent to Crete with the active encouragement of the government. Initially, the rebels were extremely successful, inflicting approximately 20,000 casualties in the first year of fighting. Since the Turkish and Egyptian forces could not engage the insurgents in open battle, they took out their ire on the civilian population. The reports of atrocities, and in particular the self-immolation of over 400 men, women and children in the besieged monastery of Arkadi on 21 October 1866, aroused great sympathy in Europe and the United States. But once again the hard realities of Great Power politics were to prove cold comfort to the cause of Greek irredentism.

Other groups in the Balkans, in particular the Serbs under Prince Michael Obrenovic, sought to gain advantage and so made demands on the Porte for concessions. This led to extensive bilateral negotiations between Greece and Serbia that resulted in the signing on 26 August 1867 of a treaty with 17 clauses, the most important of which dealt with the size of the military contingents each side would provide in the event of war with the Ottoman Empire, the territories each side would acquire if the war was won, and the formation of confederated states in some areas if necessary. Russia was also using the pretext of the Cretan rebellion to extend its influence in the Balkans. This served to heighten Franco–British sensitivities and pushed them toward adopting measures to maintain the status quo.

By early 1869, the military tide was turning as the Ottoman fleet, through its blockade of the island, was depriving the insurgents of much needed supplies. Simultaneously, the diplomatic currents had also turned against the irredentist cause. With the assassination of Prince Michael and the continued opposition of King George, the Serbian alliance fell apart; France, Great Britain and Austria were pressuring Athens to compromise; the Sultan was threatening to declare war on Greece; the Russian Empire was adopting an ever more conciliatory tone. Finally, the volatility of the issue domestically had brought down three governments in three years. Compromise was the only solution. In the Paris peace talks of 1869 it was agreed that Crete would remain part of the Ottoman Empire but that there would be significant changes in how the islanders were to be governed and in their legal status within the

Sultan's domain. The reform package was referred to as the 'Organic Laws'. Cretan unification, however, remained a key issue for the next 40 years.

An uneasy calm had reigned on Crete from the late 1860s.[14] There had been periodic outbursts of nationalist agitation, particularly during the 1877–8 wars in the Balkans, discussed previously. Nonetheless, the expanded scope for local rule awarded to the Christian population in the wake of the first Cretan revolution had eased tensions somewhat. The so-called Halepa pact of 1878 had addressed many of the Cretans' grievances and had provided for much local autonomy. It was the erosion of those powers in the 1890s that brought revolution to the island once again. In 1895, for example, the Porte announced the suspension of all civil liberties for the Christian population. As civil unrest escalated, reports of atrocities began to be circulated. Then in 1896 the Cretans rose in open rebellion once more.

The news sent shockwaves through Athens. Secret nationalist groups like the *Ethniki Etaireia* (Nationalist Society) collected money and arms and men to aid the rebellion. Mired in economic turmoil, the rebellion provided the hard-pressed Deliyiannis government with a means of diverting popular discontent. The nation readied for war.

Yet again, however, the issue lay in the hands of the Great Powers. But at this juncture the configuration of national interests among them had shifted. The German Empire had decidedly thrown its weight behind the Porte as had, increasingly, Austria. Russia was still keen to take advantage of any Ottoman reversals so long as doing so did not threaten their influence in the Slavic areas. Britain and France looked warily at any moves that changed the balance of power in the region and so threatened their vital trading interest.

Active Greek support for the Cretan rebellion elevated tensions between Athens and the Porte and, as we saw earlier, ended with the disastrous 1897 war. In the broad settlement that ended that conflict Crete's status was changed. It was to become an autonomous polity under the sovereignty of the Ottoman Empire, but governed by a High Commissioner, Prince George of Greece, and a chamber of Christian and Moslem deputies. In Chapter 6, we shall examine in more detail the period of Prince George's limited rule.

No issue more dominated Balkan foreign relations during the last decades of the nineteenth century than Macedonia. The definition of the region referred to as Macedonia in modern times defies precise delineation (Preface and Fig. 4.1). Under Ottoman rule it did not constitute a single administrative district, but instead was composed of three Vilayets: Thessaloniki, Monastir and Uskub (Kossovo). Delineating its geographical boundaries is also difficult because there are no topographical features that create a single coherent unit. As a working definition, we could define Macedonia geographically as the territory bounded on its western side by Lakes Ochrid and Prespa, the Shar, Rila and Rhodope Mountains and the Crna Gora to the north, the river Nestos (Metsa) to the east and the Pindos Mountains, Mount Olimbos and the Aegean Sea to the south. But we need to bear in the mind that the area thus defined contained a variety of different geographical regions.

Neither was there a single cultural or ethnic group, the distribution of which we could employ to demarcate an area as constituting Macedonia. For centuries the region was home to Jews, Moslems, and Orthodox Christians, to Ladino, Greek, Serbian and Rumanian speakers. Many and diverse were the groups that made up the 'Macedonian Salad' of the nineteenth century.[15]

What is incontrovertible is that the region, however loosely defined, is one of the most important in the Balkans. Macedonia contains some of the richest farmland in a part of the world where arable land is at a premium. Geographically it is the southern gateway into the Balkans, and thence into Central Europe. Macedonia also stands at the crossroads of the major overland communication routes that link Asia and Europe. The region was home to one of the most important commercial and manufacturing centres in the eastern Mediterranean – Thessaloniki. In addition to this jewel of the east, there were other towns of economic importance in their own right, such as Florina, Monastir, Edessa, and Kozani. From antiquity to the present, then, Macedonia has been one of the most important regions in the eastern Mediterranean.

At the time of the war of liberation in 1821, some Greek leaders fervently hoped that when the war was won, the resulting state would have Macedonia as a core region and that Constantinople would be the new polity's capital, or if that city could not be liberated, then the honour would have fallen to Thessaloniki. Such was not to be. Though many in the region participated in the rebellion, at the war's end there was never any serious possibility of Macedonia being included in the settlement. Through the middle years of the century there were bouts of unrest, usually related to the operation of Greek bands in the border zone between Greece and the Empire, but none of them posed a serious threat to Ottoman suzerainty over the region.

There were, nonetheless, some important developments during this period. The first was the accelerated economic development of Thessaloniki. The city grew dramatically in size, the volume of commercial traffic through the port increased substantially, and industrialization commenced. The second was the increased migration of Greeks from the kingdom into the region; some of these were peasants in search of land and others were irregulars in search of booty. Almost all of them were imbued with the spirit of Greek irredentism. Tension between Greek and Slavic speaking groups escalated. One reflection of this was the numerous petitions by Slavic community leaders to the Patriarch and the

Porte for permission to have the Bulgarian language used in church. These overtures were rebuffed until 1870.

In that year, a firman from the Sultan created a Bulgarian Church called the Exarchate, and it further stipulated that the Exarchate leadership could establish a church in any community in which two-thirds of the people professed allegiance to the new organization. Along with the new churches, of course, would come new Bulgarian-speaking schools. Shortly thereafter, the Orthodox Patriarch responded by declaring the new church schismatic. A battle was now under way for the hearts and minds of Macedonian Christians between the Exarchate, the Patriarchate, and in some areas, the Serbian Orthodox Church. Across the region, people were being forced to choose between one of the rival churches, and it was through making that choice that they began to espouse a specific ethnic identity. The stakes of making such a decision soon got much higher.

We discussed the Russo–Turkish war of the late 1870s earlier in this chapter, focusing our attention in particular on the role of the Greek irregulars in Thessaly and Epiros. The war, however, had a much greater scope than just that theatre of operations. Massive uprisings also occurred in Serbia, Bulgaria and Macedonia. The treaty of San Stefano, which not only created an autonomous principality of Bulgaria but also included in it the lion's share of Macedonia, shook the Greek world. The revised settlement imposed by the subsequent Treaty of Berlin restored most of southern Macedonia to the Ottoman Empire. But it also served to escalate the struggled between the rival Christian nationalist movements.

Pavlos Melas, a prominent Greek nationalist who lost his life fighting in Macedonia, captured the feeling of many of his compatriots when he stated that Macedonia constituted the lungs of the body of the Greek nation: without it, Hellenism would expire.[16] Over the last two decades of the nineteenth century, fierce rivalries developed between partisan groups like the Greek nationalist *Ethniki Etaireia* and the pro-Bulgarian and Macedonian groups such as the International Macedonian Revolutionary Organization (IMRO). In a struggle over culture, language and identity, each side sought to 'Hellenize' or 'Slavicize' inhabitants of the region. They endeavoured to establish as many areas as possible in which they could claim that their group predominated numerically. Maps could then be produced that showed the spatial distribution of ethnic groups and this would strengthen each side's claim to the area.[17]

Recent studies have demonstrated that the process of identity formation in Macedonia was complex and which of the competing identities a person subscribed to was based on a variety of factors.[18] Given the intensity of emotions that accompanied this struggle, it is not surprising that violence often erupted. Open conflict between the rival bands became even more prevalent and the level of violence inflicted on the local communities became even more horrific after 1897.

The Greek Kingdom's disastrous war against the Ottoman Empire and the shifting currents of Great Power foreign policy positions opened a window of opportunity for the pro-Bulgarian and pro-independence groups in Macedonia, and they were quick to seize on it. IMRO and exarchist bands stepped up the level and intensity of their efforts to 'win over' areas to their side. After his appointment as metropolitan bishop of Kastoria in 1900, Germanos Karavengelis spearheaded the efforts of the Greek patriarchists to confront them. The situation on the ground, however, cannot be seen as simply a struggle between patriarchists versus exarchists. There were divisions among the exarchist groups over whether there should be an independent Macedonia or one attached to Bulgaria, and this split occasionally erupted into open conflict. Among the patriarchists, there were some whose vision of Hellenism was shaped by perceptions emanating from the Patriarch in Istanbul, while others were wedded to a view coming from Athens. Albanian nationalist groups were also rising up in arms and their activities added an additional complicating factor. The final player was, of course, the police and military forces of the Ottoman Empire. The conflict, then, was many-sided and the fighting, conducted largely by guerrilla bands, was fierce. Purported atrocities by all sides contributed to the volatility of an already explosive situation. The fighting became even more intense and widespread after an IMRO uprising in August 1903 that centred on the city of Ilinden in western Macedonia. The revolt involved both guerrilla bands and Christian peasants. After a two month-long conflict, it was brutally suppressed by Turkish troops, assisted by some Greek patriarchist bands. Fearful of a wider Balkan conflict and repulsed by the horrors of the Ilinden affair, the emperors of Austria and Russia persuaded the other Great Powers of the need to intervene. Following a meeting in October 1903, they imposed on the reluctant Porte a series of reforms known as the Mürzsteg Programme. Some of its most important aspects were the appointment of two officials, one Austrian and one Russian, to monitor the programme's implementation; the reformation of the gendarmerie whose leadership would be made up of officers from each of the Great Powers; and the redrawing of administrative boundaries to produce districts with the most ethnically homogeneous composition possible.

For a Greece scarred by the catastrophe of 1897, the conflict in Macedonia, especially after 1903, provided a source of national hope. The Greeks, as did others, misread the administrative reform of the Mürzsteg Programme as a signal that the Powers might be supportive of the division of Macedonia along ethnic lines and that this move was but a prelude to those districts' incorporation into the appropriate national state. Funds and fighters in increasing volume began to flow into Macedonia. While maintaining to the Great Powers that it was not responsible for the escalation of the conflict, the Greek government was clearly involved. Attachés and consular officers attached to the Greek embassy in Thessaloniki were instrumental in directing the activities of the Greek bands. Greek military officers and warriors who fell in the conflict, like Pavlos Melas, were elevated to the status of national heroes. At a time of national malaise, the 'Macedonian struggle' provided a focus of national unity and purpose.[19] When in 1908, however, the Committee for Union and Progress, led by a group known as the Young Turks, staged a 'revolution' in the Ottoman Empire and inaugurated a period of reform, the fighting in Macedonia subsided and the Greek dream of fulfillment of the Megali Idea in Macedonia was dashed – for the time being at least. The disappointment at this setback to the irredentist cause would contribute, as we shall see shortly (see pages 116–18), to a major political upheaval within Greece.

Understanding a state's foreign policy over any length of time is always difficult and requires simplification of complex realities. In the case of Greece during the nineteenth century, the Megali Idea formed a type of ideological core that implicitly or explicitly shaped foreign policy decisions. Greco–Turkish relations could never be 'normalized' until the question of the unredeemed was solved. The issue clouded all aspects of interaction between the two – political, diplomatic, and economic. Greek attitudes toward nationalist movements to the north were formed on the basis of their effect on Greek irredentism. Relations between the Great Powers also ebbed and flowed depending on the needs and dictates of the Megali Idea. No other issue exerted as great an influence on the development of the Greek state and society during the nineteenth century, and by that era's end the dream of a 'Greater Greece' seemed more distant than ever.

NATIONALISM AND IDENTITY

One of the most 'remarkable achievements of modern Greece is to have forged in a relatively short period of time – let us say one hundred and fifty years – an extremely cohesive nation state of which Greek national identity, despite all political cleavages, is the cornerstone. And it has forged this out of what was geographically, historically, culturally, linguistically and up to a point even religiously, a diverse population whose allegiances and loyalties up until the beginning for the nineteenth century were small-scale and localized'.[20]

Before the war of liberation, there really was no Greek national con-sciousness. As we saw earlier, there was an awareness, either acute or vague depending on a person's station in life, of being a member of the Millet-i Rum, of being a Christian (Orthodox), and of speaking the Romaic language. But such awareness did not constitute a consciousness of being ethnically Greek. Instead, peoples' primary identity was rooted in their local village community and in the nexus of real and fictive kinship networks that bound them to others. In the remainder of this chapter we explore how a Greek national identity was forged both within the Kingdom of Greece and among the Greek communities of the Ottoman Empire.

Religion played an important but complex role in the construction of Greek national identity. From the time of the revolution, there were marked tensions between the Church, the leadership of the national liberation movement, and the people. The ideological foundation that undergirded the movement was rooted in western European Enlightenment thought, a key element of which was secularism. For thinkers such as Voltaire, for example, religion was the bastion of the *ancien régime* and was synonymous with ignorance and oppres-sion. Greek intellectuals like Adamantios Korais thus argued for the creation of a secular Greek state and for a new Greek society that drew its inspiration from the glories of pagan antiquity.

Yet the masses who rose to the banner of rebellion did so first in the name of religion and only secondarily from a sense of local grievance and discrimination. This was to be, after all, in theory at least, an uprising of the Millet-i Rum. What transpired then was a revolt based on religious divisions led primarily by liberals with the intent of creating a secular state. Another strand of tension developed when the Patriarch of the Orthodox Church and *Ethnarch* of the Christian population denounced the uprising and excommunicated its leaders.

A third level of complexity regarding Greek identity appeared during the war and this one revolved around the legacy of ancient Greece. During the long period of Ottoman domination, Renaissance Europe had appropriated the Classical age as its own legacy, seeing in fifth century Athens the primordial roots of its own civilization. It was the allure of the Classics that drew many Philhellenes to support the cause of the Greeks. Out of this situation, the roots of two opposed Greek identities thus emerged, one as 'Hellenic' that empha-sized western values that derived from antiquity and that de-emphasized the importance of Orthodoxy, and the other as 'Romioi', Roman, that emphasized the oriental characteristics and traced its roots to the Orthodox Byzantine Empire.[21]

With the establishment of the Kingdom of Greece and the enthronement of a foreign, Catholic ruler, these tensions over identity and national consciousness had to be resolved, if the new state and the 'nation' that constituted it were to endure. In other words, peasants who conceived of themselves as Christians (*Christianoi eimaste*) and speakers of Greek had to be reformed to think of themselves as members of the Hellenic nation who were both Christians and Greek-speaking. As part of this process there had to be a 'transformation of Orthodox religious identity to secular national identity'.[22] The process was neither easy nor quick, but over the course of the nineteenth century it was achieved.

There were two especially important means by which it was accomplished. One focused on the appropriation of Orthodoxy by the Greek state in such a way that the ecumenical aspect of it was downplayed, and by so doing it wedded religious identity with a Greek nationalism centred on Athens. It was from this construct that the Megali Idea emerged. The second dynamic revolved around the purposeful construction of a public culture that emphasized the Hellenic as opposed to the Romeic dimension of Greek identity. Through a process of acculturation of this ideal, Greeks began to internalize deeply an Hellenic national identity that coexisted with but took precedence over the Romeic one. Let us begin with the first dynamic.

In 1833, the Kingdom of Greece declared the Orthodox Church of Greece to be independent of the Ecumenical Patriarch in Istanbul. This was the first step toward the 'Church be[coming] an accomplice of the state in its mission to spread the cohesive nationalist creed'.[23] For the masses, however, this created a dilemma: which church was the true representative of Orthodoxy? Not surprisingly, between 1833 and 1850, when the Patriarch finally recognized the autocephalous Church of Greece as legitimate, there were numerous episodes of unrest among the peasantry in which defence of Orthodoxy played a role and there were anti-Protestant riots against foreign bible societies as well.[24] But already in the 1830s, initiatives were underway to incorporate religion into a national identity.

It was not an accident when in 1838, the government selected 25 March as the national holiday commemorating the war of liberation. That this was the day on which Archbishop Germanos raised the banner of rebellion is a perfect example of an invented tradition, since both his actions and the timing of them are open questions. But by combining the celebration of the birth of the nation with the Christian festival of the Annunciation, the bond between religion and nationalism was drawn even tighter. The day on which the announcement of the coming of Christ was made thus became now also the day on which the birth of the new nation was foretold.

The 1840s witnessed two additional key developments. The first was the revolution of 1843, discussed in the last chapter. There was a religious dimension to both its causes and consequences. Religious secret societies that espoused irredentism in the name of restoring the Orthodox Empire of the Middle Ages provided crucial support to the movement to force a constitution. Moreover, in the deliberations that shaped the new charter, the issue of the relationship between national identity and Orthodoxy was a topic of great importance. The declaration that the next king of Greece *had* to be Orthodox further tightened the connection. Henceforth, the head of state, who was also the head of the Greek Church, was expected to be Orthodox. The constitutional debates also exposed the deep division between autochthonous Greeks, those born within the territory of the kingdom, and heterochthonous ones, those born elsewhere. The new constitution privileged the former at the expense of the latter. We examined some of the reasons for this in the last chapter.

What we need to appreciate now is what this said about Greek identity. Both groups were Greek speaking and Orthodox, yet a distinction was now formally drawn over what constituted the criteria for full membership in the Hellenic nation-state. This was the context for Ioannis Kolletis's speech in which he sketched out the vision that would become the Great Idea. He was in fact repudiating the heterochthon-autochthon distinction, by arguing that the struggle for *national* liberation encompassed all Greeks inside and outside the boundaries of the current kingdom, out to the limits of the old Orthodox Byzantine Empire. But note that he also seamlessly elided the religious dimension into the idea of a Hellenic national identity.

A series of events in 1871 and 1872 symbolize, I believe, the solidification of a Hellenic national identity and definitively situated Athens as the centre of Hellenism. From the moment that Athens was selected to be the capital of the new kingdom, there had been a palpable sense that it needed to become *the* centre of Hellenism. Over time the need for it to play that role became even more urgent. In 1861, for example, the newspaper *Athena*, noted 'the capital of Greece, Athens, is the focal point and center of light and culture for two ... concentric nations, the nation of liberated Greece, and the larger nation of greater Hellenism, which is still under foreign rule.'[25] The jubilee year in the life of the Greek kingdom was 1871. The festivities planned for the celebration of the fiftieth anniversary of the start of the Revolution were to commemorate the war but also to recognize the progress that Hellenism had made over the previous decades. A central element of the celebration was to be the transportation and the interment in Athens of the body of Patriarch Gregory V. He was, you will recall, the Patriarch at the start of the Revolution who was killed during the anti-Greek pogrom in Istanbul. As historian Alexander Kitroeff observes, 'to associate the Patriarch with the commemoration of the revolution was a decision laden in irony, because the Patriarch had excommunicated the leaders of the revolution in the Peloponnesos upon hearing of the revolt in 1821'.[26] And yet in 1870 the decision was made to feature the re-interment of the cleric's body in Athens as a central element in the jubilee. The entire ceremony was redolent with symbolism. The body was transported to Greece in a Greek warship named *Byzantion*, the casket was greeted at Piraeus by the Church hierarchy who conveyed it to Athens where it was received by King George and Queen Olga. Huge crowds attended at every stage. Just as in antiquity, the re-interment of the bones of the Athenian hero Theseus symbolized the emergence of democratic Athens, so did the transportation of the bones of the Patriarch represent the emergence of Athens as the centre of modern Hellenism.

But there was an additional element to the jubilee ceremony: the wedding of Orthodoxy to the Revolution. The following year at another public ceremony, a statue of the Gregory V was unveiled at the University of Athens. It joined one of Rigas and, in 1875, one of Korais as well. Here was the 'holy' trinity of the Hellenic Revolution and revival: one who had espoused an ecumenical, secular new Greece, another who believed in secular Greece whose taproot was the Classical age, and a third who opposed the Greek Revolution. Yet in the invented tradition of nationalism, they became united as symbols of Hellenic liberation. Orthodoxy as religious identity had now been transformed definitively into a secular Greek national identity.

There were, however, other dimensions to the process of turning peasants into Greeks. A very important one was language. The so-called 'language question' in Greece has a long and contentious history, and the issue was only resolved as recently as 1976. In this section, I provide just a brief survey of it, highlighting how it relates to the formation of Greek national identity. For most of its history there has been a situation of *diglossia* in Greece. Two different versions of the same language, one spoken and the other written, existed side-by-side. At the time of independence the language spoken by Greeks was called *dimotiki* or demotic Greek. While related to ancient Greek more closely than, say, modern Italian is to Latin, it was still very different from the ancient tongue, and from the language of the Church.

Not surprisingly given that it was a living language, over the centuries Turkish, Albanian and Slavic words became incorporated into the popular spoken vernacular. Because the spoken tongue highlighted the cultural distance between modern Greeks and antiquity, particularly in the eyes of western Europeans, intellectuals like Adamantios Korais pushed for the introduction of a new, pure form of the language that would emphasize the Hellenic heritage of a liberated Greece. Some argued for the wholesale reintroduction of ancient Attic Greek as the official language of the new state.

The compromise, a language called *Katherevousa*, was a hybrid of the ancient, *koine* (the language of the New Testament and the liturgy), and demotic Greek. Katherevousa was to be the language of the new Greek state and resurrected Greek nation. It did in fact become the written language of public discourse, in government, in the newspapers, and in education. But there remained an inherent tension between it and demotic Greek. Each of them suggested a slightly different version of Greek identity, one – katharevousa – emphasized the Hellenic, the other – demotic – the Romeic. The two competing visions were not reconciled and at times led to violent clashes. Nonetheless, language played a crucial role in the invention of Greek national identity.

Related to both language and religion in this process was history. After all, all national or ethnic identities have at some point to evoke the past to give pedigree and legitimation to a group's claims to common roots. As in the other areas we have discussed so far, in the case of Greece there were two competing visions of the past – the Hellenic with its lineage ground in the Classical age, and the Romeic with the Byzantine Empire as its taproot. Greek history became a particularly contested terrain during the 1830s. In addition to all of the aspects we have analysed so far, in 1830 a new one was introduced. In that year the German philologist Jacob Fallmerayer published a study in which he claimed that the Greeks of his day were not racially descended from the ancient Greeks, but were instead Slavs. Not only did this deny to the Greeks any claim on antiquity as their heritage, but it also divorced the Byzantine Empire from it. The legacy of Classical antiquity thus belonged to the west, of which the modern Greeks were *ipso facto* not a part.

For the next few decades, Greeks responded to this challenge in a number of ways. The immediate response among historians and linguists was to mobilize data to support the idea of a connection to antiquity. Folklore studies developed in Greece as urban intellectuals scoured the countryside looking for survivals of ancient customs, practices, stories, and beliefs that resembled ones described in ancient texts. Archaeology in Greece, both by Greeks and foreigners, was called on to produce the 'symbolic capital' that demonstrated the linkage between the Greeks of 'today' and those of the distant past.[27]

These efforts did not wholly or even partially bridge the chronological gap of the Middle Ages. The historian Konstantine Paparrigopoulos accomplished that task. Starting in 1860 he published a five-volume *History of the Hellenic*

Nation from the Ancient Times Until the Modern, in which he reconciled the dual identities of the nation and gave them a historical grounding. There was, he argued, a direct and unbroken history of the Greek nation, or *ethnos,* divided into three phases – Classical, Byzantine and Modern. Each phase built upon the other. Greeks were neither eastern nor western, but both. They could legitimately lay claim to the pagan/secular and liberal legacy of ancient Greece as well as the ecumenical, Orthodox Christian one of Byzantium. 'In this manner, Paparrigopoulos delineated the modern Greek heritage. He created a unity out of the Greek past and, of equal importance, a unity of all the Greek people.'[28]

Finally, through the conscious modification of popular culture, the state and the intelligentsia facilitated the internalization by the masses of this invented Greek identity. This new vision of Hellenism was literally inscribed on to the landscape. In rebuilding the towns that had been destroyed during the Revolution, city plans were designed specifically to make the new urban areas look western. Built on a grid system and adorned with public buildings and houses in the Neoclassical style, the new towns were to give concrete form to the new Hellenic national identity by obliterating all traces of the Ottoman past and reviving the memories of the Classical past.[29] With like purpose in mind, the names of hundreds rural villages were changed from 'Slavic' or 'non-Hellenic' names to names which were 'totally' Greek.

From the 1870s onward, there was an explosion of clubs and associations. During the height of '*syllogomania'* (association-mania) as it was called at the time, numerous voluntary associations (sports clubs, reading societies, drama clubs, athletic associations, working men's clubs, etc.) developed. Some were intended explicitly to propagate the national mission; in others, furtherance of the national mission was a by-product. All of them, however, furthered the creation of unified national identity.[30] Print media and literature were called on to propagate the vision of the new national identity. Popular posters combined visual images that drew on various elements – historical, pagan mythical, and religious – that thus reinforced the central elements of the national identity. The visual arts, theatre, literature and music were implicated in one way or another in helping the craft the national identity.[31]

Lastly, and perhaps most importantly, public education became a major vehicle for transmitting this as well.[32] The history texts used in elementary schools told a simplified version of Paparrigopoulos's story of national continuity.[33] In the secondary schools, students spent more time studying ancient Greek than any other subject. Not only was nationalism embedded in the school curricula, but as Kalliataki Merticopoulou has recently shown, whether or nor parents sent their children to school was affected by their perception of the importance of education to the national cause.[34] Religious instruction was also part of school curricula.

Thus, through architecture, education, art and literature, in public festivals and celebrations, Greeks came to internalize the new national Hellenic identity that incorporated both the Hellenic and the Romeic, both the heritage of the classical world and the Orthodox Christian one. So successful was the process that, as Just, Herzfeld, and others have noted, all sense of it being an 'invention' was lost. Instead an identity grounded in 'history' became timeless and primordial. As a popular expression has it, 'we have always been Greeks'.

5 Greek Society in the Nineteenth and Early Twentieth Centuries

Greek society underwent many profound changes during the nineteenth century. There were, however, substantial continuities with the Ottoman past as well. In this chapter, we explore the social history of Greece during its first century of existence. Social history differs from its sister disciplines of political and economic history in the way in which it views the importance of time. Political history and economic history lend themselves to sequential narrative analysis, resembling in this way a motion picture where one frame follows another to tell a coherent story: events can be linked into a consecutive sequence and chronological relations of one episode to the next can be appreciated. Social history marches to a different chronological drummer. Social changes appear in the historical record less as events than as processes, and consequently it is difficult to delineate them as discrete moments in time.

The sources for social history are also not well suited to a sequential analysis; the records of society in the past are patchy and filled with gaps over both time and space, especially for the largest groups in society – peasants and workers – who for the most part have left us few written accounts of their lives. For these reasons, social history often appears less like a movie and more like a series of snapshots taken at different points in time. These problems are all evident in the case of Greece where the sources available, for example, on peasant life, are disparate and incomplete. The rich anthropological literature on Greece, while based on the recent past, can help us to transcend the limitations of the historical sources, but we have to be careful that we do not create an impression that Greek society, especially rural society, has not undergone profound changes over the last 200 years. Therefore, in spite of the obstacles that confront us, without a history that includes the peasants – male and female – the labourers, the sailors, the street vendors and the beggars our understanding of Greek society will be incomplete.

I begin with an examination of the basic structures of Greek society during the nineteenth century, such as demography and household structure. Since Greece was predominantly a rural society, we shall next move on to discuss various aspects of village life. We also need to examine how the people worked the land and how agrarian practices changed over time. Then, using gender as our organizing axis, we can explore the social worlds of men and women. In the penultimate section of the chapter, we move from the country to the city.

One of the most important social developments in Greece during the second half of the nineteenth century was the remarkable growth of Athens and its port city of Piraeus at the expense of both the countryside and the other cities of Greece. Once again, we shall begin our discussion with the structural aspects of urbanization and then move to the experiential – how did the move to the city affect peoples' lives? In Greece, as it did elsewhere in Europe, rapid urbanization generated a host of 'social problems': crime, violence, prostitution, poverty, sanitation and the like. We shall examine how the Greek state responded to these pressing social issues. Finally, I examine the great exodus of Greeks to the United States and elsewhere at the end of the nineteenth and the first two decades of the twentieth centuries.

DEMOGRAPHIC CHANGE[1]

The revolutionary war had been a long and bloody affair. Caught between the savage scorched earth policy of Ibrahim Pasha and the continual depredations of the Greek irregulars, the peasantry suffered horribly. Though it is impossible to determine the exact numbers of fatalities, we can be sure that tens of thousands died. Yet, if the earliest demographic data available after the war are to be believed, a combination of in-migration from the Greek communities outside of Otto's kingdom and a vigorous rate of population growth among the indigenous Greeks recouped the war losses in a relatively short time. Table 5.1 and Fig. 5.1 provide an overview of population growth from 1833 to 1920.

Focusing first on the kingdom as a whole, it appears that the years immediately after the war, roughly from 1832 until 1835, witnessed a modest but steady growth in population. This was followed by a very sharp increase during the late 1830s and 1840s, that saw population size expand from about 650,000 in 1835 to almost one million in 1848. Indigenous growth rates remained at moderate to high levels for the remainder of the nineteenth century. Table 5.1 also shows the impact on the size of the population of Greece of the addition of the Ionian Islands in 1864 and Thessaly and Arta in 1881. The territorial expansions that resulted from the Balkan Wars and the First World War are reflected in the census of 1920, as a result of which population had risen to just over five million people.

All told, these figures suggest a 655 per cent increase in the population of Greece as a whole, and a 295 per cent increase within the territory of 'Old

Table 5.1 Population Growth in Greece, 1821–1920

Population	Country	Peloponnesos	Central Greece	Aegean Islands	Ionian Islands	Thessaly
1821	766,470	389,709	206,356	161,412		
1828	600,000					
1835	674,180					
1843	915,000					
1848	987,000					
1853	1,036,000					
1861	1,096,810	552,414	318,535	225,861		
1870	1,436,140	611,861	356,865	238,784	228,631	
1879	1,638,850	709,245	441,033	259,056	229,516	
1889	2,187,300	813,154	556,254	235,050	238,783	344,060
1896	2,434,000	902,181	758,385	234,747	235,973	385,520
1907	2,632,000	937,366	897,773	230,378	254,494	448,610
1920	5,021,790	915,204	1,125,073	222,347	224,189	491,150
		Crete	Macedonia	Thrake	Epiros	Other Islands
1920		346,584	1,090,432	199,470	213,784	263,240

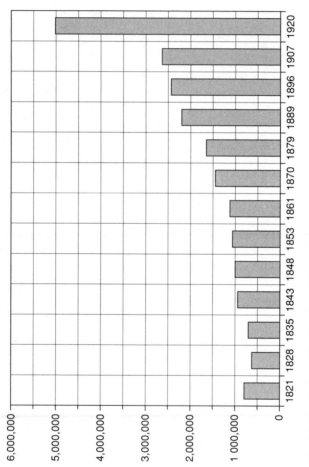

Fig. 5.1 Population of the kingdom of Greece from 1821 to 1920.

Greece', i.e. those areas that constituted the kingdom in 1832. The actual growth rate was even higher than these figures suggest because they do take into account the half million Greeks who left the country between 1880 and 1920 – about whom more will be said shortly. To place the Greek case into a comparative framework, over the same period the population of Spain grew by 183 per cent and that of Italy by 185 per cent, while the major powers of France and Great Britain expanded by 127 per cent and 233 per cent respectively. The Greek population, then, was clearly one of the fastest growing in all of Europe for much of the nineteenth century.

A number of factors control the population growth rate. At a very basic level, of course, the primary one is the ratio of the birth rate to the death rate. Quite simply, if more people are born than die, population increases. The birth rate, using the standard measure of births per 1,000 persons, in 1860 was 38.6, while the mortality rate was 26.5. The birth rate rose over the next few decades reaching its zenith during the 1880s (40.8/1,000), while the mortality rate fell at a corresponding rate, sinking to its nadir of 20.3/1,000 at the turn of the century.[2] In the absence of national level data before 1860 we have to rely on archival studies of specific localities, and the few studies that have been done suggest that figures of the same magnitude pertained before 1860 as well.[3] So more Greeks were being born while the rate at which others died fell. Why?

The key demographic variables controlling the birth rate are the female age at marriage, life expectancy, fertility rate, artificial fertility control, the percentage of women and men who marry, and the infant mortality rate. If, for example, few women marry and they marry late in life and die shortly thereafter, and if many of the children they give birth to die, then the birth rate will be low. What transpired in Greece during the nineteenth century was the development of a high-growth demographic regime.[4]

One critical contributing factor to this development was the low age at marriage for women. From the available data, it appears that throughout the century women married in their early twenties. The average age at marriage for men was late twenties. Over the course of the century, both of these figures fluctuated, but the trend was for the vast majority of women, over 90 per cent, to be married by age 26 and the average age for men declined to 26–27, with over 80 per cent of men having taken a bride for the first time by age 30. Simultaneously, life expectancy for both men and women increased from 35.7 in 1860 to 45.2 by the 1920s. Effective artificial birth control was not widely practiced by Greek couples and so a natural fertility rate predominated.

Two additional factors of importance were first that almost all Greek men and women married, meaning that everyone contributed to the reproducing population, and second that the infant mortality rate was falling. According to one study, for example, the infant death rate fell from 198.2 in 1860 to 148.1 by the 1920s.[5] We can conclude, then, that almost all Greek men and women married; they married somewhat younger and lived longer than their forebears, and in the absence of birth control, they produced more children, a greater percentage of whom survived to adulthood.

The result of this confluence of factors was clearly attested to in the 1920 census, which showed that fully 42 per cent of Greek families had more than five children and 15 per cent had eight or more children. Population expanded and Greek families grew larger. It was the combined effects of the developments discussed above that created the engine of growth that produced the profound population increase in Greece during the nineteenth century. Some of the more important social consequences of this growth will be examined shortly. I want to turn next to an examination of the nature of family and household in nineteenth century Greece.

THE SPITI: FAMILY AND HOUSEHOLD STRUCTURE

Throughout history, Greeks have drawn no difference between the house in which they reside and the people who reside there with them. In antiquity, the word *oikos* captured this dual sense of house and household, while in the modern era the word used most often is *spiti*. *Oikogenia*, a word whose origins is evident, is employed to capture the sense of family, but in everyday speech one hears people most often use spiti when they talk about their family.

As in other agrarian societies, the household constituted the primary social unit on which the communal and the national social structures were built. It was both the centre of production and reproduction, and the most basic unit for the socialization of the young. The following observation by anthropologist John Campbell about the importance of the household in the recent past holds equally true for the nineteenth century: 'A man's categorical obligations are ... to his family [spiti]. Outside his family he may have other roles ... Yet where there is conflict between loyalty to the family and duty to another group or service, the former has precedence'.[6] Household interests come before all others in the Greek peasant worldview. However, no household is an island unto itself. The spiti was also the locus for the union of two groups of kindred – the husband's and the wife's. We shall see repeatedly throughout this chapter just how central the spiti was in Greek society. It is important at this juncture to examine the structure of the household and the processes by which it was formed.

The most basic question we need to answer about the household is simply what did the average one look like? Was the typical Greek household large, consisting of many generations or groups of brothers and their families living under one roof? Or was it more like the structure normative today, in which the household usually consists of a married couple and their unmarried offspring? Answering this question is not as simple as it might initially appear. First there is yet again the problem of the paucity of information. We need fairly detailed census data or other types of family records in order to reconstruct the structure of households. Second, we have to be aware that the average household may have been prevented by demographic factors from achieving its culturally idealized final form. Nonetheless, we can venture some generalizations.

The first point of significance is that no single form of household or family structure predominated in all regions and among all classes in the Greek world. Table 5.2 presents the data derived from studies of different communities during the nineteenth century. We can see clearly from the table the variety of forms manifest both between communities and even within the same community.[7] Among the pastoralists in the Epirote village of Syrrako, for example, about half of the households contained only a nuclear family (by which we mean parents and their offspring). Another 45 per cent consisted of extended families, in which there was a nuclear family that was joined by one or more relatives, or joint families, in which one or more married siblings, usually brothers, and their families co-resided. This pattern flourished frequently in the past among groups that practiced large-scale animal husbandry. The reason for this would seem to be that larger, more complex households were better able to pool resources and to manage labour in a way better suited to the needs of shepherding, especially where transhumance was involved.

Theodore Bent, an English traveller, for example, visited an extreme

Table 5.2 Household structure in various regions. The figures represent the percentage of households recorded for each structural type.

	Syrrako 1905		Aristi 1905	Hermoupolis 1879	Mykonos 1861
	Pastoralists	Permanent			
Solitaries	2.0	12.6	8.8	13.6	11.2
No family	0.6	5.4	1.3	7.2	4.0
Nuclear	50.1	46.2	28.9	72.4	76.8
Extended	21.1	21.5	25.2	4.5	3.9
Joint	23.9	11.7	32.0	0.5	3.8
Other	2.3	2.6	3.8	1.8	0.3

example of this type of household on the island of Gatharonisi (today called Agathonisi) adjacent to the island of Patmos in the eastern Mediterranean in 1865. He found that only one family inhabited the entire island and that it consisted of an elderly couple, three married sons and their families, three unmarried sons, one married daughter and her family, and six other unmarried daughters. All together 22 people shared bed, board and flocks on this remote islet.[8]

A similar tendency toward forming joint or extended households flourished among the richest and the poorest Greeks on the Ionian Islands. Complex households were found among sharecropping families which were attached to the great feudal estates on the islands of Kerkira (Corfu), Zakinthos, and Kefallenia, and among the aristocratic families who owned the plantations.[9] In the case of sharecroppers, as with pastoralists, it appears that it was the ability to muster a larger labour force that explains why two or more nuclear families would chose to co-reside. Also by continuing to live and work together after the death of their father, brothers were able to keep intact the leasehold that was bequeathed to them as their inheritance.[10]

The reason why aristocratic families formed complex households was related to property and patrimony as well. Like nobility elsewhere in Europe, the Ionian bluebloods practiced unigeniture, a system of inheritance whereby only one child received the family's property. In exchange for obtaining legal ownership of the family's villa, plantation and townhouses, the primary heir was obligated to house and support his younger siblings. It was, therefore, not uncommon on the islands to find four or more brothers and sisters and their families living together along with their domestic servants in one mansion.

The villagers of Aristi in Epiros also showed a similar tendency toward forming more complex households (57.2 per cent), but for quite different reasons. The people of Aristi were not pastoralists but agriculturalists in an area where arable land was scarce and what there was of it was of poor quality. Like many upland communities in Greece where a very delicate balance between people and resources existed, village men would temporarily migrate as itinerant labourers, artisans or merchants. In the case of Aristi, they specialized as innkeepers and bakers, and men from the village worked in cities all across the Balkans. The female-headed households of the absent men would combine with siblings or in-laws on a temporary basis or co-reside in some other arrangement that produced joint households.

The pattern manifested among the permanent members of Syrrako typifies the more normal Greek peasant household in which the entire family worked the land on a more or less continuous basis. The nuclear household was overwhelmingly the most frequently occurring form among the peasantry and there were relatively few joint households. Extended households formed, if they occurred at all, when a widowed parent continued to reside in the family's house. Because of the differences in age at marriage and in the average life expectancy between men and women, this meant that almost invariably it was the mother who lived out the rest of her life with one of her married children. The comparatively higher number of solitaries among farming households represents widows and widowers who either chose not to live with one of their children or whose offspring had left the village.

This general pattern in which the nuclear household predominated was the norm among peasants in most of southern Europe. Newly wedded peasant couples created a new household by combining the land that the husband received as his inheritance with the property that the woman brought into the union in her dowry. Among peasant families, the formation of a joint household between siblings does not appear to have been common, and when it did occur it was in all likelihood as an emergency measure. Finally, contrasting with the patterns we have discussed so far, all of which involved rural folk, was the one that emerged in nineteenth century cities.

The cosmopolitan port city of Hermoupolis on the island of Syros manifested a pattern of family structure typical of urban areas elsewhere in Europe in which the nuclear household predominated. A variety of factors shaped this practice. With the exception of Thessaloniki, all of the cities of Greece were essentially new foundations, and thus, the result of in-migration usually of people from the countryside. These young migrants would marry, and in the absence of already established households to which they were related, families would set up a dwelling of their own. This practice was facilitated by the ease with which families could build illegal dwellings in the city. Also, elderly parents would more than likely have remained in their rural village and so the possibility of creating extended households was lessened. Finally, the number of 'solitaries' appears to be the same as among the peasants of Syrrako, but for different reasons. The sizeable number of people living alone in the city was not widowed men and women but rather merchants who had set up house temporarily.

In nineteenth century Greek society, then, there were three predominant forms of family structure. The most common pattern pertained among the Greek peasantry among whom the nuclear household was the normative form. Another pattern, most common among pastoralists and sharecroppers, featured a greater proportion of extended or joint households. And finally, there was an urban pattern in which nuclear households were the over-whelming favourite. Related to the structure of the household and to how the household operated as a social unit was the pattern of residence.

Three different types of post-marital residence pattern have been observed in Greece. Not too surprisingly each of them was related to a number of factors, such as household structure, the nature of the kinship system and the way property was transmitted to the next generation.[11] One prominent post-marital residence pattern was virilocality or patrivirilocality. In the regions where this was the custom, the newly married couple would set up residence either in the household of the husband's father (patrivirilocal), thus creating a complex household, or they would build a house in very close proximity to the father's abode, often even in the same compound. Over time, this custom produced a spatial geography characterized by clusters of men related to one another by blood. It was found most frequently among pastoralists and in other areas like Crete and Epiros, regions with a tradition of autonomy and militarism that placed a premium on having numerous fighting men connected to one another like the Mani and the central mountainous regions of the Peloponnesos, and in places such as the Ionian Islands where share-cropping created common economic interests between agnatic kinsmen.[12]

This system placed great emphasis on the kinship relationship between men and agnatic kin groups often formed tightly organized groups. Property transmission focused on men as well. Upon the death or retirement of the *pater familias*, the adult sons would share equally in the inheritance, but there were considerable social pressures placed upon them to continue to operate their holdings as a unit. Women traditionally did not receive land as part of their dowry or share in any inheritance. Instead, they received their share of the parental estate in their dowry, usually in the form of a trousseau that included cash and moveable property.

The second post-marital residence pattern practiced in the past was uxorilocality. In this case, the married coupled went to live either with the wife's family or in close proximity to them. In other words, uxorilocality is more or less the mirror image of the system that we just discussed, only in this instance the focus was on kindred women rather than men. Kinship lines tended to be traced bilaterally, in other words along both the husband's and the wife's families, and strong bonds were formed between kinswomen. Regarding the intergenerational transmission of property, the custom was for one of the daughters to receive her parents' house as part of her dowry, but the practice regarding which girl, if there were more than one daughter, varied. In some places it was the eldest, in others the youngest, and in others it was decided on the basis of filial affection. This custom was seen most frequently on the Aegean islands or in other maritime communities where the men would be absent for long periods of time.[13]

The third system fell somewhere in between the other two, and while it had a long history, it really developed into the predominant custom only during the nineteenth century. In this instance, couples practiced neolocality, in which the newly weds would establish their own household spatially distinct from either's parents. Since the parents would more than likely be leaving behind a house, one of the children would receive it as their patrimony, usually in exchange for agreeing to care of the aged parents. Property transmission among agriculturalists tended to be partible, meaning that each child received an equal share of the parental estate, and women frequently received land as part of their dowry. This was the practice among the vast majority of peasant farming families across Greece. It became the custom in the newly emerging urban areas as well, with an apartment or a similar dwelling space substituting for arable land.

Whether large and complex or simple and nuclear, the spiti was at the centre of Greek life. Before examining the traditional social roles that men and women played in their household, I want to examine first the place of the spiti in the material world posing two questions: what sort of community did most Greeks live in and how did the household operate as a unit of production in the past?

FARMS AND VILLAGES

The visitor to Greece today is immediately struck by the degree to which cities, especially Athens, dominate Greek society. Such an impression is amply supported by a glance at the most recent census figures, which show that over one half of the entire Greek population resides in the greater Athens area alone. Yet the predominance of cities and their urban lifeways is a relatively recent phenomenon. For most of its history, Greece had been a country of rural folk who lived in villages. For example, according to the first census that recorded occupational information, that of 1861, 74 per cent of adult men were agriculturalists who earned their livelihood from working the land. More-over, the pattern remained fairly consistent through time. By 1920, for example, the proportion of heads of households listed as farmers had barely changed, dropping only to 70 per cent. Before examining the agrarian systems of nineteenth-century Greece, we need to make a few observations about where Greeks lived and how that built environment of the village helped shape their social world.

Table 5.3 gives a very clear idea about the distribution of human settle-ments in Greece before the arrival of the Asia Minor refugees in 1922 (see Chapter 7) but after the incorporation of the northern regions of Epiros,

Table 5.3 Distribution of population in Greece by settlement size

Size of settlement	Frequency	Population
0–1,000	10,050	2,703,530
1,001–2,000	510	689,010
2,001–3,000	107	263,690
3,001–4,000	38	119,670
4,001–5,000	23	101,610
5,001–10,000	33	230,210
10,001–50,000	26	466,150
50,001–100,000	1	51,590
<100,000	3	593,280
Totals	10,791	5,218,740

Thrake and Macedonia at the end of the Balkan Wars in 1913 (about which, see Chapter 6). In 1920, almost 52 per cent of the entire population resided in villages containing less than 1,000 individuals, and villages of this size accounted for nearly 94 per cent of all human habitations. Hidden with these aggregate figures is the fact that the majority of villagers (approximately 35 per cent) lived in villages of less than 500 people, and over 150,000 people lived in settlements of fewer than 100. The typical village had a population of either 200–300 or 600–700 people. If we consider that settlements with between 1,000 and 5,000 inhabitants were also populated predominantly by peasant families, then over 70 per cent of the population lived in villages. The data also suggests that by 1920, the population distribution of Greece was sharply divided between rural villages and larger cities, and that towns (i.e. settlements with between 5,000 and 10,000 people) were of relatively modest importance. Moving back in time, the picture of Greece as a land of rural villages only becomes more apparent. The general pattern can be exemplified through a more detailed examination of one well-studied region in the Peloponnesos.

Karytaina is an upland district in the central Peloponnesos. Mountains and hills divide the region into numerous basins where the best arable land is concentrated. In terms of its physical geography it resembles many areas of Greece. In 1879, Karytaina contained a population of 56,017 people residing in 140 settlements (Fig. 5.3). As a glance at the distribution map indicates, the region was blanketed by a dense network of villages, 93 per cent of which were occupied by fewer than 1,000 people and fully 80 per cent contained less than 500 inhabitants. Assuming that the average household contained five people, then the overwhelming majority of inhabitants lived in villages of 100 or fewer families. Indeed, almost 10 per cent of the settlements were hamlets in which fewer than 10 families lived.

Fig. 5.2 'Interior of Typical Peasant House, 1877'. This drawing by the Illustrated
London News' *'roving correspondent' depicts the interior of a peasant house in
the Argolid. As well as suggesting the rustic construction of the typical house, it
also conveys a vivid sense of the importance of gender in rural Greece.*
*[*Illustrated London News, *28 February 1877.]*

The farther back in time we go the more pronounced the pattern becomes.
In 1829, according to the census conducted by the French expedition to the
Peloponnesos, the region contained 34,223 people residing in 127 villages with
an average size of 269 people per village. Twelve of the villages held less than
50 people, and a sizeable number of hamlets were occupied by only one or
two families. Going back to the Venetian census of 1700, it appears that
Karytaina was occupied by only 11,773 people who lived in villages with an
average population of 97, and almost one half of them were inhabited by fewer
than 50 people. In sum, accepting that the settlement history of Karytaina was
fairly typical of the rest of mainland Greece, then it would seem that for most
of its history Greece has been a land of villages, and often very small villages
and hamlets. As a consequence of this, the physical and social environment
that shaped peoples' lives was that of the small face-to-face community.[14]

It is impossible to describe *the* typical Greek village. Village design varied
from region to region and from place to place within regions depending on a
variety of localized factors. The same can be said for house design as well. In

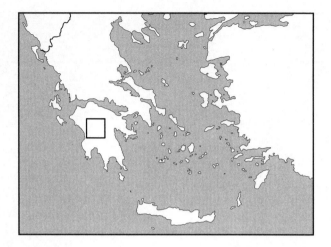

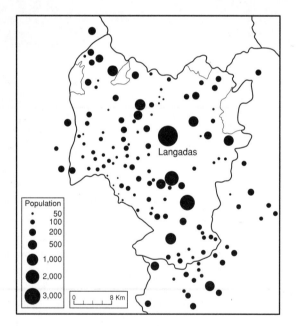

Fig. 5.3 Settlement distribution in the Karytaina region of Arkadia in 1879. (Based on V. Panayiotopulos, Plithismos kai Ikismos tis Peloponnisou, 13os-18os Aionos *(Athens, 1985), map 13, p. 211.)*

addition to the purely physical factors, there were social ones as well, especially wealth, that influenced village and house construction. We can, however, posit some generalizations regarding the common factors that influenced the physical layout of villages.

First, given that so much of the Greek landscape is hilly or mountainous and that arable land was at such a premium, villages tended to be built on hillsides and slopes rather than on farm land. Second, because of the very hot, dry summers, villages were sited with an eye to water sources. Some other recurring features were the presence of a church and an open space or square around which the village's houses would be clustered. Regarding house design, the fact that these were functioning farms also created some recurring features such as storage facilities, spaces for penning animals, and areas reserved for food preparation.

Here is a lengthy description of a village and its houses of the poorest class in rural Greece, that of dependent sharecroppers (see below pages 94–7), that vividly captures the nature of one type of rural settlement:

> Let us look more closely at a village of the first category [sharecroppers]. I will take one with which I am tolerably familiar, Achmetaga, in the island of Euboea, as typical of a village occupied by Metayers, and it will serve for a model of any other such village in Attica and central Greece. The houses grouped round the little church are all one-storied oblong cabins built of the stone which is almost every- where ready to hand, from thirty to thirty six feet in length by about twenty-four feet in width. Two-thirds of this area are devoted to the dwelling part, while the other third is reserved for the stabling of the beasts in winter; and there is seldom any partition wall to screen it, for the peasant likes to keep them in sight ... The family live in common, men, women, and children together; often, indeed, several generations of them, in the habitable end, which has a dried-clay flooring, or in some cases wooden planking raised a foot or two above the ground. The fire, on a hearth of stone, is against the wall in the more recent and better-built cottages which boast of a chimney, though in many villages it is still in the middle of the room, the smoke escaping as best it may through the holes in the roof. Furniture there is generally none, unless it be a rude cupboard, or a wooden chest, or, perhaps, a few shelves to

hold their simple cooking utensils. In one corner is a stack of rugs, mattresses, and cushions. These laid upon the ground form their beds at night. The mattresses, stuffed with maize husks, are covered with a rough carpet material which the women weave, and so are the square cushions, which serve as seats by day when the simple meal is spread upon the ground. Sometimes there is a table, but not often, in the genuine peasant's huts ... Strings of onions and bunches of golden maize hang from the rafters, and a large earthenware water-cooler, with a number of smaller red jars and bowls of classic pattern, make up the humble equipment of the cottage. No house is complete without its ikon, generally a picture of the Panaghia or Virgin, but occasionally representing the saint whose name the householder bears, or in whose especial protection family tradition has confidence. Sometimes a little rude shrine is built up round the picture, and in front of it is always a lamp, which many families keep burning night and day, often stinting themselves of oil to keep the saint supplied. Outside the door is the oven, a beehive-shaped structure of clay, which is heated well-nigh red-hot with wood, after which the fire is raked out, and the dough wrapped round with leaves is introduced for baking. There are also generally without supporting posts for a primitive loom. Sometimes the loom is arranged with cross-bars between two young trees, behind which the lower hind-posts are driven into the ground, so that the weaver sits in the shade of the trees at work, or else a little thatch is built to shelter her from the sun; for the houses are only occupied at night or during bad weather, and village life is entirely in the open air.[15]

This description captures well the simplicity and rudeness of the houses and villages of the poorest stratum of Greek society. But it also conveys some very important insights into the multifaceted functions that the house served. It was the centre for agricultural production, home to both peoples and animals, and a religious centre as well.

Contrasting with the crude village and the simple one-storey stone or mud hovels of the sharecroppers were the larger and more elaborate villages and houses found among freeholding peasants. Whether in the mountains or on the plains, villages of peasants who owned their own land tended to be more elaborate and their houses were usually larger and more complex than those of sharecroppers. In mountainous or hilly regions, the houses were well-built of stone masonry, usually two or more stories in height, and space within them tended to divided into separate activity zones, often based on gender. The ground floor was reserved for keeping animals and storing equipment; the first floor was the primary dwelling space for the family, and the third storey usually contained more storage space and the sleeping quarters.[16] In some regions, this basic form was augmented by a stone tower or some other similar type of defensive structure and it usually incorporated a walled off courtyard. Houses tended to be inward looking, and through their design they demarcated sharply between domestic and public space. The house provided the family with protection from the outside world, but it also articulated them to it.

FARMING THE LAND

Greece was a land of farmers, and so in order to understand their society we need to examine the agrarian systems that both shaped their lives and formed the backbone of the national economy. An agrarian system consists of a number of related elements, the most important of which are land tenure and ownership, technology, labour arrangements and production aims.

Scholars of the rural economy during the nineteenth century have tended to focus only on type of agrarian system and then to assume that it aptly characterized the entirety of the Greek countryside. Some, for example, have reconstructed a rural past dominated by small, independent peasant proprietors who used a primitive technology not much different from the one described by the poet Hesiod in the eight century BC to produce the bare subsistence needed to feed their family. For scholars of this persuasion, the rural economy was 'pre-capitalist' and was responsible for the retardation of the Greek economy. Others accept the primacy of the small family farm, but they see it as having been capitalist and market orientated in its production goals. Some argue that the lot of the average peasant family was a grim one, marked by poverty, poor yields, debt, and low wages for the relatively little paid work that was available. Others paint a rosier picture of family farming; in their view, most peasants were relatively well off. They argue that land was readily available, that rural wages were high, and that social mobility was a desired and attainable goal.

Historians on both sides agree that Greece was different from other

European countries, especially Spain and Italy, in not having a landed aristocracy that controlled vast tracts of land and in not having to contend with the onerous legacy of feudalism. In fact, some pretty much dismiss the plantation form of agriculture as irrelevant to the Greek case, allowing only for a couple of notable exceptions like Thessaly.[17]

While the debates make for interesting reading, they are largely misdirected because in each case the participants have a propensity for portraying the agricultural landscape of Greece as monolithic, whereas it was anything but uniform. Aspects of all of the scenarios are correct, but what needs to be appreciated is that there were a number of agrarian systems in operation simultaneously and that the fortunes of those operating within any one of them varied tremendously on a case by case basis. We can identify, I suggest, three primary agricultural systems and within each there were also a number of variations.

The first type of farm was the single-family peasant household estate. In its general characteristics, it resembled peasant farming from anywhere else in Europe and is the archetype that commentators from modern anthropologists to nineteenth century travellers and politicians have focused on.

The salient features of the peasant agrarian system are the following. First, the labour force was drawn only from household members. The adult head of the household provides the primary source of labour; as his sons got older they would assist him in the fields until such time as they left the paternal estate to start their own household or moved abroad. Female members of the household would assist in the fields on a seasonal basis, to help with harvest or with weeding – the latter back-breaking task was especially considered to be 'woman's work.' Second, the production aim of the farm was first and foremost to meet the subsistence needs of the household. In practice this meant that farmers would cultivate small amounts of numerous crops. So, each farmer would cultivate a few olive trees, some plots of wheat and barley, maize and legumes, a scattering of fruit trees, and a couple of plots of vines. The family's land holdings would be fragmented into numerous small plots scattered across the landscape. This practice reflected the family's strategy of risk minimization; because by scattering their crops across a range of micro-environments, they reduced the risk that a single natural trauma would destroy all of their crops.[18]

The technology and tools required by such a farm were rudimentary, and most of them would have been simple wooden hand tools. The high labour intensity and the relatively modest productivity of this technology was more than balanced by its suitability to the terrain and soils of Greece, and the production goals of the peasant farm. The peasant household would also have possessed some livestock. There would be the mandatory donkey, a few sheep and goats for milk, cheese, wool, hides and meat, and, if the family was sufficiently wealthy, a team of plow oxen.

Though subsistence may have been its primary production goal, no household could get by without some connection to the market. There was, for example, a range of goods that the family could not produce on its own – salt, tea, coffee, gunpowder (if the man of the house could have afforded to acquire a firearm), and metal for tools – and so the family had to purchase them from the local market town or from the itinerant merchants who traversed the countryside.

There were those agencies like the Church and the State who made claims on the household's resources and who often required their payment in cash. Finally, there was the family's need to provide the wherewithal for dowries for its daughters, to underwrite the costs of weddings and funerals, and to cope with all of those unexpected expenses that arise during the lifespan of any family.

Consequently, all peasant households had to devise strategies for generating some cash income. For many, it was the production of a cash crop, in some areas this was the currant grape, in others it was tobacco or cotton; most farmers also tried to produce a surplus of consumables like olive oil or wheat (substituting maize for the dietary needs of the family) that they could sell in local towns.[19] Greek peasant farms, then, were neither anti-market nor fully commercialized. Instead their goal was as far as possible to meet their basic needs and to get ahead as much as they could, as long as by doing so they did not place the family's future at risk.

The type of farm we have discussed so far was the ideal. And there were of course many families that achieved that ideal. But the vagaries of fortunes over time meant that many families failed to meet the ideal, while others exceeded it. One key in determining which it of the two it would be was land. As we saw in Chapter 3, the land dotation scheme enacted under King Otto was fraught with difficulties and susceptible to corruption, and produced a stark disparity between a relatively small number of sizeable estates and a much larger number of peasant minifundia. A second major redistribution of national lands occurred in 1871, and new laws that endeavoured to clarify the complex, not to say Byzantine, land tenure arrangements that had developed in the countryside over the ages, also accompanied it.[20]

The aim of this legislation was to secure firm legal ownership of the land for as many families as possible. It was estimated that over 50,000 families occupied and cultivated land to which they did not have verifiable legal title. This placed them in a very vulnerable position vis-à-vis creditors; it made them less likely to make long-term investment in the productivity of the land; it meant that they had to pay the state a burdensome usufruct tax in addition to the other mandated exactions. Giving them legal title to the land, it was hoped, would solve all of these problems. But the main emphasis of the 1871 laws was to provide land to the landless and to allow those who owned only a small amount of land to expand their holdings. Learning from the mistake of the earlier scheme, the land parcels were not purchased through auctions, in which the prices could rise outside of the range that peasants could pay, and instead government assessors set the prices.

The 1871 laws were largely successful in creating new peasant farms. But some of the old problems persisted. Corruption by assessors led to a maldistribution in some areas. Even where the system worked fairly, this second round of land distribution still left thousands of households in possession of land holdings insufficient to need their basic needs. The great interannual variability of crop yields in Greece meant that even farms that could sustain a family during a good year soon fell prey to debt and all that went with it after any one of numerous bad years.[21] The consequences of the continuing small size of the average peasant holding and its continued vulnerability to debt were first the persistence of what agricultural economists refer to as 'pluriactivity',[22] meaning that household members needed to undertake economic activities like seasonal wage labour or they were compelled to cede part of the produce of their land to creditors, effectively becoming share-croppers on their own land.

In sum, while the family farm was the predominant unit of agricultural production, there was a great range of variability within the peasant agrarian system. Some households were able to take advantage of the opportunities that arose and became wealthier; many others fell into a cycle of debt and dependency that left them destitute. Moreover, the continually increasing size of the rural population, that we discussed earlier, served only to exacerbate the fragility of many families' situations.

The second category of agricultural production, tenant farming and share-cropping, was in some ways related to the tenuousness of the peasant agrarian system. There were three predominant varieties of sharecropping in Greece during the nineteenth century. Two were inherited from older arrangements that existed for years in regions that were added to the kingdom later in the century, the Ionian Islands and Thessaly, and the third developed in Central Greece and the Peloponnesos after independence.

The Ionian Islands had been possessions of the Venetian Empire for centuries, and during that time a system of feudalism had been introduced. In the northern islands of Kerkira and Lefkas the emphasis had been on the production of olives, while on the more southerly islands of Kefallenia and Zakinthos the preferred crop was the currant grape, but on all of them, the organization of production was roughly the same. In exchange for their support of the regime, noble Ionian families had been given title to feudal estates by the Venetians, including not just the land but the people on it as well.

What was entailed under this feudal system was that peasant proprietors were given the right to work specified parcels of land in perpetuity under the following arrangement. One-fifth of the land was given to the tenant as *emphthyeusis* land that they were free to cultivate and whatever they grew was theirs to keep. The tenant was required to cultivate the remainder of the land with crops mandated by the landlord, and the harvest was divided in one of two ways. If the landlord supplied everything (equipment, tools, seeds, cuttings, etc.) but labour, then the split was two-thirds to the owner and one-third to the tenant. If the peasant supplied all of the materials needed to produce the crop, then the split was fifty-fifty. The tenants were also required to sell their share of the currant crop to their lord, and they had to have their grain and olives ground at mills controlled by him for an additional payment of 10 per cent of the crop.

Under the period of British rule from 1815 to 1864, a new wrinkle was introduced whereby annual contracts were issued specifying which of the above arrangements would obtain and what the exact division of the estate's production would be.[23] The tenants who enjoyed feudal tenure kept possession of the land in perpetuity. So, for example, in the dowry contracts that Ionian Island aristocrats drew up for their daughters it was clearly specified that she and her new husband did not take over occupancy of land but only the share owed by the peasant family.[24] When Greece took possession of the islands in 1864, it inherited the feudal regime. But not for long: after a series of tumultuous rural revolts, feudalism was abolished, but the remnants of the sharecropping system remained in place.

A not dissimilar situation occurred when Greece obtained Thessaly in 1881. In this case, wealthy Greeks, often from the diaspora, purchased the çiftlik estates from the departing Turkish owners. Depending on the status of the land under Ottoman law, the land was either held in freehold or the new owner enjoyed a form of feudal right. In this case, the owner was required to contribute nothing to the production process yet was awarded one-third of the total production from the land.

In Boiotia, Evvoia, and the Peloponnesos, the nature of the sharecropping system depended on whether the tenant willingly took up occupancy on the landlord's land or whether they had fallen into debt. In the former case, the tenant enjoyed access to a house (subject to the payment of one bushel of grain as rent) and a garden, and the family supplied all of the seed, equipment and labour in exchange for a two-thirds share. In cases where a debt was involved, creditors would take over legal possession of the farm but would leave the owner on their land. They would then provide the seeds or other supplies needed to produce a crop and in exchange for doing so they would take the produce equivalent to their investment plus 15 per cent of the remainder. Sharecropping was a despised practice. As we saw earlier, villages of sharecroppers tended to be the poorest and meanest in the land. But for many driven by debt or their inability to acquire in any other way, it was a necessary evil. Given the increasing size of the rural population and the increasing pressure on the land, it was young men and women from share-cropping families who were often the first to seek alternative work off of the farm, migrating either to the cities or abroad.

The plantation of Sotirios Sotiropoulos exemplifies the last category of agricultural enterprise we find in nineteenth century Greece.[25] Sotiropoulos came from a wealthy family and was very active in national politics, holding various ministerial portfolios during his career. He owned an estate in Messenia that consisted initially of 15 hectares, 12 of which were planted with currant vines; in 1861 he acquired an additional 9 hectares by a combination of purchase and debt foreclosure. On his plantation were also 250 mulberry trees for the production of silk, 40 pear trees, and three vegetable gardens. He grew wine grapes on another one hectare plot and set aside one half hectare as a drying ground for his currants. On another part of the grounds he had built a villa where his family resided during the summer months. Sotiropoulos was an absentee landlord. In comparison to the latifundia of Sicily or southern Spain, this was a small plantation; nonetheless within a Balkan context, it was a sizeable estate, worked by hired workers.

Sotiropoulos employed an overseer who along with his family lived on the estate year round. They were permitted to grow food crops in the gardens, were provided with a house, and were paid a monthly wage. Two unmarried hired workers also lived on the estate with them. The job of the three men was to tend the vines and the other tree crops throughout the year and keep up the villa. A gang of 15 workers was hired for a two-week period during the spring to assist with the job of hoeing the vineyards, and a group of 30 or more was employed in July or August to harvest the grapes. Plantation owners often also hired small gangs of armed guards to protect their field during the summer months. This was explicitly a commercial farm, the aim of which was the production of cash crops for an international market. It provided a nice complement to the peasant sector of the economy by providing a source of wage labour and a cash income. Smallholders, like those we discussed earlier, could supplement the income from their minifundia or obtain cash for dowries by working on commercial estates like this one. This type of plantation was found in the northern and western Peloponnesos, the Ionian Islands after 1871, parts of Boiotia, and Thessaly.[26]

THE OTHER GREEKS: SHEPHERDS, SAILORS AND ARTISANS

Historians are fond of reproducing the following passage from the memoir of the old warlord Theodore Kolokotronis as an accurate assessment of the isolation in which most Greek peasants lived:

> There were men [in the villages] who do not know of a village more than one hour distant from their own. They thought of Zakinthos [the southernmost Ionian Island] as we now speak of the most distant parts of the world. America appears to us as Zakinthos appeared to them: They said it was in France.[27]

The impression sentiments like this created was that rural men and women were born, lived and died without ever transcending the narrow confines of their village and its surrounding fields.

When anthropologists began writing about the remote villages they studied during the 1950s and 1960s, they either implicitly or explicitly reproduced this assessment. The view of the Greek village as isolated in space and frozen in time, has thus had a long history. But at best it is misleading and at worst inaccurate.[28] For one thing, as we have already seen, villages were enmeshed in very extensive networks of settlements that spread over fairly wide regions.

There were frequent and regular movements of men and women between villages for *panagyris* (festivals) and weddings, for commerce and marketing, and for the mundane aspects of social life like visiting relatives, helping kinsmen, and finding spouses. Furthermore, each region had one or more towns or large villages that connected the various villages and hamlets together by providing markets for goods like coffee, tea, salt, gunpowder and the few other items that peasant households could not produce for themselves and that served as administrative centres, including the courts. In addition to this fairly constant movement of people on a regional level, there were numerous occupations and sources of livelihood that required people to move about regularly and often.

We saw in the last section that many peasant households could not be sustained by the production from their farms. This meant that they had to seek ways to augment their household incomes. In some cases, groups of male kinsmen – brothers, fathers and cousins – and in others entire families would make a circuit around the Peloponnesos or central Greece working as seasonal wage labourers harvesting grain or picking grapes. In some regions, especially those involved in the production of currant grapes, peasants would move on a seasonal basis between the village where they lived most of the year, usually in an upland area, down to the coastal zone where they had acquired vineyards.[29]

Another strategy for generating an extra household income was for men to acquire craftsman's skills as smiths, knife sharpeners, carpenters, and masons. They would then traverse the countryside offering their skills in small villages and hamlets that were incapable of supporting a full time artisan on their own. In some villages, usually ones located in particularly inhospitable areas, almost all of the men in the village would become specialized craftsmen. Such was the case with a number of settlements in Arkadia, which produced some of the finest masons in the Balkans, and whose handiwork is still on display in many of Athens' nineteenth century public buildings. Becoming an itinerant merchant was another way to make ends meet that required men, and sometimes their families, to take to the road periodically.[30]

Adding further complexity to myriad of movement across the countryside were those groups whose livelihoods kept them much more constantly on the move. Two in particular stand out. The first one was the transhumant shepherds. There were certain ethnic groups, like the Sarakatsanoi, who specialized in large-scale animal husbandry. Twice a year, they would undertake a relatively long-range movement of their flocks, moving from the lowland and coastal plains where they spent winters to the upland pastures for the summers. In addition, while situated in their seasonal camps, they would be constantly moving their animals around the locale to take advantage of the available food supply.

The other group consisted of caravanners. Some Vlachs, for example, made a living out of transporting goods overland on donkeys. Given that through most of the Balkans, the road networks were poorly developed and that railroads did not come to play an important role until much later on, the easiest way to move goods long distances overland was on the backs of beasts of burden. This form of transportation was even more important in moving goods between lowland ports like Patras, Missolongi, Arta, and Nafplion to upland towns and between upland towns as well. Finally, in terms of livelihoods that required mobility, each year thousands of men answered the siren song of the sea and flocked to the ports to join the merchant marine.

Lastly, from the 1870s onwards, there was a massive exodus of young men and women from the countryside to Athens, Piraeus and other cities, and from the 1890s on to the United States as well. Those who migrated to the cities often traversed back to their natal village and so this added another source of mobility of people across the landscape.

In sum, the image of the nineteenth century Greek villagers as ensconced in their little villages, isolated from and ignorant of the wider world, is grossly inaccurate. No village was an island unto itself. The Greek countryside was a fairly dynamic place characterized by a relatively constant movement of people across it and periodically punctuated by the larger scale arrival and departure of work gangs, itinerant merchants and artisans, donkey caravans, shepherds with their families, and flocks, and of course, the dreaded bandit gangs which continued to be menaces to society until late in the century.

THE SOCIAL WORLD OF MEN AND WOMEN

So far we have examined the key structures of Greek society – household forms, family organization, means of livelihood and the like. It is now time to move beyond the purely structural and try as best we can to reconstruct the experiential. How did men and women during the nineteenth century think, act and behave in their daily lives? What cultural factors shaped their inter- actions with one another? What social ideologies underpinned their ideas about what it meant to be a man or a woman in Greek society at that time? In endeavouring to answer these questions, the deficiencies of the historical sources become all too obvious.

The contemporary, i.e. nineteenth century, accounts of 'traditional' society by Greek urban folklorists contain many fascinating details, but their utility is limited by the political agenda of the scholars and their class bias.[31] The vivid descriptions left to us by foreign travellers can be very useful, but they too have severe limitations. One of the most important was that foreigners frequently lacked any local knowledge – from language to customs – and so their view was shaped by their past experience of rural folk in their homeland. Another was that their perspective about modern Greeks was almost invariably shaped by the foreigners' studies of ancient Greece, and this meant they were almost always disappointed when the reality of village life failed to match their image of Classical Athens. Finally, the brevity of their stay in one place meant that they never developed a rapport with the local people that would have enabled them to probe beyond their superficial exposure to Greek society.[32]

It is on the topic of rural society, however, that the rich anthropological studies of rural Greece in the more recent past can be most valuable to us: provided that we are careful not to allow the past and the present to fold together and produce a picture of a seemingly unchanging rural society. One very important area in which there is meaningful continuity from the past to the present is the role of gender in shaping the social world. I begin with the world of men.

At the core of nineteenth century notions of masculinity was the concept of *timi*. This term is usually translated as 'honour.' Honour has become such a loaded term that we must employ it with care. A better way of conceptualizing timi is as reputation. A man of honour or timi was someone who was held in high esteem by his peers, by the other men in his community. And it appears the attribute that more than any other provided the yardstick by which a man's reputation was measured was *control*. A man should demonstrate at all times a firm command over all of those things that mattered in lives of Greek peasant men: land and property, animals and the people in his household. We should also add that he needed to demonstrate control over himself as well. Exercising control of resources defined his role as *nikokyris* (literally, lord of the household). He was to see to the material needs of those residing in his household. This included the mundane wherewithal of daily existence but also entailed ensuring that there would be enough goods to vouchsafe the future survival of his sons and daughters.

A man was to use every means at his disposal, deception, prevarication, intimidation and even violence to defend the social standing and enhance the material welfare of his household. A popular metaphor at the time compared the plebeian household to the celestial order, with the head of the household playing the role of the Supreme Being. In carrying out his 'divine' duties, a man was to manifest complete control of everything in his spiti, and he was to ensure harmony within it as well. His reputation among his peers was based on their collective assessment of how well he lived up to this culturally inscribed set of expectations.

To be sure, the ideal of a man as absolute master of the domestic realm and of the household being as harmonious a realm as the celestial order was often far from reality. As in any society, conflicts between brothers and between fathers and sons were not uncommon occurrences, and the court records are replete with examples of litigation between members of the same household and even of homicidal violence in the house.

Take the case of young man on the island of Lefkas in 1853 who went to his family's olive grove one evening and cleaved his father's head with an axe. At his trial he broke down and confessed that he had slain his father because the *pater familias* was threatening to disinherit him if he went through with his plans to marry a girl of whom his father disapproved. The son hoped to strike before the father could visit the notary and change his will. The incident itself is not especially remarkable. Interfamily fights over land, dowries and inheritances were not uncommon. What is noteworthy here was the reaction to this heinous deed.

Before the killer met his fate at the end of a rope, he was forced to march through his village and then from his village to the town of Lefkas wearing a placard around his chest that branded him as a 'father killer'.[33] While violence and conflict within the household did occur, it was socially reprehensible. Violence directed from the spiti outward in defence of its interests, however, was not only acceptable, but even mandatory, if a man did not want to lose face.

A central element of nineteenth century masculinity, then, was the ethos of vengeance. Charles Tuckerman, the United States Minister to Greece in the 1860s, captures well the essence of this ethos:

> [To a Greek man,] a wound of honor or a family insult burns like a compressed and slow consuming tow. In coarser natures it urges to desperate measures, and the traveler in the interior of Greece sometimes sees men with their hair and beards growing long in token that the wearer has an enemy to meet; nor will it be cut or shaved until he has met insult with insult, or blood with blood.[34]

This ethos meant that if a man or his family were insulted or wronged in any way, he had to respond with aggression or risk seeing his reputation diminished. But the type and the amount of socially accepted violence differed depending upon the context. One of the most common forms of honour-related violence was the knife fight, the essence of which is captured in the following tale.

On a hot summer's eve in 1836 Tonia Theodoros was sitting in his small village's wineshop on the island of Kerkira. Men gathered, as was their wont, for a few glasses and some conversation. Theodoros and a co-villager named Mokastiriotis, to whom he was not related, got into an argument, the cause of which none of the five witnesses could remember. Suddenly, Theodoros called Mokastiriotis a fool and a braggart. Mokastiriotis loudly replied that he would rather be a fool than 'the lord of a house full of Magdalenes'. Theodoros erupted from his chair, drew his pruning knife, and demanded that Mokastiriotis stand and face him like a man. None of the other men in the room intervened as the knife-fighters traded parries and thrusts. Finally,

Theodoros with a flick of his wrist delivered a telling blow that cut his victim from the tip of his chin to half way up his cheek. As blood flowed from his face, Mokastiriotis fell to his knees cursing his assailant. When asked by the presiding magistrate at the Police Magistrate's court in the town of Kerkira why he caused the fight, Theodoros sternly replied that no man would call his wife and daughters whores and get away with it. His reputation would not allow it. As a man, he would not stand for it.[35]

Thousands of similar episodes took place all across Greece. Men engaged in ritualized knife duels in order to defend their reputation. Most frequently the insult that inaugurated a duel was to call a man a cuckold or to brand his wife as a *Magdaleni* (a word in Greek that could mean either an adulteress or a prostitute), which would, of course, make the man a cuckold. Calling into question a woman's sexual reputation cut so deeply in this culture because it struck at the heart of masculinity: a man's ability to control the most important element in his household – his wife's or his daughter's reproductive behaviour. A man who could not control that aspect of his domain was, in their view, no man at all.

When confronted with such an insult or any imputation that the women of his household were anything less than chaste, a man either had to rise to the challenge and fight, or be humiliated. This form of violence was socially sanctioned and accepted. Take the episode from 1852 involving a flower vendor in Athens who, while selling flowers at the parade grounds one Sunday afternoon, saw a man approach his wife, and make advances to her. Grabbing his knife, he confronted the man and in the ensuing fight stabbed him through the heart.

Not only did the assembled crowd not intervene in the fight, they made no effort to stop the vendor and his wife from leaving, and some of the male onlookers even commended the man for the precision of the fatal stroke.[36] Finally, by allowing two men to settle their dispute with a mano-a-mano duel served another function as well: it prevented disputes over honour between two men from expanding into violence that would involve all of their kinsmen. Another consequence of the ethos of vengeance was the vendetta.

In the world of Greek men during the nineteenth century, the shedding of the blood of another initiated a vendetta in which the family and the kin of the deceased were required to shed the blood of the killer or one of his kinsmen. The following case from Athens in the 1850s is not atypical.

An old man, a veteran of the War of Independence, learned that his eldest son had been killed in a fight in a wineshop. Inquiries by himself and his kinsmen convinced him that the fight in which his boy had died was not fair. Blood vengeance was sworn. The old man waited for 40 days during which time peacemakers, including the police, failed to broker a peaceful resolution. Meanwhile throughout this period, the grieving man neither shaved his beard nor cut his hair. Came the forty-first day after the killing, with his red blood boiling and his white hair longer, the old warrior took vengeance. He slid four flintlock pistols and two curved sabers into his silk sash, went to the house of his foe and slew every man in the place.[37] He killed everyone so that the vendetta would not go any further. If he had not massacred them all, then the kinsmen of the deceased would have been bound by blood to exact vengeance on the old warrior or his kinsmen.

In theory a feud would persist until the men on both sides, save one, were killed. Few did though. Usually a form of arbitration would take place and one side would pay blood money to the other, and not infrequently the families would exchange marriage partners to seal the pact.[38] The vendetta and the feud, even as the state authorities tried to stop them and the urban bourgeoisie denounced them, remained features of Greek society well into the twentieth century.

There was one other circumstance in which the community of men absolutely demanded blood: seduction and betrayal. The story is told about a young man from a village in the Peloponnesos who courted a young girl from a good family and betrayed her. The couple became betrothed and, as was often the case after a match had been formally made, they became intimate. On the eve of the wedding, the groom got cold feet and ran away. The bride's family swore revenge. They soon learned that the absconding lothario had joined the merchant marine. Since the code of honour demanded that the bride's brothers could not rest until they had caught up with the man and killed him, they set off in pursuit. Eventually they tracked him to Portugal and on the Lisbon waterfront they cut him to ribbons.[39]

A well-known homicide from the island of Kefallenia gives us some sense of the degree to which this form of interpersonal violence was socially sanctioned. Two brothers from a 'good' (read, honourable) peasant family learned that one of their sisters had become pregnant out of wedlock. They discovered, by means we can only imagine, that it was the son of the wealthy family in whose house she was servant who had seduced her. To avenge the deflowering of their sister, on a balmy summer's eve the two brothers waited until the young man was home alone. They climbed on to the balcony that led to the upstairs dining room where the man was enjoying his evening repast, and they shot him repeatedly.

The more important element of the story is what occurred afterward. Over 20 people, servants, gardeners and others attached to the estate who were working in and around the house witnessed the killing, and yet under intense questioning by the police not a single person would reveal the brothers' identity, and some even commented that the deceased had got what he deserved.[40] It was very common for a wall of silence to descend on Greek villages when the police arrived to inquire about slayings that popular custom determined to be legitimate. And even if it was not, people believed that vengeance was the prerogative of family and kinsmen, and not the state.

From the foregoing one gets the impression that violence was highly prevalent during the nineteenth century, and compared to most other areas of Europe at the time, it was. Yet it was not violence so much as it was aggression that was crucial to honour. A related dimension to the code was that a man should act on his own to achieve his goals. To rely on others, to be dependent, was a sign of weakness, was 'to be like a woman'. Yet the reality, of course, was that such a situation was impossible. Wealth and class stratified Greek society by the nineteenth century. Even within the hamlets and small villages and certainly within the large ones, there were households that were larger and wealthier than the others.

So while men shared an ethical system that emphasized equality, their world was one rife with inequalities. How did they reconcile ideology and reality? One mechanism involved honour itself. As I mentioned earlier, a man's reputation was made or lost through the assessment of his peers, i.e., those co-villagers and neighbours and kinsmen who subscribed to the same ethical system. This process determined boundaries between those who were part of the group that mattered, Us, and those that did not, Them – the bourgeoisie, the landlords, the bureaucrats, etc.[41] The ideology of equality pertained to those in the group.

Peasants coped with the reality of inequalities in a number of ways. One was to make useful outsiders insiders through the practice of fictive kinship, blood brotherhood and godparent-hood for example.[42] Reliance on men who shared the same blood, even metaphorically, did not diminish a man's reputation. Finally, men formed strategic alliances with those from the higher strata of society in which they willingly adopted the subservient position in order to obtain material benefit and protection. These bonds between a client and his patron provided the weaker partner with an important insurance policy in the unsure environment of rural Greece. Because the dominant party came from a higher social class and because the client benefited from the arrangement, to become a client did not diminish a man's stature among his peers. The key here was that the client obtained goods and services that increased his family's fortunes, and so it enhanced his reputation as a man who could take care of his own. Thus, there was often intense competition between peasant men to forge a bond with a powerful figure.

The social world of men, then, was marked by intense and often violent contests over goods, resources and reputations. We can now examine the social world of women.

> Man is endowed with strength to meet life's challenges whereas a woman's strength is toward the tending and feeding of the child. Powerful is the man who takes risks; weak and cautious the woman. He is clever and has imposing and sweeping plans. She is a demon and loses herself in details.[43]

Thus did a late nineteenth century woman's periodical summarize some of the differences between men and women. During the nineteenth century the roles and prescribed behaviours of men and women were sharply defined, in theory at least. As examinations of gender roles in more recent times have suggested, there is often a gap between what the cultural rules mandated and how real people acted in their daily lives.[44] This certainly seems to hold true for the past as well. Let us look first at the ideal.

In reconstructing women's roles in the past the paucity of sources present a formidable obstacle. Not only is there the usual problem of the thinness of the sources but compounding it is the fact that the lion's share of them was penned by men. Nonetheless, using the information found in the travel literature, in the memoirs and commentaries by women, folksongs and folktales, and official documents combined with the ethnographic studies, we can get some sense of both the image and the reality of women's lives in the past.

The first element that stands out was the spatial segregation of women from the outside world. The house was the domain of women, and especially if they were young and unmarried, they were not to leave it without good cause. Second, modesty and shame provided the moral framework that dictated women's comportment and the Virgin Mary (in Greek, the *Panayia)* was supposed to be her model. Third, the woman was to be the source of sustenance in the household; it was her job to prepare the food and to see to the material needs of her family. Fourth, she was also to be the source of spirituality; women were supposed to keep the family icons and attend church. All of these aspects emphasize the positive roles that woman played in society. But men believed there was a dark side as well. Women were believed to be closer to nature and to have the ability to perform magic and witchcraft. Since women lacked self-control, they were always at risk of falling to prey to their baser, sexual instincts. Thus the great concern among men about their wives' reputations. In short women's roles in society were shaped by their domestic duties and their need to ensure that their reputations remained unsullied.

The reality of women's lives was more complex and varied greatly between classes. The daily lives of peasant women were dominated by domestic duties. Preparing her family's food, especially bread, took up a considerable portion of her day. Fetching water was also a very time-consuming task that was gendered as women's work. The care and nurture of children was obviously of importance as well. The women of the household were also to spin and weave the cloth consumed in the household and they were to produce the goods that constitute the trousseau that the daughters of the house would include in their dowries. And while these activities were mainly conducted within the house, there were a variety of activities that took them out into the world.

The labour needs of the peasant household, for example, invariably required women's participation. In large villages and in towns, unmarried women were often employed as domestic servants and perforce had to venture out into public. Lastly, there were a whole variety of female dominated social gatherings that took place in public. Female seclusion then was an unrealizable ideal, except perhaps among the upper classes for whom women's labour was not vital. What was crucial was that women comported themselves in public in a way that conformed to cultural expectations and that the reason she was out in public needed to be related to one of her domestic roles.

Finally, women were supposed to be active defenders of their own and their family's reputations.[45] There was an ethical code for women similar to men's honour and, like men, women engaged in contests over reputations. But whereas men often waged their combat with knives, women employed words. Gossip and slander were the weapons of choice and the stakes were high. If a woman did not contest malicious gossip about sexual comportment, the cleanliness of her house, or her devotion to the church, her sons might have a harder time to find a good match, her daughters might require a much larger dowry to secure a husband, or her spouse might find himself drawing the blade to defend her and his reputation.

In sum, the social world of the little communities of Greece in the past was shaped by the gendered roles of men and women. But in many ways, those roles served a common purpose – enhancing the material wealth and social reputation of the households that men and women made together.

So far we have examined Greek culture largely in a village context, and given that throughout the nineteenth century, Greece was predominantly a society of rural dwellers, that is appropriate. But there was another important development during the long nineteenth century that had a profound impact on society and that was urbanization. By 1920, a sizeable portion of the Greek population resided in Athens and its port city of Piraeus. This began a process that by would end with the greater Athens being home to almost one-third of the country's population and lead to a situation in which one megalopolis effectively dominated the life of the nation.

ATHENS ASCENDANT

From its foundation as the new capital in 1834 Athens was a peculiar city. Unlike many nineteenth century cities, Manchester or Birmingham or Lyon for example, it did not develop as an industrial centre that grew by attracting manufacturing and workers. Nor was it similar to cities like London, Paris or Madrid that enjoyed a long tradition of being a national capital. Indeed, in spite of its antiquity, modern Athens was literally a new city. Granted, during the period of Ottoman rule, Athens had served as a regional marketing and administrative centre, but it could by no stretch of the imagination be considered a conurbation in any meaningful sense of the word. In addition, it had suffered greatly during the war of liberation, and was reduced to ruins at the contest's end.

Looking at the sprawling metropolis of over five million people today, it is hard to imagine that, but for the chance of fate, it could have remained a sleepy little provincial backwater. This proposition seems even more outrageous given the prominent position that ancient Athens plays in the imagined identity of modern Greece. Nonetheless, the observation is accurate. As late as the middle of the nineteenth century, a caustic observer of the Greek scene, Edmond About, noted that if the capital of the kingdom was moved elsewhere, back to Nafplion or to Korinth, Athens would in short order become a ghost town of little consequence.[46] Though cast in his usual hyperbolic fashion, About's point is a telling one. Athens became the premier city of Greece because it was selected to be the capital, and not the other way around. And this had a very profound impact on the way it developed as a city. Before examining the character of the new city's development, we must first get a picture of its demographic development.

Table 5.4 charts the growth of Athens and its port of Piraeus from 1821 to 1920. As we can see, on the eve of the revolution Athens was a modestly sized provincial town. The population was roughly split between Moslems and Christians, and though it operated as a market town, many of its inhabitants were farmers. A few huts hugged the shore around the bay of Phaleron, but

Table 5.4 Population growth of Athens and Piraeus, 1821–1920

	Athens	Piraeus	Total
1821	7,000		7,000
1836	17,600	1,001	18,601
1840	18,535	2,033	20,568
1850	24,278	5,286	29,564
1860	41,298	6,452	47,750
1870	44,510	10,963	55,473
1880	84,903	24,883	109,786
1890	114,355	36,000	150,355
1900	123,001	50,200	173,201
1910	167,479	73,579	241,058
1920	292,991	133,482	426,473

Piraeus, as we know it, did not even exist. Between the mid-1830s, when it was made the kingdom's capital, till mid-century, Athens grew from 17,600 to 24,278 and Piraeus was established as the main port to service the new city. During this first phase of growth, Athens expanded through in-migration of wealthy diaspora Greeks, office holders, and the new clerical middle class and those members of the lower social orders needed to provide services to them. In other words, the initial expansion of Athens involved disproportionately members of the middle and upper classes.

A second, and far more profound, period of urban expansions began during the 1860s and then took off during the 1870s and 1880s. Between 1870 and 1890, Athens and Piraeus grew by 271 per cent and manifested annual growth rates of an astonishingly high 5.17 per cent. Unlike the early phase of urban in-migration, this second growth spurt was fuelled by the movement of rural peasants and workers moving to the city in search of work. As we saw earlier in this chapter, the Greek rural population grew at a fairly consistent and high rate for much of the century, but economic growth did not keep pace, nor could the material conditions of the countryside provide for the increasing numbers. The pressure on land and the oversupply of labour created a rural pressure cooker that could only be relieved by a rural exodus. By the fin-de-siècle, Athens and Piraeus had become a large urban complex that was radically different in character than it had been even at mid-century. As it grew in size and complexity, so too did Athens change in character.

King Otto and the Bavarian Regents decided to make Athens the capital of the new kingdom because of its connection to the glories of classical antiquity – a connection that was openly visible in Athens more than in other cities like Nafplion and Argos. A series of architects were employed to draft blueprints for the construction of a city that would both pay homage to the past and reinforce the connection of Greece to the west. Neoclassical public buildings in marble, like the Royal Palace, the Royal Academy, and the Parliament building, began to adorn the wide boulevards like Ermou Street and Panepistemiou Street. When the seat of government shifted to Athens in 1834, hundreds of people flooded Athens in search of housing. One newspaper of the time bemoaned how old Athenian families, some even with pregnant women and infant children, were being turned out into the streets to make way for the rich and the powerful, for the bureaucrats, officeholders and government hangers-on.[47]

Conforming to the grand vision set out in the various master plans, splendid townhouses adorned with neoclassical facades soon began to appear on the major streets and avenues around the new centres of power. As home to the cultured elite and as the centrepiece for the 'westernization' of Greek society, Athens quickly became a very cosmopolitan city. The latest styles in clothes, for example, would soon find their way from the salons of Paris, London and Milan to the shops of Athens. On the city streets, then, one would see side-by-side living vestiges of the legacy of Ottoman rule along with self-consciously crafted displays of Europeaness.

Alongside bourgeois Athens, another city developed. This other place was home to the lower classes of society. After all, the upper and middle classes could not get by alone. They needed servants and shopkeepers, haberdashers and hairdressers, carters and coachmen. Carpenters, masons, and other construction workers were needed to meet the demand of contractors. Dockworkers and deliverymen were needed to shift the ever-increasing volume of goods that now began to appear at Piraeus. People, especially from the Cyclades, began moving to Athens to fill these roles. With the influx of migrants, land and housing prices in Athens soared. In addition, because this was to be a planned city, permits were required to build within the city limits. The high cost of accommodation and the tight restrictions on building new houses put lower class people in a bind.

The story is told of an old woman who was standing in an Athenian street, staring at a plot of land with tearful eyes. In her hand she held a piece of paper. An elderly gentleman approached her and inquired what circumstance had driven her to such a state. She needed to build a house for her family, she replied, but she did not have the permission of Athens' planning board and did not expect to hear back from them for many months. And in the meantime, she bemoaned, they would have nowhere to live. Not to worry, the man replied, I know the architect. Give me your petition and I'll see what I can do. Within days she received her building permit. She was a lucky woman indeed.

Fig. 5.4 'Bootblacks in Athens'. The massive influx of young men and women from the countryside to Athens during the last two decades of the nineteenth century could not be absorbed by the under-developed industrial economy of the time. Many men found work in low-level service occupations, like shining shoes, as depicted here. The urban migration stream would soon flow out of the country to the United States. [H.A. Franck, I Discover Greece, *New York, 1929, photo facing p. 172.]*

Not many people could get King Ludwig of Bavaria, the father of their own King Otto, to intervene on their behalf.

Most people who found themselves in that situation simply disregarded the law and built illegally, risking a confrontation with the authorities.[48] Or they built outside of the city limits and thus were not covered by the planning laws. Some threw together shacks to house their families. Others built multiple dwelling houses with an eye to renting one or more of them to newcomers at very steep rents. The housing difficulties rose to crisis levels during the 1870s and 1880s as tens of thousands of people poured into Athens and Piraeus. The central core of bourgeois and 'respectable' Athens became ringed with poorer neighbourhoods. Piraeus, in particular, developed as a working class city because this was where the hard jobs of working the docks and of carting the goods were concentrated, but also because it was in and around Piraeus that industry began to develop.

As Athens and Piraeus grew in size and complexity, the usual 'social problems' that accompanied nineteenth century urbanization developed. The rates of crime and violence, for example, soared. During the period of peak in-migration the greater Athens area experienced one of the most profound increases in homicide ever recorded.[49] For the years 1888–91, when the homicide indictment rates in cities like London, Paris, Berlin and Amsterdam were less than two killings for every 100,000 people, Athens recorded a rate of 107! The overwhelmingly young and male migrants to Athens and Piraeus brought with them the propensity to violence inculcated during their rural upbringing, except that circumstances in the city brought their violent tendencies more frequently to the fore.

Thrust together in a hostile environment, men from various regions of the country found themselves in new contentious situations. Absent, however, were many of the social control mechanisms that existed in the village – limited though they were. Kinsmen were not there to pull disputants apart; nor were the village elders who might prevent disputes from reaching violent ends – though as we saw above, they were often unsuccessful mediators. And in the struggle to create new social hierarchies, men became, I would suggest, hyper-sensitive to slights real or imagined on their honour. Thus, as we saw earlier, much of this violence took place in taverns and cafes. One episode reported in the newspaper *Avgi* epitomizes the new street violence.[50] Two men were standing in line to get water at a pump. One cut in front of the other. They exchanged angry words. One pulled a razor and slit the other's throat.

The numerous wars and irredentist conflicts waged by Greece during this period introduced another dimension: cheap firearms. The impression is that pistols came to account for the majority of homicides in this period.

Along with violence, other public order issues emerge. Street crimes like robbery and larceny became a constant problem in Athens.

> In every house great precautions are adopted against robberies. These a few years since[,] were frequently committed. A band of ten or fifteen robbers has been known to enter one of the largest houses in the city, by the connivance of the porter, and to plunder it of all its valuables. The poorer class of houses is entered with comparative ease.[51]

Beggary and vagabondage, and prostitution also became issues of social and political importance. Other social problems emerged as well. Infant abandonment, for example, became a grave concern.[52] As did a whole variety of environmental issues like the need to supply water, build sewers, provide streetlights and pavements, and regulate traffic. All of these issues required direct state intervention, and in responding to them the power of state over civil society and the capacity of the government to intervene in peoples' lives, often at the expense of civil liberties, ominously expanded.

Harilaos Trikoupis, as in so many areas of late nineteenth century Greece, led the reform movement. In each of his long administrations, for example, Trikoupis enacted reforms of the criminal justice system. With regard to the police, he initiated a variety of comprehensive reforms that helped to modernize the various forces. He appointed the ruthless Bairaktaris as chief of the Athens police and gave him sweeping powers to deal with urban crime. Bairaktaris doubled the number of police in Athens, increased their pay, and inaugurated more careful screening and training of recruits. Law 2509 of 21 July 1892 gave the Athens' chief of police the power to use regular army troops to patrol the city, and Bairaktaris employed this tool vigorously. Trikoupis also suspended *habeas corpus* on two occasions and allowed known offenders and 'shiftless young men' to be rounded up, detained without trial and exiled to deserted or sparsely populated Aegean islands – often for a considerable period of time.[53] While helping to deal with the immediate problem of urban crime, these actions set dangerous precedents for the future. He was just as active in other areas as well, passing laws regulating housing, sanitation, and public welfare. He built new hospitals and orphanages and refurbished older ones. And while these measures did help to alleviate some of the most pressing problems caused by rapid urbanization, many more remained unsolved.

COMING TO AMERICA

'There are few manufacturing plants and none of any great importance ... Female and child labor are very generally utilized in Greece, whenever they can be made serviceable ... There is not much hope for a laboring man to save money in Greece, where three to four drachmas a day are good wages and where seven drachmas are regarded as a high wage for a master workman.' A laborer earning five drachmas per day will pay ten drachmas per month for a room for himself and his family. 'The workman's breakfast consists of bread and black coffee; his luncheon of a piece of bread, or if he can afford it, a piece of bread and some black olives, which he usually takes with him in a little round, covered box. Sometimes he buys a half cent's worth of inferior grapes, or a tomato. Thus his lunch would cost, say, six cents for bread and two cents for olives.' At night the family dines on a few cents' worth of rice, boiled together with wild greens and olive oil, and bread, or wild greens boiled in olive oil and eaten with bread, or some similar inexpensive dish ... Meat is eaten by the laboring classes as a general thing three times a year: Christmas, Easter, and on the so-called 'Birth of the Virgin,' which the church has set down for the month of August. Such a family as I am describing, the average laboring man's family of Greece, rarely if ever see such things as butter, eggs and milk. There are 180 fasting days in the Greek religious year, which are rigorously observed by the laboring class, without, however, causing any marked degree of abnega-tion in the matter of diet.' People living under conditions of this sort are ripe for emigration, especially if, like the Greeks, they are of a stock which has always displayed great readiness in severing home ties. All that is needed to start an enormous exodus is some immediate stimulus, some slight turn in the condition of affairs, provided that a favorable outlet presents itself, and the process of migration is not too expensive or difficult. As an American gentleman of long residence in Athens remarked, 'The wonder is, not that the Greeks are now emigrating to America in such numbers, but that they did not begin long ago.'[54]

This passage from the first study of the Greeks in America captures the key factors that inaugurated and sustained the massive exodus of Greeks at the turn of the century. Between 1890 and the 1920, over half a million people, almost 90 per cent of them men between the ages of 18 and 35, left their homeland and migrated to almost every corner of the globe. Some crossed the Mediterranean and moved to Ethiopia, the Sudan, Tanganyika, and South Africa; others gravitated to places where long-standing Greek communities existed like Britain and Russia; but the vast majority looked to both the northern and southern hemispheres of the New World, and above all the other places combined, they immigrated to the United States. During the decades around the turn of the century, more than 500,000 men moved to the United

States. Many returned to Greece; others stayed and carved out a living, eventually bringing over a bride from their *patrida* (homeland).

The factors driving the exodus are for the most part the same ones that caused the shift in population from the countryside to Athens. Relative rural over-population, a scarcity of labour and low wages made it simply impossible for households with more than one or two sons to make ends meet and to provide for the continuation of the family into the next generation by providing dowries and inheritances that could sustain new households. The 1890s collapse of the currant market, which pushed Greece into bankruptcy as we saw in the last chapter, devastated the rural economy. Larger estates that employed thousands of wage labourers either went out of business or dramatically scaled back production, thus putting more people out of work. Sharecroppers who paid their rents in currants now found themselves defaulting on their payments, and many were evicted. Small private land-holding peasants who grew currants as their cash crop with which to pay their taxes and to meet household expenses were devastated. A new wave of men and women were driven out of the countryside looking for work. The slow pace of industrialization meant that there were not sufficient jobs in the cities to absorb the rural refugees. In addition, as the passage cited above suggests, many of those who had been part of the migration flow to Athens and Piraeus during the 1870s and 1880s and who found jobs and established families suffered as well during the depression of the 1890s. Some determined to stay and fight for better conditions by joining the labour movement or one of the emerging left wing political parties. Others chose to seek a better life in America.

Three different migration flows brought people from Greece to the United States. The largest one consisted of men and a few women who had either already lived in the cities for some time or who had recently arrived there but could not make ends meet. According to the best available figures over 63 per cent of the immigrants to the States were either unskilled workers or servants.[55] Another stream swept up people who moved abroad directly from the countryside. Included in this group would be those 16 per cent who considered themselves to be farmers and some of those who listed their occupation as labourer. There was a third and smaller group that consisted of merchants and skilled workers. Most of these folks moved from the city, and constituted the majority of those who moved as couples or as complete families.

The move abroad, or what in Greek is referred as *xenitia*, was financed in one of three ways. In some cases, men paid for their own passage with funds that they had been able to save or to borrow from kinsmen. In a large number of instances, agents called *padrones* would make an agreement with young men whereby the agent would provide them with passage to America and in return the men would be obligated to work for whomever the padrone contracted them out to. Obviously this system was susceptible to corruption and abuse, and many Greek migrants recalled the horrors of the transatlantic crossing that were only compounded when they arrived in the United States to be shipped in cattle cars to the western frontier to work laying railroad track or digging in mines. The last mechanism for emigration consisted of chain migration. In these cases, one member of a family who had made the sojourn previously would send money back to Greece to pay the passage of a kinsman. In this way more than one member of a kingroup could move abroad without falling into the clutches of a padrone.

The mass migration of the late nineteenth–early twentieth century had a profound impact on the development of Greek society. Could it be otherwise when a country loses almost 40 per cent of its adult male population? But the impact of the exodus had both positive and negative dimensions. The most important of the positive results was the massive amount of money injected into the Greek economy by remittances sent home by foreign emigrants.

It is estimated that on average Greeks sent home approximately $5,000,000 each year between 1903 and 1914. The huge outflow of people relieved the population pressure and underemployment in the countryside: perhaps too much so. Some large landowners found themselves having to bring in migrant farm workers from Albania to meet their labour needs. Wages in some industries also rose as companies competed for workers. The levels of interpersonal violence were reduced substantially as the most violence prone sector of society migrated to the United States, where they were equally violent.[56]

But there were numerous negative consequences. Factory owners and others replaced male workers with women or children, to whom they paid low wages. The demographic growth of the country slowed. The number of men in their prime eligible for service in the military fell. Large sections of the countryside went out of cultivation, and numerous small villages became deserted.

Many of the migrants would eventually return to their homeland, but from the turn of the century onward a new chapter in the long history of the Greek diaspora had been opened.

6 From a Nation United to a Nation Divided

No single figure casts as long a shadow over the history of Greece in the twentieth century as Eleftherios Venizelos. For a quarter of the century, he dominated the political life of the nation. He led Greece to some of its greatest accomplishments and was part of its most cataclysmic defeats. He came closest to fulfilling the *Megali Idea*, but was partly responsible for the dream coming to an end. He did more than anyone else to foster the social and economic development of Greece; but he also brought it to the brink of civil war. During his era, he was both the most loved and the most despised man in Greece.

In this chapter, we return to a more conventional narrative mode in order to tell the story of how Greece rebounded from the disasters that occurred at the end of the nineteenth century and then went on to score some of its greatest domestic and international successes a few short years after that, only to be plunged back into chaos by an event that is still referred to simply as the 'Catastrophe.' Since Venizelos played so prominent and important a role in the events that first united Greece and then divided it, our story centres first on the Cretan leader.

NATIONAL MALAISE AND VENIZELOS'S RISE TO POWER

Eleftherios Venizelos was born in the city of Khania on the island of Crete in 1864. Reared in a professional family, he studied at the University of Athens and in 1887 received his degree in law. In addition to his career as a lawyer, he went on to become a journalist and a politician. Possessing an agile mind, a deep intellect and a charismatic personality, in the words of a recent biographer, 'he was alternately an audacious revolutionary and a thorough constitutionalist, liberal by education and principles but intolerant by temperament, a popular agitator and a sober statesmen, an outlaw and a prime minister.'[1]

We examined in Chapter 4 the story of the Cretan struggles for liberation from 1832 onward, and we saw that though the ultimate goal of the Cretan insurgents (union with Greece) remained unfulfilled, their actions caused the Great Powers to pressure the Porte into granting greater autonomy to the island's Christian population. Given his natural aptitude and his ardent patriotism, not surprisingly, the young Venizelos quickly became a leading figure in the Cretan liberation movements. He entered politics in 1889 as an assemblyman in the short-lived Cretan assembly.

Between that date and the second Cretan revolution of 1896–97, Venizelos was very active writing articles and making fiery speeches in favour of unification. While the end was always clear, the liberation of Crete and its union (*enosis*) with Greece, his views on the means for achieving them were not. He opted for a strategy of 'guns and negotiations' (*doufeki kai pazari*), though how these two were to be balanced and carried out was never really clear. The outcome of the war of 1897, however, changed that situation.[2]

The settlement between Greece and the Ottoman Empire in the aftermath of the 1897 war seemingly granted major concessions to Greece regarding Crete. The treaty granted autonomy to the island, under the leadership of a High Commissioner; it reduced the Sultan's dominion over the island to a purely symbolic level; it established a Cretan assembly composed of 138 Christians and 50 Moslems; and it created a locally devised and operated judicial and criminal justice system. The Great Powers selected King George I's son and namesake, Prince George, as the High Commissioner. Venizelos emerged as the leader of the liberal faction on the island. He helped to draft the constitution and became the first Minister of Justice. In spite of the concessions made to the islanders, their ardent desire for unification was not dampened. If anything, the bestowal of autonomy and the appointment of a member of the Greek royal family only stoked the fires of nationalism and elevated the Cretans' hopes that unification was imminent.

Many Cretans found Prince George high-handed and overbearing, and even though he was an advocate of unification, they believed that he was not doing all he could to push the process forward. The reality was that the Great Powers had no intention of altering the status quo on the island. After a series of confrontations with the High Commissioner, Venizelos resigned from the government and in 1905, at the head of a small band of armed followers, he raised the banner of revolt. From his mountain stronghold he declared unification of Crete with the Kingdom of Greece. A few days later the Cretan assembly followed suit and demanded that Prince George bring the issue before the representatives of the European powers. George was caught in a dilemma. He knew that it was futile to press the Powers, but he would lose the support of moderates if he did not pursue the matter. He also realized that Venizelos's actions directly challenged his authority, but he was loath to order the Greek gendarmerie to fire on other Greeks. Finally, the Great Powers intervened and Venizelos was forced to capitulate, but he did so on terms which were fairly favourable to his position and which had not been cleared with Prince George. The settlement made it obvious to all that Cretan unification was only a matter of time.

The results of this episode were long lasting and important. First, the Prince had lost face and his position on the island became untenable. He resigned accordingly. Thus began a lifelong antipathy between the royal family and Venizelos. Second, the Cretan leader emerged as national hero in the wider Greek world. It was because of the reputation he earned as nationalist leader on Crete that Venizelos was able to enter the stage of Greek politics on a national level in 1910 when he answered the call of the military coup that had taken place in Athens in 1909. He would stay in the limelight for over two decades.[3]

The so-called 'Goudi coup' of 1909 had deep and multi-stranded roots. We have already touched on some of the more important ones, like the financial collapse of 1893–95, the military debacle of 1897, and the vacillating fortunes of the national struggle in Macedonia and Crete. Together, they helped to create an ongoing crisis of the entire political system and they fostered a *fin-de-siècle* malaise that infected much of Greek society. Following Harilaos Trikoupis's departure from politics and his death in Paris in 1896, there was a void in the leadership of the pro-western reformist faction. The conservative Deliyiannis had been discredited by defeat at the hands of the Ottoman military and, after he was stabbed to death in 1905 by a gambler upset at his proposals to crackdown on public gambling, his party also plunged into disarray.

A new generation of political leadership was developing but there was no unifying force equivalent to Trikoupis's reform-mindedness and Deliyiannis's populist conservatism. Instead, four figures emerged from the older parties, but none of them proved able to fill their predecessor's shoes. Giorgios Theotokis took over control of the Trikoupis party, but he lacked the dynamism to control the party's old guard and his cautious moderation alienated the younger, more reform-minded newcomers. Kyriakoulis Mavromichalis and Dimitrios Rallis split the Deliyannis party, and Alexander Zaïmes, Deliyannis' nephew and a moderate centrist, was able on occasion to siphon off enough members of the two main parties to form a viable third party. In the end, neither of the two traditional parties nor any of the old guard among the political leadership proved able to mobilize sufficient support among the people nor to gain the steadfast backing of the palace to rule the country effectively.

The result was political gridlock, the nature of which historian Victor Papacosma captures well:

> Party propaganda, extravagant promises, bribery and patronage flourished. Since party discipline was non-existent and individualism rampant, deputies continued to shift parties for politically selfish reasons. Parliamentary obstructionism remained standard practice with politicians, generally adept in oratory, often filibustering up to three days to block legislation. At other times sizeable groups of deputies absented themselves from the *Boule* so that quorum requirements necessary for business could not be met.[4]

Government was almost at a standstill.

Fragmenting the political scene even further was the emergence of new political groupings based on a variety of ideologies ranging from anarchism to popular radicalism to agrarian conservatism. Turned off by the nature of the old parties, many men who once would have formed the parties' new cadres now looked elsewhere. Some, like Stefanos Dragoumis, Dimitrios Gounaris and their colleagues, eschewed partisanship and argued instead for political, economic, and social modernization. They were dubbed the 'Japan' party because they aimed to reform Greece in manner reminiscent of what the Meiji dynasty had recently accomplished in Japan. Others argued that it was in fact modernization and the importation of 'western' ideas that were creating Greece's problems. They urged that society should return to a society in which the Orthodox Church was the dominant institution.[5]

At the same time political parties and movements began to develop that were both secular and stood in opposition to the old guard. In those regions where an industrial workforce had come into existence, workers' centres were founded. These helped to create class-consciousness among labourers and they provided a forum in which workers were exposed to the writings of leading socialists and Marxists.[6] Even in the countryside radical organizations began to take root among the poor sharecroppers and rural labourers. Finally, a last cultural response to the national malaise that cut across boundaries of class and political ideologies was romantic nationalism. The struggles in Macedonia and Crete exerted an almost mystical hold on large segments of the Greek population.[7] The vacuum in public life created by the collapse of the old parties was quickly filled by an odd assortment of new movements, almost all of which challenged the status quo.

Just as important as the rise of ideological opposition to the old order were the numerous episodes of actual disorder in the streets. Periodically this manifested itself in mass, violent actions. In November 1901, for example, perhaps as many as 50,000 people took to the streets of Athens to protest; the demonstrations soon led to clashes with the police and the military, during which at least eight people were killed and scores more wounded. The cause of the riot was the publication of the Bible in demotic, or popular, Greek.

We saw in Chapter 4 how important the language question was in regard to Greek national identity, and the so-called 'Gospel' riots indicate the strength of feeling over this issue. But there were other factors involved as well and they speak to the issue of the national crises of the early twentieth century that interests us here. Advocates of Katharevousa saw the translation of the Bible into popular Greek as a betrayal of Hellenism and as part of a Pan-Slavist plot. Those who supported the translation argued that it was only demotic Greek that could unite the entirety of the nation, both those within in the kingdom and those who had yet to be redeemed. Thus nationalism, Hellenism, the Megali Idea, cultural identity and the Macedonian issue all came together at a time when many believed that their government was impotent to protect the national struggle, and the result was mass violence over an issue that seemed trivial to the rest of Europe.[8]

Numerous other violent public demonstrations occurred over the next years only served to heighten the sense of national crises. There was, for example the '*sanidika*' demonstration (so called because of the planks or *sanides* torn from kiosks and used by the rioters as weapons) in December 1902 in which members of various artisan and merchant guilds rioted in protest at the failure of the November elections to produce a working government. A few months later, uprisings by tens of thousands of peasants protesting the deplorable state of the rural economy rocked the Peloponnesos and required the intervention of the army before order could be restored.[9] Even the royal family was not spared in 1905, when guild members besieged the palace demanding an audience with the King to protest the government's recent tax hikes.

Contributing to this unrest was the poor state of the economy. New international loans and ever-increasing taxes were required to pay the bills. Migration to the cities, and especially to Athens and Piraeus, and emigration to the United States, as we saw in the last section, were creating social dislocation on a massive scale. Finally, there was a widespread and pervasive sense among the people that none of the existing political parties could deal with all of these problems. Nor did they believe that the monarchy could.

Politically, as well as there being a void created by the absence of a strong party or leader, there was also a crisis of legitimacy regarding the monarchy. Crown-Prince Konstantine partly bore responsibility for the national humiliation in Thessaly, and by extension, his father also had to share in the blame. The reign of the Glücksburg dynasty was at its lowest point ever. After an unsuccessful attempt on his life and the ever-increasing evidence that he had lost the support of much of the population, King George even considered abdication. The military was angry over what it saw as unfair criticism. The high command believed that blunders by the politicians had forced them to fight a war for which they were ill-prepared and under equipped. The relationship between the monarchy and the military had for some time been a cause for concern. As Commander-in-Chief of the military, the King could play a very active role. Thus, favourites of King George and his sons often had a fast track to promotions while other, more qualified officers did not. Disgruntlement spread in the officer corps because of favouritism and the consequent lack of mobility for qualified men, the absence of good leadership in the armed forces, the vacuum of political direction, and cuts in military spending.[10]

The result of this situation was the formation of clandestine societies within the military. The most important of these was the *Stratiotikos Sindesmos*, or the Military League. A series of events beginning in 1907 led to the decision of the League's leadership that the intervention of the military into politics was required. The first of these was the situation regarding Macedonia. Britain was continuing to put pressure on Greece to stop the activities of the Greek bands. When during the summer of 1907 Britain entered into a pact with Russia, fears were raised that a solution unfavourable to Greece would be forthcoming. The following year the Young Turk Revolution brought into power a reform minded Ottoman government that promised major modifications to the administration of the region. This held out the promise of ending the troubles that beset the region and could lead to Macedonia remaining as an integral part of the Empire. The radical nationalist turn of the Young Turk government in the spring of 1909 threatened to plunge the region back into sectarian violence at a time when it was clear to the Greek military leadership that the current government in Athens was unprepared to deal with it.

These events came on the heels of another disastrous year economically and the consequent increase in civil unrest. Finally, the impending trials in a court martial of some of their colleagues in the military for having presented the government of Prime Minister Dimitrios Rallis with a list of demands provided the final pretext for action. Rebuffed yet again by the government, Colonel Nikolaos Zorbas and First Lieutenant Theodore Pangalos, prominent members of the League, gathered 5,500 troops at the garrison at Goudi and on 28 August 1909 used them to stage a *coup d'etat.*

After bloodlessly over-throwing the government, the Military League issued four demands:

- a written acknowledgement from the government that it had received and accepted the memorandum of reforms which they had issued;
- formal assurance that the parliament would not be dissolved;
- amnesty for all those who had taken part in the coup or who had been dismissed for political reasons in the months leading up to it;
- the dismissal from the military of those officers who had opposed the League.

Rallis refused to accept these terms and resigned. King George appointed a caretaker government and did the best that he could to keep up the appearance that the monarchy was still in charge, but the Military League held the reigns of power.

The Military League had a very narrow agenda, limited primarily to issues involving the armed forces and irredentism. The coup initially met with wide support, not because the Military League furthered the interests of a single class, but rather because they symbolized action at a time of national malaise. Once in power, it became apparent that the League leaders were unsure how to proceed. King George was very concerned about his position; the Great Powers had never supported the coup and reiterated their firm support of the monarchy. Moreover, the coup imperiled Greece's relationship to the international financial community. As a consequence of these developments, the leadership of the Military League finally recognized that it needed to return the reins of power to civilian politicians. The dilemma for them was who would best be able to step in and not lead the nation back into the 'politics as usual' of the previous period?

The choice finally fell on Eleftherios Venizelos for three primary reasons:

- he had demonstrated his *bona fides* as a nationalist leader through his recent activities on Crete;
- those activities had resulted in the resignation of Prince George as High Commissioner of Crete and so Venizelos was seen as an opponent of the monarchy;
- he was not associated with any of the old political parties and the old political system, known as the *palaiokommatismos*, and thus was seen as someone who could break the gridlock of pre-coup politics.

Once he became the spokesman for the military, Venizelos engineered the dissolution of the parliament and called for an election to obtain a mandate for a new government. The so-called 'revisionary' parliament was returned in August 1910 with no clear victor. While this was occurring, elections were held on Crete and Venizelos was elected première there. Having established himself in Athens as a force to be reckoned with and having been the driving force behind Cretan unification, his prestige in the Greek world soared. Venizelos returned to Athens in September and was greeted by enthusiastic crowds and wary politicians. No-one was quite sure what to expect from the Cretan. Rather than fire, he breathed the language of moderation. Seeing that Venizelos was the only politician who could control the military, King George gave him his support. The monarchy was thus saved and Venizelos's stature grew even more.

THE FIRST GOLDEN AGE OF VENIZELISM

Eleftherios Venizelos became the focal point of a new party – the *komma ton Fileftheron*, or the Liberal Party. It would be the dominant political force in Greece for 20 years with a legacy that would persist long after that. After some initial political machinations, Venizelos won two resounding victories in national elections, garnering 260 out of 346 (75 per cent) seats in the election of December 1910 and 145 of 181 (80 per cent) in a second election 14 months later.[11] The period from 1911 to 1916 is often referred to as the 'First Golden Age' because of the striking successes that Venizelos and the Liberals would achieve both domestically and abroad.

The popular base of the Liberal Party was diverse. It drew on younger, educated professionals seeking advancement. Trikoupists, who saw the party as a continuation of their old movement, flocked to the Liberal banner. For a variety of different reasons urban merchants and artisans, industrial workers, and factory owners also gave their support to the new regime. The party's evident nationalist orientation helped to solidify support across the board. Unlike the conservative parties that refused to recognize that class divisions had developed in Greece during the previous 20 years and the various parties of the Left that had adopted explicitly class-based orientations, the Liberal Party recognized class differences but endeavoured in some way to address the needs of all of them.[12] Thus, in the period between 1910 and 1912, Venizelos and the Liberals passed a bevy of legislation at a frantic pace.

During the first six months of 1911, for example, no less than 53 constitutional amendments were passed dealing with the procedures and powers of the judiciary, the legislature, and even the monarchy. New bureaucratic organizations, most importantly a new council of state and a consultative committee for drafting legislation, were established. The eligibility requirements for parliament were altered; the age of qualification was lowered; commissioned officers in the armed forces were barred from holding office, as were civil servants and directors of banks and public companies. The powers of the state were expanded. The administration of public education was taken out of the hands of local authorities and placed under central control. The state's ability to confiscate private property was eased, requiring only that the state show 'public benefit' rather than compelling 'public need'. One amendment rendered to the state the capacity to suspend fundamental civil rights, such as protection from arbitrary seizure, the right to a trial by jury, the need to show cause for a search of a person's body or premises, the freedom of the press, and the right to public assembly. These latter amendments show the autocratic side of the charismatic Cretan.

In the months that followed, Venizelos demonstrated his populist side by pushing through an impressive array of legislation, over 330 separate laws. Many of the new regulations dealt with social issues. He passed a variety of new laws dealing with work place conditions and the delineation of workers' rights. For example, legislation was passed which fixed wages for women and children, regulated child labour, established the six-day working week, and created a labour relations board. Trade unions were legalized and joint trade associations (these were management controlled workers unions which employees had to join as a condition of employment) were outlawed.[13] 'Feudalism' and the archaic law of summary seizure for debt were abolished. He legislated for the creation of a national health insurance system. Land reform and land redistribution schemes were passed and implemented. He attempted to simplify the Byzantine tax system by introducing a graduated income tax; many of the most onerous and regressive indirect taxes were removed from the books. Seen as a whole this was the single most comprehensive agenda of social reform legislation in Greek history. Moreover, it had something for everybody, and so stole the thunder of the parties both to the Left and the Right.[14]

Recognizing the circumstances that had brought him to power, Venizelos was careful to address the needs of the armed forces. Not only was he cognizant of the potential interference of the military, he saw clearly that Greece needed strong armed forces both to achieve his own dream of Cretan unification and to further the cause of Greek irredentism elsewhere. Consequently, he embarked on a programme of reform and restructuring of the military. He introduced compulsory military service and increased the size of the army to 150,000. Massive expenditures were made on the latest arma-ments from Germany and elsewhere. French advisers had been brought in to staff the new officer training college he founded. The monarchy was allowed its traditional connection to the army, but its role became more ceremonial than real. The Greek fleet was expanded and modernized and its officers sent to study with English Royal Navy experts. Paying for the reforms and the mil-itary expansion was made possible through the financial management skills of Stefanos Dragoumis. He managed to raise revenues through tax reform which, when combined with new loans and renegotiated terms on existing loans alongside higher revenues, led to cash surpluses in the treasury by 1912. The nation had been rearmed and Venizelos would soon put the refurbished military to use.

In his first years of office, Venizelos oversaw the reinvigoration of Greece after the financial collapse of the 1890s, the national humiliation of the Greek military on the plains and hills of Thessaly, and the malaise and discontent of 1900s. His social reforms addressed fundamental questions and problems that, if left unanswered, threatened to erupt in massive unrest – as had occurred in many other parts of Europe. His fiscal reforms brought a semblance of financial stability in the wake of the chaos of the previous decade. His military reforms had rearmed the nation and set it on a footing to compete for power in the Balkans.

THE BALKAN WARS

In the short span of less than two years the Balkans would be convulsed in a major regional war, from which Greece would emerge victorious and with its territory substantially enlarged. At the heart of the Balkan Wars were three issues:

- the disposition of Macedonia;
- the problem of Crete;
- liberation and autonomy for the countries still under Ottoman rule, in particular Albania.

Through the first decade of the twentieth century the problem of Macedonia had remained an issue of national and international significance. As discussed previously, during the late nineteenth and early twentieth centuries rival factions, in particular IMRO and the *Ethniki Etaireia*, which continued to be active even after its formal disbandment in 1897, struggled to define the ethnic and cultural identity of the region. Language, religion, and education were for a time the chosen battleground, but soon the conflict took on a more violent aspect. The situation was complex: some wanted total unification with Greece, others wanted a separate Macedonian state, and still others wanted Macedonia to be included in a Serbian or Albanian or Bulgarian state. Villages and even households were split, and deciding which cause one espoused was increasingly a matter of life or death. *Makedonomakhoi*, guerrilla warriors from all around the Greek world, flocked to Macedonia to join the fighting. Matching them were fighters from all the other sides. In spite of the hyperbolic propaganda produced by the various factions, it is clear that atrocities were being committed and that no one group was any guiltier than the others.

Athens was actively supporting the irredentist movement in Macedonia. Money, materials and men were being surreptitiously sent northwards. The Metropolitan of Kastoria, Germanos Karavangelis, spearheaded the Hellenic cause in Macedonia. Greek bands totalling approximately 2,000 men waged constant guerrilla war against IMRO and other exarchist bands. Terror was a tactic used by both sides against non-combatants. An economic war was also waged. In Thessaloniki, for example, exarchist shop owners found themselves facing boycotts aimed at compelling them to sell out, or even worse, they became subject to terror tactics intent on the same goal. The result was that the city became more of a Greek city. To be sure, Jews and Turks still outnumbered Greeks, but the Slavic population was decreasing and consequently the exarchist forces were losing access to the main port of the northern Aegean. The situation was becoming increasingly tense.

The Great Powers became more involved in the Macedonian problem through the first decade of the twentieth century. Britain in particular endeavoured to find a workable solution to the question. Russia had expressed continued interest in the Slavic cause, which in turn caused concern in Austria. Pressure was brought to bear on Greece to curb the activities of the *Makedonomakhoi*. British Foreign Secretary Sir Edward Grey, in a series of speeches in the British Parliament, began to explore the idea of an independent Macedonian state. The Young Turks Revolution of 1908 changed the situation dramatically. The initial response to the Young Turks was very favourable. Their promise to decentralize rule, to create a true multi-ethnic state, and to hold elections, which included the Christian population, generated great enthusiasm. Bands from all sides came forward and surrendered their arms. Negotiations between Athens and Istanbul were cordial and held the promise of success. The respite in the conflict was short lived. After a failed counter-coup in 1909, a nationalist faction of the Young

Turk movement came to power and they reverted to an older, authoritarian model of rule. Gone was the promise of decentralization; gone was the pledge of self-rule; gone was the guarantee of multinationalism. In Macedonia and on Crete, the new regime was even more intransigent than the Hamidan dynasty it had overthrown. War clouds loomed.[15]

The Cretan problem also continued to stew through the first decade of this century. The protectorate status of the island was simply unacceptable to the nationalists who wanted *enosis* at any cost. The matter came to a head with the accession to power of Venizelos. The Turks threatened war when he took up the office of Prime Minister. Tensions increased further when the assembly on Crete voted to send representatives to the new parliament of 1912. The British fleet intervened to stop them reaching Athens, and after they were released, Venizelos forbade their admission into the session. Nonetheless, the response from the Porte was clear: the issue of Crete could lead to war.

The final cause of the Balkan War lay with the nationalist issue in the Balkans. Bulgarians, Albanians, Serbs, and Montenegrins all sought to advance their respective nationalist causes. A rallying cry of the day was 'the Balkans for the Balkan states'. The way forward seemed to be through a form of Pan-Slavic movement, or failing that at least through some configurations of bilateral cooperation. Such an arrangement of major importance was signed on 13 March 1912, between Serbia and Bulgaria. It was a mutual defence pact, obligating each to assist the other in case of war. The treaty also divided northern Macedonia between them. It assumed that the fate of southern Macedonia would be decided between Bulgaria and Greece.

The response in Athens to this development was to sign a bilateral agreement with Bulgaria and to open negotiations with Serbia. Venizelos, however, was cautious about these developments. He feared that Greece was at that moment the least prepared to go to war and that it was the one with the most to lose; he was thinking here of the massive Greek population in Asia Minor. But Macedonia was very much on his mind as well. This made the Bulgarian treaty particularly important because, in spite of long negotiations and general agreement on numerous other issues, no consensus could be reached on the fate of the region. Essentially, the three Balkan powers agreed to cooperate militarily against the Porte, but after that each was expected to grab what they could, any way they could. While the treaties set the stage for war against Turkey, they also left too many vital issues unresolved for peace to endure.

The Balkan Wars lasted from October 1912 until August 1913. The three powers declared war on the Turks on 18 October 1912, having marshalled combined forces of over 1,290,000 men. Venizelos's modernization plan paid rich dividends. The Greek military forces were larger, better equipped and well trained. Within a matter of weeks, the Greek army pushed back the Turkish army, taking Katerini, Elassona and Kozani by October 25. Along the north-western front, Greece successfully moved deep into Epiros. Bulgarian and Serbian forces were also successful and by early November the Ottoman forces were faltering on all fronts.

At this point the major division among the allies that all had feared emerged: who would possess the great city of Thessaloniki? A headlong rush by both Greek and Bulgarian forces began, and the Greeks got there first. On November 8, only a few hours ahead of the northern rivals, the Greek military entered the city. Crown Prince Konstantine rode on horseback at the head of the first division through the streets of the city, until he arrived at the Konak Palace where he received the sword of surrender from the commander of the Ottoman forces. In a ploy to strengthen Greek claims to the city, King George and Venizelos hastened to join the army. All across Greece the news of Thessaloniki's 'liberation' was greeted with outbursts of jubilation. Special masses were celebrated to commemorate the event. But could the gains on the battlefield be translated into success at the bargaining table?

By December, the Porte, Bulgaria and Serbia were ready to sue for peace. Greece, however, in spite of its gains was reluctant to do so because Ioannina had yet to capitulate. Negotiations dragged on through January 1913, but then broke down. The Young Turks stormed back into power through a coup, and the fighting recommenced. Of the three Balkan powers, Bulgaria was faring the worst. After some initial successes, it had over-extended its forces to the north-east and so had lost a valuable opportunity to stake a claim to Macedonia. Serbia and Greece quickly sought to take advantage of this and in June signed a bilateral agreement in which they divided Macedonia between themselves.

The Bulgarian response was to attack both, with disastrous consequences. The war between the erstwhile allies was brief. It began on 28 June 1913 and was for all intents and purposes over by mid-July. The Greek forces success-fully drove the Bulgarian army out of southern Macedonia; the Serbian forces were likewise victorious in the north. Also, Rumania and Turkey took advantage of Bulgaria's troubles and joined the fray. In spite of Great Power intervention, Greece and Serbia were victorious. The Treaty of Bucharest (10 August 1913) gave Greece major territorial gains.

Under Venizelos's skilful guidance, and as a result of his extensive military reforms, Greece reaped the rewards of success in the international arena. With the addition of southern Epiros, Macedonia, Crete, and some of the Aegean islands, the size of the country was increased by 90 per cent, including some of the richest agricultural land on the peninsula. The population rose from approximately 2,700,000 to 4,800,000. In addition, from the Greek perspective, the great Hellenic cities of Ioannina and Thessaloniki had at last been reclaimed. There were still over three million unredeemed Greeks in Thrake, Asia Minor, Cyprus, Albania, and Pontos, but nonetheless the gains of the Balkan War had brought the Megali Idea closer to realization than ever before. But the Greek victory was somewhat bittersweet.

In March 1913, King George fell prey to an assassin's bullet. A Greek madman espied the aged monarch out on his daily afternoon walk along the waterfront in Thessaloniki, approached him, and shot him in the back. The murderer, Alexandros Schinas, said he killed the King because he would not give him some money, but most Greeks believed that the killer was a Bulgarian agent. Ironically, just before he was slain, George had decided that he would take the opportunity of the forthcoming jubilee celebration of his coronation to abdicate in favour of Konstantine.[16]

Though mournful on the death of their old King, Greeks greeted the coronation of Konstantine with special enthusiasm, seeing in it momentous portents for the success of the Great Idea. A new rallying cry was heard across the country and beyond: 'A Konstantine founded it [the Byzantine Empire]. A Konstantine lost it [with the fall of Constantinople in 1453]. And a Konstantine will get it back'. Unfortunately for Greece this was not to be.

THE NATIONAL SCHISM AND THE GREAT WAR

The outbreak of the First World War shattered the internal stability that had been achieved and left in its place bitter divisions that would last for generations. The division of Europe into competing alliance groups, with the Triple Entente (Britain, France and Russia) on one side and the Triple Alliance (Germany, Austria, Italy and eventually the Ottoman Empire) on the other, had ramifications throughout the Balkans.

Greece found itself in a difficult situation. It had a number of reasons for opposing the Alliance. First, Turkey's membership in the Alliance alienated Greece, which still sought ways to incorporate the unredeemed Greeks of the east into the motherland. Second, Bulgaria had aligned itself with Turkey and the Central Powers and it was still exploring ways to take back Macedonia. Third, Greece had treaty obligations that bound it to Serbia and the Serbs were at loggerheads with the Austrian Empire over Bosnia. Finally, the Entente Powers had been the ones who had most consistently supported Greece in the past and so could make a claim on past friendships.

One the other side of the ledger sheet were the close connections between the royal house of Greece and the German monarchy. The reigning queen of

Greece, Sofia, was the sister of Kaiser Wilhelm. In addition, there were close connections between the German military establishment and the Greek leadership, many of whom including King Konstantine had been trained in Germany.[17] These competing interests exploded when war erupted, and Greece was compelled to choose a side.

King Konstantine, in spite of his brother-in-law's best efforts, sought to keep Greece neutral. His sympathies were clearly with the Alliance but he also realized that Greece's interests could best be served by remaining outside the fray. Venizelos, on the other hand, was staunchly pro-Entente. He was by inclination more sympathetic to Britain and France. Moreover, British promises made shortly before hostilities broke out completely convinced him that Greece's interest lay with the Entente. As he noted during secret talks with David Lloyd George, Winston Churchill and John Stavridi, Greece '. . . with the friendship of England and France would become a power in the East which no one could ignore'.[18] In January 1915 Britain made the following offer: if Greece would enter the war and send troops to assist the hard-pressed Serbs and contribute to the proposed invasion at Gallipoli, at the end of the war Greece would agree to give Kavala, Drama and Serres to Bulgaria, and would receive in exchange territorial compensation in Asia Minor. Calculating that the Entente would win the war, Venizelos saw this as an offer he could not refuse.

A royal council consisting of Venizelos and a number of previous prime ministers, the members of the general staff of the armed forces and the King was convened to craft the country's response to the various offers being floated to Greece by Britain. The Greek people, meanwhile, were making their feelings known with massive public rallies in support of the Entente. Initially, Konstantine agreed with those politicians who urged acceptance of the British offer. After the resignation of some military commanders and at the urging of other members of his staff, he changed his mind.

This was a very difficult time for the King. In addition to the growing crisis within he his government, he was also extremely ill. Already suffering from pleurisy and pneumonia, he contracted blood poisoning after surgery to remove some of his ribs. It took the miraculous healing powers of the holy icon of the Virgin Mary from the island of Tinos to bring Konstantine back from death's door.[19] Faced with an intransigent monarch backed by the General Staff, Venizelos resigned on 6 March as Prime Minister. The King appointed Dimitrios Gounaris as the new Prime Minister, but the real power in parliament still belonged to Venizelos. So began the constitutional crisis that came to be called the *Ethnikos Dikhasmos*, or the National Schism.[20]

In June of 1915 Greeks went to the polls and sent Venizelos and the Liberals back into power with 185 out of 316 seats. The King, however, refused to accept the results and it was not until August that he allowed the new government to be formed. Machinations had gone on through the summer with the result that by early autumn Bulgaria had decided to capitalize on Serbia's seemingly imminent defeat and so declared war on it. Sofia also claimed Macedonia and Thessaloniki as its own. Venizelos demanded that the army be mobilized in compliance with the treaty with Serbia. Konstantine reluctantly agreed on the stipulation that the army would fight only if Greece, not Serbia, was attacked. In response, Venizelos allowed French and British troops to be landed in Macedonia, establishing a northern front. He had moved so quickly that Konstantine had little time to react. Venizelos escalated tensions further by requesting a parliamentary vote on a declaration of war on Bulgaria, and by extension against the Triple Alliance. The motion was carried by a 37-vote margin. The next day the King called Venizelos to the palace and demanded his resignation. A constitutional crisis had erupted.

Having just won a major victory at the polls, the Liberals and their followers refused to accept the King's order. Technically, the Greek constitution did give the monarch the right unilaterally to dismiss a government; in this case, the King felt that he was better qualified to make the crucial decisions about war and peace. Be that as it may, the spirit of the constitution was that he should only do so when the popular will of the nation was in doubt. In this case it was not.

The June election had been fought precisely on the issue of war or neutrality. New elections were called for December. The Liberals, along with the vast majority of the electorate, boycotted them with the result that the newly elected government had no base of popular support. Relations between Venizelos and the Liberals and Konstantine and the monarchists continued to deteriorate as each staked out a harder line. Popular opinion vacillated depending on circumstances.

For example, when French and British troops landed in Macedonia in October 1915 over the protests of the King, popular sentiment was with him as most Greeks saw the allied manoeuvre as a breach of Greece's sovereignty. But the tide of public opinion soon shifted. After Konstantine balked at allowing the allies to transport Serbian troops overland from Epiros to the Macedonian front, the allies started to grow increasingly impatient with the royalist government. When pro-monarchist military leaders surrendered Fort Rupel in eastern Macedonia to the Bulgarians and so allowed the region to fall to the Triple Alliance, public opinion was outraged. The allies were now convinced that the King and his government were untrustworthy and that Venizelos was their only hope for getting Greece behind the war effort. Also outraged by the surrender were numerous members of the officer corps, who now threw their support behind the Venizelists. The crisis was becoming critical and there was widespread uncertainty as to who actually spoke for the nation.[21]

In the autumn of 1916 Greece stood on the brink of civil war. Venizelos had previously withdrawn to Crete where he waited for an opportunity to reassert himself. It was not slow in coming. Simultaneously, military officers loyal to him formed a clandestine organization, the National Defence (*Ethniki Amina*), based in Thessaloniki and aimed at bringing down the King and restoring the government of June 1915. They staged a coup and called on Venizelos, who was in Athens at the time, to join them. Escorted by a French cruiser, he went first to Crete where he officially announced his support of the coup and then he visited many of the Aegean islands to gauge the level of support he enjoyed on them. Finally, in late September 1916 he arrived in Thessaloniki and formed a 'provisional' government. Greece now had two competing governments.

The allies meanwhile were putting great pressure on the King to capitulate. After much equivocation, they recognized the provisional government. When allied troops were fired on at Piraeus, France and England set up a blockade of all ports under Konstantine's control. Beginning on 7 December 1916 and continuing for 106 days no goods were imported or exported at central and southern Greek ports. 'During the dark months that followed thousands of unemployed Greeks were thrown into the streets to beg for food. Even in the villages there was starvation . . .'.[22] Many people became more sympathetic to Konstantine's position because of the hardships created by the Allied blockade. The rupture within the political system also took on a geographical dimension and inaugurated a division between 'Old' Greece to the south and 'New' Greece in the north. The significance of this north–south division would only increase in the decades ahead. The political division also led to partisan violence. Under the leadership of Ioannis Metaxas, former acting Chief of the General staff, aide de campe of Konstantine and future dictator of Greece, a reactionary paramilitary unit, the 'League of Reservists', was founded and it embarked on a systematic campaign of terror and repression against Venizelists who had remained in Athens and against anyone who did not support the monarchy. A pattern of violent, partisan reprisals had begun, and once started it would prove very hard to stop.

By late spring 1917 matters were coming to a head. The provisional government in Thessaloniki had grown in strength and enjoyed a considerable degree of legitimacy both at home and abroad. The allied blockade rendered the King's position precarious. Newspapers that previously extolled his principled stance against foreign interference now began to question the wisdom of his obduracy in the face of his peoples' suffering. Allied leaders, still concerned that their projected invasion of the Balkans could be jeopardized as long as Konstantine was on the throne, began openly to call for his abdication. The French leadership, in particular, was outspoken in its support of the provisional government and its opposition to the King. British Prime Minister David Lloyd George, who had come to power in December 1916, joined them in calling for the Greek monarch's departure.[23]

Finally, on 11 June 1917, the High Commissioner of the Protecting Powers, Auguste-Charles Jonnart, delivered an ultimatum to the pro-monarchy government in Athens: if Konstantine agreed to leave Athens and appoint his son Alexander as King, he would be allowed to return to the throne when the war was over; if he did not, then Athens would be attacked and the monarchy as an institution would be abolished. Konstantine had little choice but to leave.

Fig. 6.1 'Metaxas Cognac'. This advertisement for Metaxas cognac aptly captures the flavour of bourgeois culture in Athens during the early twentieth century. Nattily decked out in his spats and bowler, this man would not seem out of place in any western European café. Note as well the widespread network of places where Metaxas cognac was 'prized' – from Paris and London to Monaco and Bucharest. (Postcard from the private collection of T.W. Gallant.)

Three days later, he announced to his bewildered followers: 'It is necessary to obey, and I must leave. I am fulfilling my duty to my *patrida* (fatherland). I am leaving you Alexander and beg you to resign yourselves and accept my decision; trust in God, whose blessings I invoke on you'.[24] Venizelos was free to throw the weight of Greek support into the allied cause.

Ten divisions of the Greek army fought with great valour in the autumn campaign in 1918 along the Macedonian front. They routed German and Bulgarian positions and pushed the front line northward at a great human cost. The hard fighting was soon rewarded as Germany and its allies capitulated. Then came the reward as Greek troops triumphantly marched into Constantinople/Istanbul. At the cost of splitting the nation, Venizelos had brought the nation into the war on the victorious side. In order to justify the cost he now had to win the peace: the wounds of war would only be healed with the fulfillment of the Megali Idea. But even then the deep cleavages wrought by the *Ethnikos Dikhasmos* could not be undone. The legacy of sectarian violence would endure.

The Inter-war Period, 1919–1940

A time of turmoil

With the cessation of the 'war to end all wars,' Greece could have known peace for the first time in years, but it did not. Instead, more war, catastrophic defeat, and an enduring legacy of social and political instability would mark the inter-war era in Greece. The combination of the Balkan Wars and the First World War had exacted a heavy toll on Greek society. The key question in 1919 was: could Eleftherios Venizelos and the Liberals gain enough from the Allies at the Paris Peace Conference to compensate for the country's sufferings? At first, it appeared that they had. Soon after the conference, Greece would come as close as it ever would to achieving the dream of the Great Idea. But the dream would soon turn into a nightmare. Military defeat at the hands of the Turkish nationalist forces would all but bring to an end the millennial-long Hellenic presence in Asia Minor. Consequent upon this military debacle would be a decade of social unrest, political chaos, and economic disaster. Then Greece, like so many other places in Europe, would fall prey to the sickness of the inter-war period: authoritarianism.

PEACE AND WAR

Prime Minister Eleftherios Venizelos went to the Paris peace talks armed with the vague assurances made to his government by the Allies during the war, all of which focused exclusively on the issue of territorial aggrandizement for Greece. The task before him was daunting and the stakes were high. Internally, political stability hinged on his coming away from the negotiations with a settlement favourable to Greece. As a politician who had risen and stayed in power largely through his successful pursuance of the irredentist cause, he had to ensure that the cause of Hellenism in Asia was advanced. Representatives of the Greeks of Asia Minor specifically were lobbying him to ensure that the sufferings visited upon them during the war – the forced relocations of many Greeks to the interior of Anatolia, the confiscation of land, and the destruction of churches – were recompensed.

The wily Cretan was up to the task. 'Venizelos quickly won a reputation for moderation, wisdom and statesmanship. This reputation, founded on passionate sincerity and strength of will coupled with charm of manner and political tact, enabled him to press Greece's claim to the utmost'.[1] He showed all of his considerable talents at these talks. He wooed leaders like Woodrow Wilson and Lloyd George. He cajoled some and threatened others. For all of his best efforts, and they were considerable, Venizelos could not escape one fundamental truth: Greece could not achieve its goals without the active assistance of the major powers and such cooperation would be forthcoming *only if* the powers perceived it to be in their best interest. But in the rapidly changing circumstances of the Paris talks, such interests were often in flux. Furthermore, in the context of the truly momentous issues that confronted the leaders of war-ravaged Europe, the affairs of the eastern Mediterranean were little more than a sideshow.

Even while the talks were in progress, military forces were required to act as policing agents and as peacekeepers in various occupied zones. Venizelos was quick to offer the services of the Greek military. At one point, for example, Greek troops assisted French forces in an operation in the Black Sea region. This paid international dividends, as foreign leaders became more indebted to him and began to see Greece as a stabilizing factor in an unstable region. Working with Lloyd George, he was able to take advantage of Woodrow Wilson's anger at Italy over the disposition of Fiume in the Adriatic and George Clemenceau's ambivalence about the region to obtain permission to occupy specified regions of Asia Minor. 'But from the start the French were half-hearted, the Italians opposed and the Americans distracted. Greece was never to have firm inter-Allied support'.[2]

Over lunch on 6 May 1919, Lloyd George, Wilson and Clemenceau decided that, acting as a proxy for the allies, Greek troops should occupy Smyrna. When the British leader informed Venizelos of their decision, the Cretan curtly replied, 'We are ready'. Widespread euphoria greeted the announcement in Greece. The newspaper *Nea Chios*, for example, exclaimed 'Glory to God. The Nation has risen ... Greece has found herself again!'[3] On the morning of 15 May, Smyrna's quayside was packed with members of the city's Greek community. Greek flags were draped everywhere. At 7:30, the first ship carrying Greek troops arrived to a hero's welcome. Archbishop Chrysostom blessed them. Liberation and unification were at last becoming reality.

On the previous day, allied troops had landed and were deployed around the city in an effort to forestall any incidents between the Greek troops and the Turkish forces still stationed there. They were unsuccessful. Within hours of their arrival Greek forces were involved in a shoot out with the Turkish troops. From the start, then, there were ominous indications that the dire warnings uttered by many of the military advisers to the Supreme Council that allowing the Greeks to occupy Smyrna was a major mistake were correct. But in the spring of 1919 nothing it seemed could stand in the way of the realization of the Megali Idea. All that remained, many believed, was the signing of the treaties that would finalize the occupation. But before discussing that issue we need first to examine the domestic situation in Greece in the aftermath of the Great War.

Greece had not suffered to the extent that so many other countries in Europe had during the First World War. The figures of casualties suffered by Germany, France, Britain and Russia are too well known to need repeating here. It is enough to note that Greece did not experience anywhere near the manpower losses proportionally that those and other countries did. Neither did Greece experience anywhere near the same magnitude of destruction as they did. Most of the fighting had been restricted to Macedonia and Thrake, and the rest of the country was largely spared from direct attack. Nonetheless, the war had had a deep impact on Greek society and its economy. We must bear in mind, for example, that the armed forces had been mobilized almost continuously since the Balkan Wars and so the losses during the Great War must be added to the earlier casualty figures. Also, these losses have to be placed in the context of the massive out-migration of young men that had been occurring since the turn of the century (see Chapter 5); granted, many men returned to Greece from the United States to fight, but their numbers did not offset the numbers of those who continued to leave. Second, the nation was becoming war weary and even the call of nationalism was starting to fall on increasingly deaf ears.

The economic situation was also dire. The agrarian sector, which was still the backbone of the economy, emerged from the war years in a depressed condition. The addition of the new lands in Epiros and Macedonia after the Balkan wars and the high prices that appeared at the start of world war led to an initial upswing in the rural economy. The combination, however, of manpower shortages, protectionism, government requisitioning, the devastation of Macedonia, and the Allied blockade soon created a crisis. Some of Greece's most important industries, such as mining, went into decline at the start of the war and never recovered; according to one estimate the size of the labour force involved in mining was halved between 1912 and 1922.[4]

Manufacturing output and profits rose because of a combination of protectionism and wartime demand, but were hard hit by the Allied blockade on account of Greece's dependency on foreign imports of coal and other vital raw materials. This led to a large and increasing trade deficit. Fiscally, the situation was grim, but could have been managed but for the Asia Minor campaign. Greece had emerged from the Balkan Wars in debt but was well on the way to paying them off, mainly through public subscription at home and from additional foreign loans. It was, however, unprepared to foot the massive expenses the First World War generated. Loans were contracted, and the Allies pledged millions of pounds in credits, against which the National Bank of Greece issued banknotes.

Nonetheless, Greece emerged from the war deeply in debt. The war years witnessed another emerging crisis: the rise and spread of labour unrest and class division. We saw in the last chapter that workers and peasants were prepared to take direct action in order to get their grievances heard. This trend of public unrest continued but with two additional dimensions. The first was that workers' movements became more organized. Trade unions and workers' associations spread through many sectors of the economy, and they grew in scale, culminating in 1918 with the foundation of the General Confederation of Greek Workers. The second development was the emergence of specifically class-based political parties; often themselves tied to the trade union movement. In 1915, for example, an all-Greece conference of socialists was convened and three years later the Socialist Labour Party of Greece was formed. As working-class movements became more organized, they became more powerful and could exert greater pressure on the Liberal government.[5]

The lengthy war years had taken a great toll on the Greek people, and even while the negotiations were going on in Paris, serious problems on the home front threatened to jeopardize the grand plans being devised there. Moreover, the Liberal administration that Venizelos had left behind in Greece was growing increasingly unpopular. Since the summer of 1917 (see above pp. 139–40), the Venizelists had wrought a terrible retribution against their political opponents. Royalists were purged from the military and the civil service. Prominent anti-Venizelists were imprisoned or exiled. These actions simply drove the wedge of division that was the National Schism even deeper into the body politic. Rifts even began to develop within the Liberal Party. Thus, even as he scored successes abroad, the Venizelists' mismanagement of domestic affairs was costing Venizelos popularity at home. Finally, Venizelos put all of his energies into winning the peace talks and neglected matters back in Greece. He would eventually pay for this neglect.

After two years of intense negotiations peace was achieved: for a short time at least. Greece stood on the verge of fulfilling the *Megali Idea*. By the Treaty of Sèvres signed with Turkey on 10 August 1920, Greece received the Aegean islands, including Imbros and Tenedos, and all of Thrake; a new territory around the city of Smyrna was established and placed under the protection of the Greek government, and, in accordance with the principle of national self-determination, all Greeks in Asia Minor were encouraged to move there. The Smyrna Protectorate was still under the aegis of Turkey but administered by Greece, and after five years a plebiscite was to be held to determine which country it would belong to. Since May 1919 Greek troops had been stationed at Smyrna and their presence had attracted many Greeks from the country-side who feared Turkish reprisals or bandit attacks. The massive shift in population, which was already informally underway, ensured that the plebiscite would produce a result in Greece's favour. The Greek presence inside the Smyrna zone was becoming solidified and Greek ascendancy in the area seemed assured. Venizelos announced in triumph that there was now a 'Greece of two continents [Europe and Asia] and five seas [Black, Aegean, Mediter-ranean, Ionian, and Adriatic]'. The irredentist dream seemed to be coming true.

The nightmare was about to begin. On the eve of returning to Greece after his extended absence (12 August 1920), two monarchist naval officers shot Venizelos as he was boarding a train at the *Gare de Lyon*. His wounds were not life threatening, but nonetheless, they incapacitated him at a time when he needed all of his vigour and energies. Already out of touch with the develop-ments in Greece, his extended convalescence isolated him even further from the domestic scene. In addition, the response in Greece demonstrated that the deep divisions created by the earlier political rift were still present. Upon hearing of the shooting, pro-Venizelist mobs attacked and even destroyed buildings that housed pro-monarchy newspapers. Prominent opponents of the Liberal Party leader were assassinated in the streets. In a society in which the ethos of vengeance runs so deep, each drop of blood spilt demanded repayment in kind. The slide to anarchy, moreover, was just beginning.

Two months later, an untoward event shattered the uneasy compromise regarding the monarchy. On the afternoon of 2 October, King Alexander took his favourite dog, Fritz, for a walk in the gardens at the royal estate of Tatoi. Startled by the barking dog, two Spanish monkeys jumped out of a tree and attacked. Alexander stepped forward to save his pet and was himself savaged, suffering severe bites on his legs and abdomen. By evening septicemia had set in. Racked by fever and beset by delirium, he clung to life for over three weeks before succumbing. A crisis over the succession quickly developed. His brother refused to ascend to the throne, leaving his father, the exiled Konstantine, as its primary claimant. A war-weary and nervous electorate brought down the curtain on Venizelos's term of office in the elections of November 1920.

A coalition of pro-monarchy parties, called the United Opposition, led by his old nemeses, Dimitrios Gounaris and Dimitrios Rallis, won 260 of the 370 parliamentary seats contested – even though the Liberals won 52 per cent of the total vote. The United Opposition had made three campaign promises: first, they pledged to end the 'tyranny' of the Venizelists by restoring the civil liberties and freedoms that the Liberals had abridged, first on the pretext of wartime necessity and then on the grounds of public order; second, they promised to restore Konstantine to the throne; and third, they swore to pursue the Great Idea even more vigorously than had the Liberals. On this last point, however, there was not complete unanimity within the coalition; some voices from the centre-right spoke out in favour of a small but stable Greece rather than a large but unstable one. Like modern-day Kassandras, their prophecies of doom in Asia Minor went largely unheeded. Repudiated by the nation at the moment of his greatest triumph, Venizelos went into self-imposed exile. Under the leadership of Gounaris, the United Opposition formed a government and took up office. One of their first actions was to schedule a plebiscite regarding the restoration of Konstantine. Following a landslide victory (999,960 in favour and only 10,383 opposed) in what was clearly a rigged ballot, on 19 December 1920, Konstantine returned to the throne of Greece.

There were four major consequences to these developments. First, after years in the political wilderness, royalist supporters let loose counter-purges against Venizelists in provincial administration, the judiciary, higher education, the civil service and the military. This acted only to perpetuate the wounds of the National Schism. In many ways the most important effects of this development were felt in the military. Almost all of the leading command posts were given to Royalist officers. Though many of these officers were competent military commanders, the change in command did have a deleterious impact on the armed forces, especially in Asia Minor, as we shall see shortly. Second, the election of a conservative government, by a minority vote at that, drove even more members of the working-class, including many poverty-stricken peasants, into the folds of leftist parties. The Socialist Labour Party of Greece's membership, for example, increased considerably. This added a new and important dimension to the National Schism. In addition to the monarchist-Venizelist cleavage, there was now a growing Left versus Right division. Third, some of the conservatives attempted to be even more fervent in their nationalism than the Venizelists had been and so adopted a more aggressive, radical line in regard to Turkey. Fourth, since many of the commitments made to Greece were personal ones between allied leaders, like Lloyd George and Wilson – who themselves would fall from power – and Venizelos, after the removal of the Cretan statesman from power these obligations also lapsed. The result was that allied support, especially that of Great Britain and France, waned, while that of Italy vanished completely.

Most importantly, the Allies made good on their threat to punish Greece if Konstantine returned: they refused to make available the millions of dollars in credit, which they had promised at the Paris peace table. When that happened, the Royalist government also found the European capital markets closed to it. Greece alone would have to foot the bill for the irredentist struggle, and it was going to be very high indeed.[6]

THE ASIA MINOR CATASTROPHE

While these developments were taking place in Greece, the situation in Turkey was also changing dramatically. By the summer of 1919, the Turkish authorities had by and large become resigned to the dismantling of their empire, but what they had not become reconciled to was the invasion by a foreign army and the occupation of a vital region of their homeland. A new movement, Turkish nationalism, and a new leader, Mustapha Kemal, emerged from the ashes of defeat and they both posed a direct threat to Greek irredentism. Kemal was a Turk from Thessaloniki who had risen through the ranks of the Ottoman army. During the war, he had distinguished himself at Gallipoli, on the Russian front and in the Middle East campaign. At the end of the war, he became one of the most vocal of the many military officers who felt betrayed by the actions of the pro-Allies Turkish government in Istanbul. In order to remove him from the scene, the government assigned him the military inspectorate of the eastern districts. Shortly after his arrival in Samsun on the Black Sea in May 1919, he launched the Nationalist Movement. It quickly grew in strength and power. From its new headquarters in Ankara, the Nationalist Movement and its leader announced their intention to reclaim the sacred and inalienable territory of Turkey from the foreign invaders. By autumn of 1920, at the same time that the changing of the guard was taking place in Athens, the Nationalist Movement had developed into a force to be reckoned with. Turkish nationalism and Greek irredentism were on a collision course.

During the winter of 1921 the Gounaris government in Athens had decided to confront the Turkish nationalist movement more aggressively. In an effort to avert a conflict, Lloyd George and his Foreign Minister, Lord Curzon, met with representatives of the Greek government in February. Already piqued that Konstantine had been restored over their objections, the British warned the Greeks that they should be prepared to make compromises because British support would not be as staunch as it had been in the past and because the French were now willing to support the Turkish demands. At the subsequent London Conference, however, it quickly became apparent that compromise between the various parties was impossible. Upon returning to Athens in

March, the Greek delegation recommended that the time for talking was over. The order was given and on 23 March 1921 the Greek military launched a major offensive. It proved to be a disaster.

Under the command of Royalist supporters, first General Anastasios Papoulias and then General Giorgios Hadjianestis, the Greek army pushed eastward along two fronts, one to the north and another in the south. The military high command aimed to employ a pincer movement to bottle up the Turkish nationalist forces in central Anatolia. On the political side of the military equation was the idea of isolating Istanbul and by so doing putting pressure on the Allies to grant even greater concessions to the Greeks. The southern front advanced more easily than the northern one, which encountered fierce resistance. Attacking along two fronts and across such a broad area was a strategy that entailed taking some very serious risks, the most important of which were spreading the Greek forces too thin and over-extending the supply lines. At one point the Greek line extended across much of Anatolia. Yet the advance continued.

Through 1921, the Greek army met mostly with success and this encouraged the strategic command to persist with their high-risk gamble. The campaign seemed to be going so well that Konstantine himself visited the front line and his younger brother George remained there as a member of the high command. But there were warning signs that all was not well. Greece was finding itself isolated from the Allies. Britain and the United States urged caution and offered to mediate a solution. France and Italy openly supported the Turkish nationalists, supplying them with arms and material. The nation's cash resources were running out as the allies withdrew their loans in protest at the continued hostilities. Internally, the Greek army was fraught with divisions between Venizelists and Royalists that impaired almost every aspect of the conduct of the campaign. After one defeat snatched out of the mouth of victory because of poor planning and inadequate logistical support, Arnold Toynbee, a reporter for the *Manchester Guardian*, noted that the Greek troops 'were angry – angry at spending so much blood and labour in vain, but even more humiliated at a defeat which broke a long record of victory of which they had been intensely proud'.[7] Finally, ammunition and supplies were beginning to run out, and there was no money to purchase more.

Kemal enticed the Greek army to progress ever deeper into the rugged heartland of Anatolia. Historian Michael Llewelyn Smith reproduces the memorandum in which the strategy was laid out. After proposing that his forces retreat, the nationalist leader understatedly observed, 'if the enemy should pursue us without coming to a halt, he would be getting farther away from his base of operations . . .. Thus our army will be able to rally and meet the enemy under more favourable conditions'.[8] This was truly an understatement. The Greek forces did in fact follow the retreating nationalist forces and the consequent overextension of the Greek line proved disastrous.

By late August of 1922, Kemal judged that the Greek position was untenable and so he launched his carefully planned counter-offensive. By concentrating all of his firepower at a few strategic points, he was able to gain overwhelming superiority. The assaults by the Turkish nationalist forces were fierce and the results swift. The Greek line was shattered. Through a series of coordinated north–south pincer movements Atatürk isolated and destroyed numerous sectors of the Greek army. A rout turned into a race as the rag-tag remnants of the Greek forces retreated to Smyrna with the Turkish forces at their heels.

The scene became chaotic as tens of thousands of Greek troops joined by legions more of civilians fled before the Turkish cavalry. All sought an escape, but exits were scarce. Most headed for the main point of departure out of Anatolia under Greek control: Smyrna. A contemporary witness, George Horton, vividly captured the scene as troops and refugees converged on the city:

> Then the defeated, dusty, ragged Greek soldiers began to arrive [in Smyrna], looking straight ahead, like men walking in their sleep .... In a never-ending stream they poured through the town toward the point on the coast at which the Greek fleet had withdrawn. Silently as ghosts they went, looking neither to the right nor the left. From time to time, some soldier, his strength entirely spent, collapsed on the side-walk or by a door.[9]

Nothing stood between the Turkish forces and the great city of Smyrna. Ships from the naval fleets of the Great Powers arrived to evacuate foreign nationals and diplomats. Greek ships arrived disembarking troops whose assigned task was to keep order in the city. Their stay was a brief, and ineffective, one. As the Turkish forces approached, the scene on the waterfront became more chaotic as people sought any means possible to flee. For most, however, it was too late.

'The Turks are coming!' This cry rang through the streets of Smyrna on the morning of 9 September 1922. The cavalry arrived first. Armed to the teeth and seemingly well rested, they swept through the city spreading panic before them. Later that evening the looting and killing commenced. Initially, the violence was fiercest and bloodiest in the Armenian quarter, but it soon spread. After Archbishop Chrysostom was humiliated and butchered by a

Turkish mob, the massacre began in earnest. Then on the evening of Wednesday, 13 September, a fire broke out in the Armenian quarter, and quickly spread. While soldiers, sailors, and journalists from around the world watched from ships anchored in the bay, the city burned. Flames rose up behind them forming a fiery wall of death as mobs of people ran to the water-front, hoping to be conveyed to one of the ships lying in the harbour. But it was an impossible task. In addition to the paucity of conveyances, the captains of the foreign warships had strict orders not to interfere. The results were horrendous. Tens of thousands of Greeks and Armenians died during the destruction of Smyrna. For all intents and purposes, the Megali Idea went up in smoke on the shores of Asia Minor.

The war, however, was not over with the devastation of Smyrna. After regrouping the remnants of the forces that escaped from Asia with newly mobilized reserves, the Greek army prepared to make one last stand in eastern Thrake. An eyewitness to the events there, Ernest Hemingway, captured well the ignominious end to the Greek adventure in Asia Minor.

> Greece looked on Thrake as a Marne where she must fight and make a final stand or perish. Troops were rushed in. Everybody was at a white heat. Then the Allies at [the peace negotiations at] Mudania handed Eastern Thrake over to the Turk and gave the Greek army three days to start getting out. The army waited, not believing that their government would sign the Mudania convention, but it did, and the army, being soldiers, are getting out. All day I have been passing them, dirty, tired, unshaven, windbitten soldiers hiking along the trails across the brown, rolling, barren Thrakian countryside. No bands, no relief organizations, no leave areas, nothing but lice, dirty blankets, and mosquitoes at night. They are the last of the glory that was Greece. This is the end of their second siege of Troy.[10]

THE CATASTROPHE COMPOUNDED

The Asia Minor catastrophe had serious and lasting consequences. Two problems immediately faced Greece. The first concerned the internal political situation: who would rule Greece? Related to this was the question of who was to blame for the disaster. The second was how to achieve peace in Asia Minor and how to cope with the flood of refugees who were pouring daily into Greece.

The first dilemma was quickly addressed. A small, dedicated band of military officers gathered on the battleship *Limnos* after the debacle and formed a Revolutionary Committee. At its head were Colonels Nikolaos Plastiras and Stilianos Gonatas, and naval Captain Dimitrios Fokas, all Venizelists of long standing. Given the chaotic conditions of the time it was relatively easy for a small, organized and armed group to take control, and this they did. Landing at the port of Lavrion on the coast of Attika with a force of 12,000 men, they staged a coup. In a letter of 26 September 1922, they demanded the resignation of the government and the abdication of King Konstantine. After hasty deliberations with his closest advisors, the King agreed that both demands were to be met.

Shortly after Konstantine left the country, his brother George was sworn in as King. The putchists set about establishing a government and purging the bureaucracy and the military of Royalists. Their next major move was to assign blame for the catastrophe. A show trial of the leaders in charge of the Asia Minor campaign was staged. General Giorgios Hatjianestis, former Prime Minister Dimtrios Gounaris, Petros Protopapadakis, Giorgios Baltazzis, Nikolaos Stratos, and Nikolaos Theotokis, together with Xenophon Stratigos and Michael Gouadas were charged with high treason. This was an act of political retaliation and scapegoating. These men were certainly guilty of ineptitude and gross incompetence, but not of treason. All eight were found guilty: six were sentenced to die, two to life in prison. On 27 November 1923, the six were hanged. With the executions the Venizelist: anti-Venizelist rift grew wider and more ferocious. The politicization of the military was furthered, and the militarization of politics ensured.

To address the other pressing problem, negotiating an acceptable peace with Turkey, the Revolutionary Committee led by General Plastiras turned to Venizelos. After lengthy talks at Lausanne, an agreement was finally reached and signed during July 1923. In it Greece agreed to cede Imbros and Tenedos to Turkey. Thrake was divided into two sections with Greece receiving the western sector. In addition, Greece also obtained the Aegean islands running along the coast of Turkey, but they were included in a demilitarized zone. In exchange for these territorial acquisitions, Greece relinquished all claims to Asia Minor. Finally, Greece and Turkey agreed to the single largest compulsory exchange of populations known to that time. All Moslems living in Greece, with the exception of those in Thrake, were to be evacuated to Turkey; they numbered over 350,000. In return approximately 1,300,000 Greeks were sent to Greece. Religion, not language or culture, was the determining factor. Also included in the treaty were certain provisions for the protection of Orthodox Greeks and Moslems who were granted special status and allowed to remain where they were: the Thrakian Moslems or the Greeks of Constantinople for example. The Treaty of Lausanne established for the most part the boundaries of Greece, which obtain to this day; in theory at least, it turned Greece into an ethnically homogenous state by removing the major minority group; and it ended once and for all the Megali Idea. It also created a massive problem: what to do with almost one and a half million refugees?

THE EXCHANGE OF POPULATIONS AND ITS COST

Even before the Treaty of Lausanne had been signed, a torrent of refugees from Asia Minor and eastern Thrake was making its way to Greece. The torrent soon turned into a flood of destitute and despairing humanity. Ambassador Henry Morgenthau would later recall:

> In one case, which I myself beheld, seven thousand people were packed into a vessel that would have been crowded with a load of two thousand. In this and many other cases there was neither food to eat nor water to drink, and in numerous instances the ships were buffeted about for several days at sea before their wretched human cargoes could be brought to land. Typhoid and smallpox swept through the ships. Lice infested everyone. Babes were born on board. Men and women went insane. Some leaped over-board to end their miseries in the sea; Those who survived were landed without shelter upon the open beach, loaded with filth, racked by fever, without blankets or even warm clothing, without food and without money. Besides these horrors the refugees endured every form of sorrow – the loss of husbands by wives, loss of wives by husbands, loss of children through death or straying, all manner of illnesses. If ever the Four Horsemen of the Apocalypse rode down upon a nation it was when this appalling host appeared upon the shores of Greece, that was trampled by the flying hoofs of their chargers and scourged by the spectral riders of War, Famine, Pestilence, and Death.[11]

Given their condition, not surprisingly, the arrival of the first wave of refugees created immediate and huge problems. First and foremost was the difficulty of finding food and shelter for them. Initially, families were settled wherever space permitted. During the autumn of 1922, 'tin towns' and tent villages sprang up around Athens and Thessaloniki. The situation of the refugees was desperate. Most had had to flee with only the few items that they could carry. Many had nothing at all. There were a disproportionate number of women, children and elderly men because of the systematic arrest and detention in labour camps of able-bodied young men by the Turks before the exchange. In the refugee settlements around Athens, for example, women over 16 outnumbered men by almost two to one. Only a major, concerted relief effort could forestall a human disaster.

The Greek fiscal situation was already dire and the state simply did not have the funds needed to deal with the situation. Various international relief organizations, like the American Red Cross and the League of Nations Refugee Treasury Fund, stepped in with food, supplies, and medicine. The Red Cross, for example, expended over $3,000,000 between October 1922 and June 1923, and the organization's timely efforts stopped at least one major outbreak of typhus and prevented others from spreading across the country.[12] But the international humanitarian relief efforts served only as a temporary solution to the much greater problem. The exchange of populations agreed to in the treaty was about to present Greece with close to one and a half million displaced persons.

The wave of immigrants who arrived in Greece through the exchange of populations was different from the previous wartime influx. More families arrived intact, though overall there was still a gender and age imbalance. They were able to bring with them personal property, portable wealth, and cash, and so were not destitute like those who had fled for their lives during the darkest days of 1922. That they were forced out of their homeland with more than the clothes on their backs did not minimize the trauma that this second wave of migrants experienced.

The Greeks from Asia Minor were a very heterogeneous group. Some were wealthy, educated, and sophisticated merchants, lawyers, and professionals who had called the Ottoman urban centres home. Others were agricultural-ists who had owned vast tracts of land in one of the rich riverine valleys or wide upland plains of Asia Minor. In addition to class and occupational differences, there were cultural ones as well. The people called *karamanlides*, for example, spoke only Turkish but because they were Orthodox Christians, they were included in the exchange of populations. They found themselves, then, enmeshed in a new country where they could not even speak the language. Settling and incorporating such a huge and diverse refugee population was an enormous challenge.

There were two main primary strategies for accomplishing this Herculean task. One focused on establishing them on farms in the countryside and the other on creating an urban labour force. The majority of the Anatolian Greeks were settled in the areas of Macedonia and Thrake left vacant by the departing Moslem population; smaller numbers were settled in Thessaly and Crete. The international Refugee Settlement Commission provided families with a plot of land, some farm equipment, and supplies. Before the war, Greek farmers in Asia Minor had been remarkably successful in growing tobacco, and this soon became the dominant cash crop in some regions. In addition, there was an appreciable increase in the production of wheat and other cereals for domestic consumption.[13]

But the agrarian resettlement programme cannot be deemed a complete success. Some settlers refused to become farmers and gravitated to the cities. Others, dissatisfied with the plots of land they had been given, abandoned them and moved elsewhere. In some areas this problem was especially acute because wealthier members of the indigenous Greek population had already purchased or usurped the better parcels of land previously owned by Moslems. Finally, the most widespread and acute problem faced by the rural settlers was debt. Unable to sustain their families on the lands provided many Anatolian agriculturalists had to borrow from the local Greek rural elite. Caught in the nexus of debt, many found themselves reduced to the status of sharecroppers or landless hired labourers compelled to eke out a living working for others.[14]

In the cities, refugee neighbourhoods developed around the makeshift camps in Athens (e.g. Kaisariani, Vyrona, Nea Ionia) and Piraeus (e.g. Nea Kokkinia, Drapetsona, and Keratsini) and Thessaloniki. The Refugee Settlement Commission devoted considerably fewer resources to dealing with the urban migrants, and so conditions for them remained difficult for longer than they did for the rural settlers. Some state and commission-funded housing was provided, but many people had to make do with hastily constructed shanties. The male refugees provided a skilled and relatively cheap work force. Women refugee workers entered the labour force in large numbers out of need to supplement their household incomes or to compensate for the lack of male wage earners. Many of those who settled in the cities had been professionals or entrepreneurs before the exchange, and they helped to invigorate the industrial sector of Greece. Cigarette and cigar rolling, carpet weaving, and textile manufacturing grew dramatically, primarily because of the Asia Minor Greeks. The Greek economy between 1924 and 1930 witnessed its highest level of industrialization to that time.[15] Nonetheless for many years, the economic condition of the refugee population was grim. Low wages, nagging poverty, and prejudice made life extremely difficult for the urban refugee population.

The refugees faced other problems as well. For many Anatolians both in the city and in the country, there was culture shock. Torn from their homeland and thrust into a largely alien society, where, as we shall see shortly, they were not particularly welcome, their sense of alienation and psychological dislocation was profound. The plaintive voice and poignant lyrics of the Anatolian singer Antonis Dalgas in his song 'Soútsa Polítiki' captured well the sense of loss and longing that his compatriots felt:

> The city [Constantinople] and the Bosphorous
> Are my dream
> There where my love lives
> There is my beloved.[16]

Within a short period of time, the rich cultures of the Asia Minor Greeks began to assert themselves, especially in music which helped to keep alive a specifically Asia Minor identity. Many refugees were also less than impressed with their new home.

> Their [the refugees] initial impressions of mainland Greek
> life were disappointing. By contrast with the towns and
> villages of their homeland, metropolitan Greece could not
> be viewed in a favorable light. This small country was
> backward, and parochial, and its people unsophisticated.[17]

To many of those in Old Greece, however, the Asia Minor and Pontic Greeks were different and inferior, and a process of cultural integration was required before they could be fully assimilated into mainstream Greek society. This proved to be very difficult and for some time they faced prejudices bordering on racism. The writer I.M. Panayotopoulos vividly captures this sentiment in the following passage from his novel *Astrofengi* [*Starlight*]. In the midst of a heated debate about the refugees, a royalist protagonist launches into this diatribe:

> Should a person leave his house to give it to one of them?
> Forget the fact that all of them smell, that they're sick and
> penniless. One and a half million people! What can poor
> Greece do for them? . . . There isn't a school, a shed, or a
> tent left unused. [They are in] theaters, cinemas, churches,
> coffeehouses – all over Greece. Everywhere! And what
> people! God protect you from them! . . . Let them stay in
> their homelands.[18]

So, regardless of their previous situation, many refugees faced prejudice and were often denigrated as 'Turkish seed,' or 'Turkish-born,' or 'baptized in yogurt' by the native population who considered them dirty, smelly, lazy, ignorant, and sexually licentious. On a number of occasions during the 1920s there were violent clashes between the locals and the refugees in the cities of Athens and Piraeus and in the countrysides of Macedonia and Thrake. The cultural cleavage that divided indigenous and refugee Greeks would take on other dimensions, mainly political, that only served to further rigidify the demarcation between the two groups. In short, the class dynamic of Greek society was altered forever.[19]

In the long term, however, the incorporation of the refugee population into the mainstream of Greek culture and life brought certain benefits; in the short term, there were numerous difficulties and challenges. Greece was now a land polarized along a number of axes. In addition to the political one based on the National Schism, there was now a rupture based on identity – indigenous (*dopii*) versus foreign/refugee Greeks; related to that was another based on geography – Old Greece (south) versus New Greece (north); and yet one more based on class and wealth distribution. These ruptures, not surprisingly, translated into profound political instability.

COUNTING COUPS

For much of the 'Roaring Twenties' Greece was racked by political turmoil. The old political division between Venizelists and anti-Venizelists ran deeper than ever before, and added to them was an equally deep division between those who wanted to keep the monarchy and those who favoured its replacement with a republic. Moreover, once unleashed, the military found it hard to stay its hand from grabbing the levers of power. In July 1923, a staunchly anti-monarchy group within the armed forces formed a group called the Military League; it grew quickly in membership and was led by a number of prominent commanders such as Generals Theodoros Pangalos, Alexandros Othonaios, Giorgios Kondylis and Admiral Konstantinos Hatzikyriakos. The extremism of the Military League soon led to the formation of opposing factions of monarchist officers and of officers who were neither republicans nor monarchists but who simply wanted to bring the schism to an end. One of these latter groups attempted rebellion in October 1923. The Plastiras government quickly suppressed it and, with its suppression, the republican movement gained further momentum. The elections for a National Assembly in December were boycotted by the anti-Venizelist parties and so the new chamber was dominated by Venizelists, but the majority of them were opposed to altering the constitution. Nonetheless, because of the growing power of the Military League and emergence of a numerically significant political party, the Republican Union, the die was cast: the monarchy had to go. Venizelos, even though he was not an avid supporter of abolition, agreed to become leader of the new government in the vain hope that he could keep the ship of state aright.

After less than one month, however, he realized that he was mistaken. The intransigent factions in his own ranks, ranging from the rabid pro-militarists on the right to the socialists on the left, made it impossible for him to command effectively. So once more he went into exile. In the wake of his departure, the Liberal movement split into a number of factions, each of which competed to gain support among the military. After a brief interlude, the Republican Union under the leadership of Alexandros Papanastasiou came to power. He appointed to his cabinet two prominent members of the Military League. Judging the time to be ripe, he brought a resolution calling for the establishment of a republic before the assembly. Some of the other Venizelist parties abstained and so the vote in favour was overwhelming (259 to 3). A few months later, the resolution was ratified in a public referendum by a vote of 69 per cent to 31 per cent. The constitutional questions, however, would not go away. Moreover, even the change from monarchy to republic could not stem the tide of unrest. In truth, however, the general public evinced little enthusiasm one way or another. For government civil servants and for members of the military officer corps, on the other hand, it was an issue of enormous – indeed, possibly even life or death – importance. Political instability through the 1920s, then, was in many ways a continuation of the National Schism, only in a different form. Between 1924 and 1928 there were ten prime ministers, two presidents were deposed and one resigned, and numerous military coups occurred. This was one of Greece's darkest hours.

VENIZELOS REDUX

In 1928 Venizelos once more stepped on to centre stage in Greek history. In August of that year, the Venizelists captured 63.5 per cent of the popular vote and 90.4 per cent of the seats in Parliament. The novelist Giorgios Theotokas captured the moment well:

> Chief, saviour, symbol of half of Greece, Satan to the other
> half, he was certainly for all the President of Greek affairs,

the axis around which the Nation was starting to whirl again. Nobody understood what he had in mind, but his presence was enough to upset everything as if this presence emitted some mysterious current, which shook all at once all the forces of the national organism, the forces of faith and heroism, of adventure and plunder, of creation and dissolution, of malice and envy. All the vital instincts which slept unused, awoke again and boiled forcefully on the rosy coasts of the Eastern Mediterranean: Venizelos! Venizelos![20]

One Royalist supporter saw Venizelos quite differently. So returned, in his view, 'a real rascal, a true traitor, a real Caligostro of politics, a Cretan liar, who, unfortunately for Greece still lives'.[21]

Weaving together an electoral coalition consisting of the old liberal base and the refugees, 91 per cent of whom supported him, Venizelos crafted an overwhelming majority in Parliament. He remained in power until 1932 and oversaw a period of political stability and economic growth. Under his banner he brought together an array of interests, including those on the left who found the Balkan policies emanating from the COMINTERN, particularly its support for the establishment of an independent Macedonian state, as sufficient grounds for repudiating the only true leftist party in Greece, the Communist Party. The leftist, populist Agrarian Party had grown in numbers but was still a minor presence. The conservative Populist Party provided the main opposition and the central issue separating the two major parties above all else was the constitutional question. In spite of a strong parliamentary base, Venizelos had to negotiate his way through treacherous waters. On the one hand, he needed to keep the hard-line anti-royalists in line, most of whom were conservative in other respects; on the other, he had to address the issues held most dear by old style liberals, leftists, and the refugees, a group which increasingly was leaning to the left.[22]

Venizelos was able to implement a number of changes, most of them funded by external loans. He introduced numerous reforms aimed at improving Greek agriculture, such as land reclamation schemes, agricultural credit programmes, cooperatives and price supports for agricultural produce. In 1929, for example, the Agricultural Bank of Greece was established with its primary goal being to supply low interest loans to farmers so as to alleviate the debt crisis. The road and rail networks were improved and expanded. Protective tariffs were raised to make indigenous products more competitive in the marketplace. Public housing projects were erected and made available to poor Greeks. A loan of over £1,000,000 was contracted for the building of public schools. The success of this programme can be gauged even today by the frequency with which one finds 'Venizelist' schools in even the most remote reaches of the country. All of these were sound measures that led to some notable progress. But all too often in their implementation these initiatives fell prey to sectarian struggles and political patronage. Typical was the case of the village of Karpofora in Messenia, where two rival cooperatives developed, one for the royalist faction and another for the supporters of the republic.[23] The schism had become deeply embedded into the fabric of Greek life and the distribution of state resources became integrally tied to political allegiance.

Venizelos also scored some notable successes in foreign policy. He successfully took part in the establishment of the Balkan Pact, a move aimed at lessening its members' reliance on the Great Powers. In like vein, he signed a treaty restoring cordial relations between Italy and Greece. The most important of his foreign policy initiatives, however, was his rapprochement with Atatürk, culminating with the Ankara Convention of October 1930 by which Greece and Turkey officially recognized the existing territorial boundaries and accepted naval equality in the eastern Mediterranean (See Fig. 7.1.)

While this agreement did achieve a workable *modus vivendi* with Turkey, it proved to be a domestic disaster for the Liberals. The treaty stipulated that the lands abandoned by Greeks and Moslems were to be considered as a commensurate exchange and so no compensation would be paid to refugees on either side. This was a bitter blow to the Anatolian Greeks and it led to their turning away from their Cretan champion.[24] Disillusioned and angry, debt-ridden and despondent, many refugees looked to parties on the Left for support.

The 'second golden age of Venizelism' also witnessed an ominous extension of the policing powers of the central state. Even in his first administration, Venizelos had been a firm believer in the need for large and well-trained police forces, and he took steps at that time to develop them. Like the military, both the rural and the urban police forces soon became caught up in the mutual recriminations that followed in the wake of the National Schism. The rise of the Communist and the Agrarian Parties during the 1920s led to an even greater emphasis on 'law and order' issues. During the dictatorship of General Pangalos in 1925–26 in particular, the police were given *carte blanche* to break strikes and to combat the increasingly leftist labour movement.

In his second term (1929), pressed by the right wing of his party, the Venizelos government passed the *Idionym* (Special) Law. This legislation gave the state far reaching powers to crack down on any form of protest. For example, it made it a 'criminal offence to agitate for an overthrow of the existing socio-political order.' Moreover, it became illegal even to propagate

Fig. 7.1 'Rapprochement'. Published in 1930, this cartoon depicts Venizelos as the master statesman bringing together Greece and Turkey. The Treaty of Ankara that he signed with Kemal Atatürk ostensibly brought peace to the region and established cordial relations between the two peoples. But as we know, it failed, and tensions between Greece and Turkey remain to the present day.
(G.I. Panagiotakis, O Venizelos stin Epanstasi kai tin Politiki, *Herakleion, 1993, p. 292.)*

ideas that could be construed to threaten the social order. The law also placed very tight restrictions on the activities of trade unions, especially on their legal rights to strike. Under the new law, thousands of labour leaders, trade unionists, and Communists were arrested or deported to remote Greek islands. A new fissure, Left versus Right, emerged in inter-war Greece, and the mechanisms of order designed to combat the 'Bolshevik' menace greased the slippery slide to authoritarianism.[25]

The financial crises of 1930 and 1931 initiated a period of political chaos and pushed Greece even further into civil conflict. Venizelos was unable to address the economic dilemma effectively, and so his fragile political coalition began to unravel. The refugee vote splintered as some became disillusioned with the lack of improvement in their lot and so they turned to the more militant parties of the left, while others abandoned the Venizelist banner because of the diplomatic overtures to Turkey that they perceived as a betrayal. Within the Liberal coalition, splits became evident as men like Papanastasiou, Kondylis, Kaphandaris and Zavitsianos broke ranks and asserted themselves, each seeking to succeed the aged Cretan.

Casting a pall over all political discourse was the constitutional issue, in the latest manifestation of the *Ethnikos Dikhasmos*. In one parliamentary debate, Panayis Tsaldaris, the leader of the Populists, proclaimed that there would be no crisis in Greece if only the nation could call on the talents of the Martyred Six (referring to the six leaders executed in 1922). Venizelos responded by stating that the nation would be solvent but for the 40 million gold pounds of credit promised by the Allies but lost when Konstantine was returned to the throne.

More significant than the parliamentary posturing was the very real threat of reprisals and purges felt in the military if there were to be a change in leadership. Unable to maintain control, Venizelos relinquished power, and elections in the autumn of 1932 produced a hung Parliament (Liberals 98 seats, Populists 95 seats, Communists 10 seats and the Agrarians 11 seats). Tsaldaris and the Populists after many negotiations were allowed to form a government. When it fell, elections were held once more, and this time the Populists won a clear majority. Plastiras would not accept this and so he attempted a *coup d'etat* in March 1933. It failed miserably. The bitterness of the old disputes rose to the surface of public life. Aggravating an already tense situation was a bungled assassination attempt on Venizelos during the summer of 1933. Another coup, in which Venizelos was directly implicated, was staged and failed. Discredited, the great man retired first to Rhodes and then to Paris.

The Populists now held power but still stability proved elusive. The

Fig. 7.2 'Inner City Blues'. This 1938 cartoon captures vividly the dark side of the Athenian underworld in the aftermath of rapid urbanization, the influx of the Asia Minor refugees, and the economic turmoil of the 1930s. (Cartoon drawing by Alexandros Koroyiannakis, Ethniki Pinakothiki Mouseio Alexandrou Soutzou, with permission.)

monarchists in his own party toppled Tsaldaris. Led by Giorgos Kondylis and General Papagos, a rump Parliament declared the restoration of the monarchy and in a rigged plebiscite, in which 97 per cent of the electorate supposedly agreed, King George II was restored to the throne. He returned to Greece on November 25, 1935. The new government scheduled elections for January; these were intended to legitimize and validate its actions. The government had, however, miscalculated the mood of the people. The royalists won 143 seats, but the republicans captured 141; with its largest vote ever, the Communist Party won 15 seats and so held the balance of power.

This development was unacceptable to the King and the Right. The political balance was precarious. Labour unrest and massive strikes in May raised the issue of public order. After the strikes were bloodily put down, the Communists were blamed for them. Emerging as a presence in government was Ioannis Metaxas. As one study observed

> Greek politicians now seemed only too ready to give Metaxas enough rope to the hang the Left, a convenient scapegoat, as it has often been in Greece; only they were

soon to discover that the aspiring dictator was reserving the
other end for them.[26]

When General Papagos seemed unable to maintain order, the King
replaced him as Secretary of War with Metaxas. Metaxas consolidated his
power base, placing men loyal to him in key positions in the military. Using
as a pretext the threat of general strikes planned for 5 August 1936, Metaxas
staged a coup. On 4 August he seized control, dismissing what remained of the
government and with the King's blessing, he suspended the constitution.
Metaxas had become dictator of Greece.

THE METAXAS DICTATORSHIP

Ioannis Metaxas was born in 1871. After studying at the Prussian Military
Academy in Berlin, he became a life-long soldier. He greatly admired the
Germanic qualities of regimentation and seriousness, which he contrasted
with the individualism and lack of discipline that he saw in Greeks. He rose
through the ranks and became a staff member during the Balkan War. He
established at that time close connections with the royal family, and in
particular with then Crown Prince Konstantine. A royal favourite, he soon
became acting Chief of Staff. He resigned in 1915 as the schism between the
King and Venizelos developed, and he spent much of the war in exile on
Corsica. He rose to the rank of general after the restoration but resigned his
commission in 1920 in protest over the Asia Minor adventure.

From then on he was a persistent but minor voice emanating from the far
right fringes of Greek politics. His various forays into electoral contests were
uniformly unsuccessful; his monarchist parties never received more than a
handful of votes. His rise to power was linked completely to his connection
to the royal family. Thus, when George took the throne in 1935 and looked for
a strong man who could hold the situation together, his gaze fell on his family's
old and trusted friend.

Metaxas's 'Third Hellenic Civilization' (the first being ancient Greece and
the second the Byzantine Empire) was a curious blend of elements borrowed
from the fascist regimes in Italy and Germany and his own idiosyncratic
notions about corporatism. Unlike Hitler or Mussolini, Metaxas had no broad
base of popular support; Greek fascism was not a mass movement. Unlike
them as well it was not based on any coherent ideology or racist dogma. At
best, his rule can be described as authoritarian paternalism. For the most part,
the Greek public neither actively resisted nor supported his regime.

Metaxas styled himself as the 'First Peasant' or 'First Worker' of the state. The virtues he extolled were hard work, selfless commitment to the state, and self-sacrifice for the public good. His goal was to reshape the national character. Pragmatically, he addressed a number of issues of importance to the working classes. He instituted a coherent programme of public works and drainage projects. He declared a moratorium on debt in the countryside. Price supports for produce were introduced. There were new regulations for the collection and distribution of subsistence grains. For industrial workers, he set wage rates, regulated working hours, guaranteed the five day working week, and passed other measures aimed at making the workplace safer. The bureaucracy was revamped and made more efficient. The military forces were purged and expenditures on men and material increased. He established a variety of national organizations, like the National Youth Organization (EON), aimed at instilling those virtues that the diminutive dictator held dear.[27]

All of this, of course, came at a price: deprivation of freedom. Strikes were outlawed, unions suppressed. Civil liberties and personal freedoms were curtailed. Opposition and obstruction of the public good became treasonable. Under the direction of Konstantine Maniadakis the secret police became all powerful. Communists and other leftists in particular were subjected to systemic repression. Over 30,000 of them were arrested and detained in prisons and concentration camps or sent into exile on remote Greek islands. Torture was routinely used to extract confessions or to make people sign documents that branded others as 'communists' or 'obstructionists'.[28] The new National Schism of Left versus Right was on track to develop into a civil war. But that fight would be delayed for a few years as international affairs intruded into the life of the nation.

The main dilemma for Metaxas was in foreign affairs. By temperament and inclination, he looked to Germany and Italy as his closest friends. And there was certainly a major increase in German economic penetration into Greece.[29] But he also realized that Greece's fortunes were closely connected to Great Britain whose fleet would always pose a threat to his maritime nation. Moreover, throughout the 1930s, it became evident that Greece's national interests in the eastern Mediterranean (concerning control of the Aegean islands and the Dodecanese for example) and in the Balkans (especially Albania) clashed directly with Mussolini's plans for his 'new Rome'. Italian expansionism in the region placed Metaxas and Mussolini on a collision course. As war approached in Europe, Metaxas found it increasingly hard to walk the fine line between the Allies and the Axis Powers. Mussolini's persistent provocations settled the issue. First came his announcement of the annexation of Albania in April. Then, as his impatience increased at Germany's continued overtures into the

Balkans, he decided to assert his independence and so he turned his attention to Greece.

At 3 a.m. on 28 October 1940 the Italian ambassador delivered an ultimatum: Greece must allow Italian forces to occupy strategic locations on Greek soil. Standing at the door in his nightclothes, Metaxas delivered his one word response: *Okhi* (No)! Greece was plunged into war. This was one of the dictator's last acts – he died three months later – and this one act did more to restore Greece's national pride than all of his other actions combined.

8 The Terrible Decade

Occupation and civil war 1940–1950

The decade of the 1940s was the most devastating and deadly in Greek history. The horrors of foreign military occupation were combined with the peculiar ravages which only a civil war can bring. The events of this decade left scars that 50 years later have yet to heal. The literature on this period is vast and growing, as more sources, government documents, personal accounts and oral histories, become more accessible. Ideology continues to shape historical interpretations as well. The brief account that follows makes no attempt at completeness, but like the rest of this book, it aims at providing the reader with a general overview of events and developments and their consequences in shaping modern Greece.

THE 'GOOD' WAR

Initially the war against Italy went very well for Greece. Even though the Italian forces had the advantage of being on the initiative, they were inadequately prepared to launch such a massive invasion. Furthermore, because of the mountainous terrain their superiority in armoured vehicles was obviated and because of poor weather they could not fully capitalize on their superior air power. On the morning after Metaxas's strident declaration of Greece's resistance to Italian aggression, tens of thousands of Athenians took to the streets to show their support of the dictator. The nation as a whole rallied behind him, and men of all political persuasions ran to join the fray. While beneficial to the nation, this development spelt trouble for the diminutive dictator. 'The danger to [Metaxas] was that his liberal and socialist opponents were even more ardently opposed to the Axis than his supporters . . .'.[1] The leadership of the Communist Party, for example, sent out a letter calling on its members to join the war against the fascist invaders, arguing that the class war against the Greek Right could only be waged once the nation was safe from foreign invaders. Many of those who had escaped incarceration by signing a declaration of renunciation saw the Italian conflict as a chance for them to redeem themselves. The war became a struggle for national liberation that cut across old political divisions and current ideological divides.

There were, however, warning signs. The first was that hidden behind the zeal of the officer corps to defeat the Italians was still remaining sympathy for fascism as a political system in general and for National Socialism in particular.[2] Second, the very high levels of German investment in Greece made some financiers and industrialists reluctant to support any moves that could alienate the Third Reich.[3] These rifts, however, would only become evident later. At the start of the war, unity was the cry.

Under the leadership of General Giorgios Tsolakoglou, commander of the III Army Corps, the Greek forces in Epiros had by early December driven the Italian army out of Greece, through most of Albania, and was on the verge of pushing it into the sea. Many Greeks saw this campaign not only as a war against the Italian invader but also as an opportunity to liberate the Greeks of 'northern' Epiros. Had it not been for the onset of a very severe winter that literally froze the army in place, the campaign would have been successful.

Great Britain at this time had no other active ally except for Greece, and Churchill was determined to stand firm with Greece; consequently, he offered Metaxas air support and troops. The dictator accepted the former but not the latter for fear of provoking Hitler into intervening. When Metaxas died in January,[4] his successor, Alexandros Koryzis, had no such hesitation, and in March a British Commonwealth expeditionary force of 63,000 men landed in Greece and on Crete. But the fate of Greece hung on decisions made not in London but Berlin. As the Italian advance faltered and edged toward failure, Adolf Hitler and the German High Command faced a crucial decision. Operation Barbarossa, the invasion of the Soviet Union, was on course for the spring and, for two reasons, the Balkan front had to be secured. First, history had shown Germany that its underbelly to the south could be exposed, and the idea of simultaneously having to fight a three front war was very unattractive. Second, the vital oil supplies to the Middle East and North Africa had to be safeguarded. Since Mussolini did not seem up to the task, the Germans decided on a joint invasion with their Bulgarian allies against Yugoslavia and Greece.

The British expeditionary force that had landed in March proved of little help due to confusion between the various military commanders, and so, because of poor coordination, the forward Greco-British line was established too far south for it to be defensible. When the German *blitzkrieg* was launched on 6 April 1941, the Greek and British forces quickly fell. One part of the German expeditionary force moved westward through Macedonia and isolated the army of Tsolakoglou from the rest of Greece. Trapped between the Italian army to its north and the German army to its south, without even putting up a fight, it capitulated to the Germans on 20 April. To add insult to injury,

Tsolakoglou offered to serve in a government of occupation, if that were the Führer's wish.

Meanwhile, the other part of the German invasion force rapidly rushed south along the east coast of central Greece toward Athens. The advancing Nazi forces demonstrated overwhelming tactical and technical superiority against the Anglo-Greek forces, which continued to fall back before the German assault. Unable to halt the advance, the Allied forces abandoned the capital. An eyewitness vividly captured the moment:

> ... cheering, clapping crowds lined the streets and pressed about our cars .... Girls and men leapt on the running boards to kiss or shake hands with the grimy, weary gunners. They threw flowers to us and ran besides us crying: 'Come back – You must come back again – Goodbye – Good luck!'[5]

It would be years later and after much suffering that Allied troops would re-enter Athens.

After a sustained air attack that caused massive damage, Athens fell to the German ground forces on 26 April. King George II, the civilian government under the newly appointed Prime Minister, Emmanouil Tsouderos, and the remnants of the Greek army fled to Crete. It remained there until the brutal invasion by German paratroopers in May successfully captured the island. The Greek government then fled to Egypt. It would be a government-in-exile for some time to come.

OCCUPATION

By June 1941 Greece was a defeated country. The German authorities were then confronted by the question of how to control this crucial part of the world. They established a puppet government under the leadership of General Tsolakoglou so that some semblance of a legitimate Greek government with which they could deal would exist. Tsolakoglou had a very difficult time convincing members of the old political order (who had not fled) to join his government and so he had to rely on inexperienced military men like himself. In the end, he also had to draw on the support of a number of far Right Greek parties, such as the Greek Fascist Party, the National Union of Greece, and the Nationalist-Socialist Political Organization of Greece.

The primary duties of his quisling administration were to maintain law and order, oversee the economic takeover of the country, and to liaise with the occupying powers. Shortly after the fall of Athens, the SS, working with the Greek police and using the infamous files kept from the days when Manidakes was head of security, began to round up known Communists, Venizelists and anyone else whom they considered to be an enemy of the Reich. Germany and its other Axis allies met with the quisling government to divide the country into zones of occupation over which Axis Powers would have administrative control.

The Germans retained control of Athens, Thessaloniki, Crete, the Thrakian border zone with Turkey, and a number of the Aegean islands. The Bulgarians were given Thrake and eastern Macedonia, which they proceeded to rule with an iron hand. The Italians occupied the rest of the country. The loss of Macedonia and Thrake to the Bulgarians was especially humiliating to Greeks. The barely healed wounds from the Macedonian struggle and the inter-war period were opened again as the Bulgarian army of occupation let loose a reign of ethnic terror that caused over 100,000 Greeks to leave the Bulgarian zone of occupation.[6] They also actively encouraged and provided material inducements to Slav Macedonians who were Greek citizens to sign Bulgarian identity cards.[7]

The Italians also used ethnicity as a means of dividing the rural Greek population, especially among the Slav Macedonians and the Vlachs. In the region of Thessaly, for example, they formed a paramilitary force called the Roman Legion that consisted almost exclusively of Vlachs. Though this strategy of divide and rule met with only limited success, the impact of foreign occupation on local society was nonetheless devastating, as the following passage shows:

> This [1941] was indeed a thrice-accursed winter . . . .. Black,
> black as pitch, was the night which this unbearable slavery
> had cast over them! And in this night of horror, the
> [Roman] Legion, greatest blight of all, lightened and
> thundered! In very truth, the Legion stormed through the
> night. Its army now amounted to more than three
> thousand men and was made up of a collection of the most
> impudent adventurers and worst vagrants in the area. Most
> of them were criminals who had managed to escape from
> the prisons when the Germans invaded the country. They
> wore arm-bands on the sleeves, carried truncheons in their
> hands, pistols in their belts, and, occasionally, light Italian
> rifles on their shoulders. They strutted, well-fed and

clothed, among the starving and ragged population and spread terror around the plain. Reports came in from every village of brutality, insults, beatings and torture; of people being hung by the arms or legs from trees in the public squares so that whole villages might witness the tyranny and humiliation. There was nowhere to turn for protection. No one dared to ask for protection for if a court decision was issued against the offenders, they would pay the victims back with more beatings and with even more ferocious persecution.[8]

In addition to predations by the occupation forces and their local surrogates, the Germans also oversaw the systematic plundering of the nation's economic resources. It was akin to a systematic rape of the Greek economy.

Fig. 8.1 'Famine in Athens'. The first to feel the effects of the food shortages of the winter of 1941 were the very young and the elderly. (Voula Papaioannou and the Photographic Archives of the Benaki Museum, with permission.)

Key commodities like bauxite and other minerals were either seized or purchased at a fraction of their true value. The bulk of the harvests of the major food crops, wheat, olives, vines, citrus, and other fruits, were confiscated for the provisioning of the occupying troops. Moreover, the Greek people were to underwrite the costs of the foreign forces. As Mussolini ruefully put it, 'The Germans have taken from the Greeks even their shoelaces and now they pretend to place blame for the economic situation on our shoulders'.[9]

This ransacking of the Greek economy combined with the British naval blockade quickly produced massive food shortages. By May 1941 there was only 21 days' worth of wheat left in the national stores. Through the summer, peasant farmers began to hoard food, refusing to send anything to the urban markets. The German leadership turned a deaf hear to the warning calls, and the Italian authorities responded that they were simply unable to help. By October, the first bodies began to appear on the streets of Athens. Famine soon spread to other regions and cities as well (Fig. 8.2). Over 50,000 people perished for want of food during January and February, and all together, by July 1942 close to 200,000 people had died. During the darkest days of winter, the Turkish Red Crescent provided some relief to over 150,000 Athenians per day. Eventually, the Wehrmacht allowed first the Red Cross and then the United States to supply humanitarian aid.

The famine abated, but a new catastrophe took its place: hyperinflation (Table 8.1). The prices of almost every commodity skyrocketed, completing the devastation of the Greek economy. Black markets flourished and profiteers and

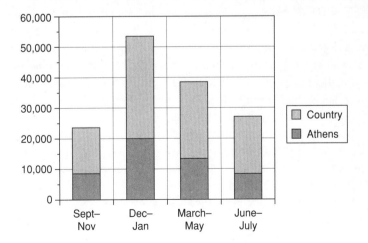

Fig. 8.2 The number of deaths attributable to starvation from September 1941 to July 1942.

Table 8.1 Hyperinflation struck Greece beginning in the autumn of 1943. The table below compares the prices of key commodities between October 1943 and September 1944; for comparative purposes the average prices from 1940 have been provided. Prices are in drachmas, per kilo of bread cheese and olives, per liter of olive oil and for a pair of shoes.

	1940	October 1943	April 1944	September 1944
Bread	10	13,000	46,000	34,000,000
Cheese	60	120,000	6,000,000	11,600,000,000
Olive Oil	50	80,000	28,000,000	4,000,000,000
Olives	26	22,000	12,000,000	4,000,000,000
Shoes	450	8,000,000		22,040,000,000

collaborators benefited from the sufferings of others. Memories of these dark days would be indelibly etched in the minds of many and the thirst for revenge against those who exploited the situation would only widen the already yawning divisions within Greek society.[10]

The brutality of foreign occupation did not stifle the will to resist. Shortly after Greece's capitulation in the spring of 1941 sporadic acts of resistance occurred, the most audacious of which took place on the night of 30 May when two youths tore down the Nazi swastika flag from a flagpole on the Acropolis. Acts of sabotage that caused real as opposed to symbolic damage also occurred in various parts of the country. During the summer of 1941 more organized resistance movements began to form. Workers and trade union leaders in Athens, for example, created the National Workers' Liberation Front (EEAM).[11] Other groups started to organize. In September, an umbrella organization was formed to coordinate resistance activities: the National Liberation Front (EAM, the *Ethnikon Apeleftherotikon Metopon*). While its primary goal was to drive the Axis forces out of Greece, an ancillary aim soon emerged: to ensure that there would be a free choice regarding the nature of the government that would be formed when the country was liberated. The old constitutional issue raised its head once more.

Very quickly the Communist Party of Greece (KKE) achieved a dominant position in EAM and in the other organizations that sprang from it, like ELAS (the National People's Liberation Army) and EPON (the National Panhellenic Organization of Youth). They were able to do so for a number of reasons.

First, the persecutions during the Metaxas years had forged an identity and a unity that gave the organization coherence. It also gave many party cadres a powerful incentive for revenge against members of the Right, some of whom were now actively collaborating with the occupation forces. Second, it possessed an organizational structure and experience at clandestine activities that meant it was the one group ready and able to undertake resistance activities. Third, with its slogans about social justice, peoples' power, and economic prosperity, the Communist Party projected a vision of a better future that resonated with impoverished peasants and destitute workers at a time of great suffering. Fourth, they were standing firm in Greece with the people in contrast to the old politicians and the King who had fled to the safety of London or Cairo. From shared suffering came unity of purpose.

The vast majority of members of EAM and ELAS, however, were not Communists, even though the leadership clearly was. Instead it drew on a wide spectrum of Greek society, and it attracted in particular many men and women who had been largely unempowered under the old style of elite politics that dominated Greece since its inception.

> EAM and its various auxiliary organizations, especially its military arm, ELAS, satisfied a need of Greeks from all walks of life not only to resist the occupiers by the modest means available, but to provide as well a populist structure of local organization and a support network untainted by the stigma of collaboration with the enemy.[12]

For the reasons set out here, the majority of people were ready to follow them, even though many did not support the KKE's political vision of a Communist postwar Greece. There were other resistance groups, the most important of which was the National Republican Greek League (EDES). But EAM/ELAS remained the dominant formation.[13]

The government-in-exile and the monarchy had little contact with the forces in occupied Greece. King George II was active in lobbying the western allies on behalf of Greece. During 1942 and 1943, he visited the United Kingdom, the United States and Canada making speeches and meeting with government officials. Using these venues he launched appeals for aid for his country, he reminded the Allies of the great sufferings that Greece was undergoing, and he emphasized the role of the regular Greek army in fighting the Axis. Rarely did he mention the activities of the resistance movement inside of occupied Greece. There were contingents of the Greek armed forces that continued fighting alongside their British and American allies. But even within the regular military, men were becoming dissatisfied with the old political leadership, and indeed on a number of occasions mutinies did take place. Already tainted by his role in the Metaxas regime, the King's position at home was made even more suspect by his absence. Already deeply fractured by the cleavages that divided them since 1915, the old political parties found themselves out of touch with the Greek people as well. Moreover, many new faces were emerging through the vehicle of the resistance movements.

> Patriots! I am Aris Velouchiotis, Colonel of Artillery. Starting today, I am raising the banner of revolt against the forces occupying our beloved country. The handful of men you see before you will soon become an army of thousands. We are just a nucleus.[14]

So spoke Athanasios Klaras to villagers of Domnitsa in central Greece in June 1942. Standing behind him were 300 armed men who more closely resembled bandits than they did an army. But men and women from Dominitsa and hundreds of other villages and towns soon proved his words true as the ranks of ELAS swelled. By late 1942, ELAS contingents had been formed in central Greece, under the command of Aris, the Peloponnesos, Macedonia, Thessaly and Thrake. The number of guerrilla warriors in its ranks grew from 2000 in February 1942 to 45,000–50,000 by September 1944.[15] ELAS became by far the largest of the resistance forces, but in order for the resistance movement to succeed it needed support from western Europe, and that meant Great Britain.

The Special Operations Executive (SOE) of the British military provided arms and experts to the Greek resistance. The SOE, operating together with fighters from ELAS and EDES, struck a major blow against Germany in November 1942 by destroying the railway bridge over the Gorgopotamos gorge in central Greece. This severed the supply line to General Rommel in North Africa. Through 1943 the Greek resistance movement, and especially ELAS, conducted numerous successful operations against the Axis Powers, so much so that some regions were effectively liberated and placed under EAM control. Paralleling the successes of its military wing, EAM grew both in size and strength, and as we shall see in more detail shortly, became a major political force. But the resistance movement as a whole started to dissolve because of internal pressures. British attempts to coordinate all resistance activities foundered because of Winston Churchill's steadfast support for the Greek monarchy in the face of the widespread resistance to restoration by people of all political persuasions in Greece. It was not long before fighting broke out between ELAS/EAM and the non-Communist resistance groups, especially EDES. Some of the animosity was based on the virulent anti-Communist feelings among some Greeks, but by and large the sectarian violence at this point was based on specific, localized disagreements and antagonisms rather than being part of a concerted effort by the Communist Party to eliminate opposition groups.[16] The struggle over the future course once the occupiers had been driven from the land was yet to come.

One source of antagonism between the resistance movements in the countryside and the old political leadership in the cities was related to the advisability of there being any resistance movements because of the brutal reprisals being visited on the civilian population. As acts of sabotage and resistance increased so did the policy of reprisals.

> There were bodies everywhere – in front of the house and inside them . . . there was a church or small chapel in the main square . . . and in front of this church lay a large heap of bodies. So far as I could see from the tangled mass of humanity there were more women and children than men there.[17]

This description of the massacre at the village of Komeno in western Greece in the summer of 1943 could be multiplied many times over.

As ELAS expanded its activities and as the occupation powers started to lose their tight grip on the country, the German Wehrmacht started to play a greater role in maintaining order and security. Then with Mussolini's fall in the summer of 1943, the Wehrmacht and SS took responsibility for nearly the entire country. There was also a change in policy towards the greater use of violence and fear against the Greek people. They implemented a policy of taking hostages in a vain attempt to undercut local support for the *andartes*. When this proved largely unsuccessful, they decreed that 50 Greeks would be killed for every German soldier lost; as a consequence of this policy entire villages were destroyed. In some cases, in order to heighten the terror among the populace, groups of people would be randomly selected, marched to a public place and shot. Finally, the German authorities in conjunction with the quisling government of Ioannis Rallis began to utilize gangs of thugs and collaborators whom they organized into units called Security Battalions. Some of those who joined were simply hardened criminals and bad men; the majority were die-hard royalist military officers and policemen, who were opposed to the resistance movements because of the constitutional issue. All told the security battalions numbered approximately 18,000 men. Divided into ten units, the Greek-manned battalions unleashed a wave of violence and terror that surpassed the actions of the SS.[18]

One of the war's many tragedies was the destruction of the Greek Jewish population. Before the war there had been vibrant and sizeable Jewish populations in cities like Thessaloniki, Athens, and Ioannina. Almost immediately after the occupation began the German authorities in Thessaloniki began the persecution of the city's large Jewish population. Initially those efforts took the form of confiscating books and manuscripts. Then Jewish men were compelled to perform labour service building roads. The ancient Jewish necropolis was destroyed and the headstones used as building material. On one occasion in the summer of 1942 thousands of Jewish men were herded into one of the city's main squares where they had to endure hours of physical torture and public humiliation. Finally in spring of 1943, the decision was made to implement the final solution. In the short span of two and one half months, 50,000 from the Macedonian capital alone were sent to Auschwitz; few returned. The communities from the rest of Greece were not spared either, and by the end of 1943, the long history of Jews in Greece had largely come to an end.[19]

In the summer of 1943, events took a new course. British policy underwent a change in direction. In order to pave the way for the allied invasion of Normandy, it was necessary to convince Hitler that the main theatre of operation was to be elsewhere, for example in Greece. The policy had merit because of the Gallipoli campaign of the First World War. The cooperation of all the resistance movements was needed if the plan was to succeed. ELAS in particular was needed because it controlled the largest army and occupied the most territory; in fact by 1943, it had liberated significant parts of countryside. Increasingly the occupiers held only the towns and cities.

The so-called 'National Bands' agreement was made in July 1943 and it gave EAM/ELAS primacy in exchange for a cessation of violence against the other groups. The dubious prospects for long term cooperation between the various resistance groups and the British were shattered in August 1943 as a consequence of a disastrous series of meetings between guerrilla leaders, the government-in-exile and the King in Cairo. The leaders of the resistance had two demands. The first was that the King agree not to return to Greece until a plebiscite had been held. The second was the assurance that EAM/ELAS representatives be given the portfolios of interior, justice, and war in the postwar government. Both demands were refused. The guerrilla representatives returned convinced more than ever that the British intended to force King George on the nation.

The immediate result of the Cairo conference was the onset of civil war between ELAS and EDES in October. Forced to choose, the British opted for EDES and so it stepped up arms shipments to them while cutting off the supply to ELAS.[20] This proved ineffective because the surrender of the Italian forces in September had left ELAS well equipped. Having stabilized its position militarily EAM declared the formation of a Political Committee of National Liberation (PEEA) on 10 March 1944 with its capital in the heart of 'Mountain', i.e. liberated, Greece. The PEEA initially enjoyed a good deal of popularity, in part because it counted among its members prominent non-Communists. To be sure, the KKE was firmly in control, but even the semblance of political ecumenicalism gave it a degree of legitimacy it would not otherwise enjoy. Moreover, with its formation for the first time since the war had broken out there was an alternative to the government-in-exile. Numerous people rallied to its banner. For many in the liberated areas of Greece, the experience of EAM/ELAS rule had been an uplifting one, as the following suggests:

> The benefits of civilization and culture trickled into the mountains for the first time. Schools, local government, law-courts and public utilities, which the war had ended, worked again. Theatres, factories, parliamentary assemblies began for the first time. Communal life was organized in place of the traditional individualism of the Greek peasant … EAM/ELAS set the pace in the creation of something that the governments of Greece had neglected: an organized state in the Greek mountains.[21]

For many women in particular the experience of the resistance movement was one of personal liberation; they became empowered as never before. As one oral informant told sociologist Janet Hart:

> Why did I join the Resistance? Eh, at the time, of course, there were the conquerors (*kataktites*) in our country … and we knew that if we did not fight, we wouldn't be able to throw out the *kataktites*. Besides that, we also had fascism on our soil too, we had the Metaxas dictatorship, and that had to change …. And, the development of us personally … as I told you, for women, it was a chance to make things better.[22]

Many women echoed those sentiments. Women took part as warriors and workers. Peasants and working-class men also found the prospect of going back to the old ways unacceptable.

Another group also rallied to the call of the PEEA. The only arm of the Greek military that had escaped from the Germans largely intact was the navy. During the years of occupation, it had been forced to play no active role. Many bridled at this inactivity while occupied Greece suffered. The formation of an alternative government provided an impetus for action. Mutinies erupted in the military forces stationed in the Middle East as men clamoured for the formation of a government of national unity which would carry the fight to Greece. British resolve to resist such a move was bolstered in October 1944 when Churchill and Stalin agreed that Greece was to be in the British sphere of influence and that the USSR would not interfere.[23]

The mutinies led to a change in Greek leadership. George Papandreou was appointed as the new Prime Minister. As a loyal Liberal supporter of Venizelos and a republican it was hoped that he would woo away non-Communist, anti-monarchist EAM supporters; as a staunch anti-Communist it was expected that he would toe the British line. His appointment was like waving a red flag, as it were, at the guerrilla forces. It nearly guaranteed deadlock. In an attempt to form a workable government, Papandreou convened in May a conference in Lebanon, the goal of which was to devise a structure for the restored government. Twenty-five delegates attended the conference, and the PEEA, EAM and ELAS were all represented, but only two of the delegates were Communists. The affair was stage-managed by the British.[24] After intense debate, an agreement was drafted, but in the course of the conference the Communist members found themselves isolated, even from the other members of their own delegation. Though the final pact assured EAM of participation in the government, the Communists did not gain control of the key ministries they sought, those relating to the military and the police. Initially, they refused to accept the agreement. But under pressure from Moscow, they finally acceded. Elevating tensions even higher was the impact of the agreement arranged at Caserta in September between Communist representatives, the government and the British authorities whereby ELAS agreed to allow British troops to land in Greece to support the Papandreou government, to place ELAS troops under the command of British General Ronald Scobie, to keep ELAS forces out of the major metropolitan areas and out of those few regions controlled by EDES, and finally they accepted that only the Government of National Unity would have the right to try and punish collaborators.[25]

The Germans began to withdraw from Greece in October 1944. For the previous five months Greece had witnessed a vicious three-sided war between the German forces and their Greek collaborators, ELAS, and the other resistance groups. The civil war abated momentarily as the resistance forces chose to harass the retreating Germany army at every turn. They also turned their wrath on the garrisons manned by the Security Battalions that the Germans had left behind. 'In an orgy of revenge,' collaborationist forces in the Peloponnesos, Macedonia, and Thessaly were slaughtered.[26] With the Third Reich's forces removed from the equation and the Security Battalions in disarray, ELAS/EAM was left as the paramount military presence in the country. Yet EAM made no concerted attempt to seize power – something it could easily have done. Why the Communist Party did not seize this moment when they still possessed a formidable fighting force and enjoyed a broad base of support with the general populace is still the topic of intense debate.[27] They would soon lose both, and with that passing, the opportunity for a Communist seizure of power had come and gone.

CIVIL WAR

George Papandreou and the Government of National Unity entered Athens on October 18. The euphoria of liberation swept all before it. Rejoicing in the streets went on for days as people tried to forget, for however brief a time, the horrible travails of the last four years and the daunting task of reconstruction that loomed before them. But fear and mistrust abounded. Too many key issues remained unresolved; prominent among them was the constitutional question. It was, however, not the only one. In a culture where the ethos of vengeance runs deep, retribution against those who had cooperated with the Axis Powers was on many peoples' minds.

When, therefore, Papandreou and the British showed little interest in pursuing and punishing collaborators and members of the Security Battalions, suspicions on the Left were raised further. As part of the agreement hammered out earlier, on 10 December, the 60,000 armed men and women of ELAS were to lay down their arms, with the exception of one elite unit equal in size to the government's Sacred Battalion and Mountain Brigade. In late November, however, Papandreou demanded a total demobilization of ELAS's forces, and this the leadership would not do. The question was: which side would relent? An on-the-ground observer captures well popular feelings. 'December 10th drew nearer, and with its approach there was the strange phenomenon of the most garrulous of people becoming silent as they anxiously awaited the outcome.'[28]

In a move designed to put greater pressure on the government, EAM called for a massive rally on December third as a prelude to a general strike in protest over the government's high-handedness. Thousands of people gathered in the Sintagma Square in the heart of Athens. Tensions ran high. Shortly before the demonstration, an explosion near Papandreou's house had resulted in a policeman's death. For reasons still unknown and seemingly without provocation, a policeman fired into the crowd. Before the world's press corps, his colleagues joined in.[29] Sixteen people were killed and many more wounded.

Open fighting exploded in the streets of Athens between the police, British troops and ELAS fighters. ELAS forces captured a number of police stations, prisons and the security force's headquarters. EAM was not, however, attempting to seize power.[30] Indeed, in cities outside of Athens where ELAS forces far outnumbered British troops, there was no fighting. It would seem that once the fighting against the British had commenced the aim was to bring down Papandreou. However, ELAS forces outside of the metropolitan areas did seize on the opportunity of the '*Dekemvriana* [December event]' to settle old scores. Napoleon Zervas and his EDES troops in Epiros were attacked and demolished, and elsewhere ELAS fighters went after known collaborators. The potential for escalation of the fighting all across the country was clear.

The situation was extremely tense. Churchill and his Foreign Secretary Anthony Eden flew to Athens in order to gain a first hand assessment of the situation. They came away convinced that the constitutional issue had to be resolved as expeditiously as possible. Under strong pressure King George II agreed to stay out of Greece and to the appointment of Archbishop Damaskinos as Regent. In a concession to the opposition, Papandreou was removed from office and replaced by the old Liberal warhorse General Plastiras. In addition to these concessions, the Communist leadership was leaning toward compromise because it was becoming evident to them that, in spite of their limited successes in December and January, they lacked the supplies to carry on fighting and if they did so, they risked losing their greatest asset, the support of the rural populace.

The Greek people had suffered greatly during the war and they wanted peace in order to rebuild their lives. But they needed resources that had to come from the west to do so. Also, as we saw earlier, during the 'Dekemvriana', ELAS forces struck out at anyone who did not actively support them. Both sides committed atrocities. Innocents were killed. The firm support that ELAS and EAM had enjoyed in the liberated zones started to dissipate. The Communist leadership sought compromise. In February 1945 a semblance of peace was restored with the Varkiza Agreement in which ELAS undertook to disarm and turn over their weapons, which they did in huge numbers, in exchange for an amnesty for all 'political crimes' and the calling of a plebiscite on the constitutional question.[31]

The Varkiza Agreement initiated what became known on the Left as the 'White Terror'. Rather than prosecuting collaborators, the Ministry of Justice and the security apparatus, itself still rife with far right wing supporters and men appointed during the Metaxas dictatorship, went after leftist resistance fighters. For example in March 1945, Mihalis Monidas and two compatriots, who had fought valiantly against the Nazis in the liberation of Piraeus in 1944, were sentenced to death for the killing of collaborators during the occupation. The amnesty on 'political crimes' seemed only to apply to members of the Right, like the infamous Security Battalions. Judges of the Popular Justice Tribunals that had flourished in liberated Greece were charged with murder. Tax collectors for the PEEA were charged with theft because they were not acting at the time as officially recognized agents of the government, i.e. the government-in-exile.

Right wing death squads and paramilitary groups, like the *Khi* (X) organization in the Peloponessos, embarked on a campaign of terror and assassination against leftists. Many EAM/ELAS members, Communists and non-Communists alike, went underground for their own safety. Through 1945 a series of weak governments proved incapable of stemming the escalating sectarian violence.[32]

Themistoklis Sophoulis, yet another of the Liberal old guard, formed a government at the end of 1945, and he announced that there would be a national election on 31 March 1946 that would be followed immediately by a plebiscite on the monarchy. This inverted the order agreed upon in the Varkiza Agreement. The Left claimed that fair and impartial elections were impossible in the climate of violence and repression overlying the land. The leftist parties, including the KKE, decided to abstain. So a war weary people went to the polls in what the Allied Mission for Observing the Greek Election (AMFOGE) called 'on the whole' free and fair elections. Without the Left, the choices open were between the People's Party, a loose grouping of the old Populist Party with Metaxasists, monarchists, and anti-Communists, a centre-right coalition, the National Political Union, of aged Liberals, or the National Party led by the old EDES warrior, Napoleon Zervas. Clearly the abstention of the Left had a major impact on the balloting and in the final analysis was probably most responsible for putting the People's Party in power. The leader of the government became Konstantinos (Dino) Tsaldaris, the nephew of the pre-war Populist leader.

The Tsaldaris regime renewed the persecution of the Left, removing civil servants and university professors from their posts because of their politics; head hunting by right wing bands was stepped up. Arrests were renewed, and soon over 30,000 men and women were interned in concentration camps or sent to island exiles. The country drifted ever closer to civil war. Far ahead of schedule, Tsaldaris demanded a plebiscite on the monarchy. Rather than waiting until 1948, as was agreed, he called for the referendum in September 1946. By a majority of 68 per cent to 32 per cent the monarchy was restored. The plebiscite was suspect. If not outright rigging, there was certainly coercion. For many Greeks the restoration represented a betrayal of everything they had fought for. As best we can judge, there was definitively widespread opposition to idea of a Communist government, but we can be equally certain that there was also widely and deeply felt antipathy to the monarchy in general and to King George II in particular, tainted as he was by his cosy relationship with Metaxas. Others joined the hardcore of former ELAS warriors who had fled once again to the mountains of Greece for safety. War clouds gathered on the horizon.

In October 1946, Markos Vafiadis announced the formation of a Communist Democratic Army of Greece (DAG). Many came forward and offered to fight. The reason for many was simple, as one partisan put it: 'For a whole year I was tortured, imprisoned, persecuted. I gritted my teeth. But eventually I could stand it no longer, I went to the mountains'.[33] Others more toward the middle of the political spectrum, as well as moderates and rightists who had fought with ELAS against the occupation forces, refused to join the new force. Consequently, the size of the Democratic Army fell from its previous wartime level of approximately 50,000 and now fluctuated between a high of 28,000 fighters to a low of approximately 13,000.

Fighting the foreign occupiers and their collaborationist lackeys was one thing, picking up arms for a Communist revolution was quite another. Atrocities and other assorted acts of violence against those who opposed or who would not join them drove many who had previously been supporters of ELAS into the opposition's camp.

The Civil War commenced in earnest during the winter of 1946–47. Markos adopted a strategy of guerrilla war, utilizing hit-and-run tactics to harass the National Army and its ancillary groups like the police and the paramilitary bands. DAG forces scored some notable successes but they were unable to capture any of the major towns. At one point, Markos attacked Konitsa in Epiros, aiming to make it the capital of the Provisional Democratic Government. The assault failed.

The Civil War was, like all internecine conflicts, marked by brutality on both sides. Villages were destroyed and civilians killed. Partisans from the Left and soldiers from the Right fought and the majority of the people were caught in between. As one victim of the war recalled, 'each side [was] as bad as the other'. In addition to the havoc wrought by the armed forces,

> people used the civil war to fight out personal animosities and hostilities, that was the worst. People who didn't like each other before or had some long standing complaint or quarrel with another, used this as a basis for killing and fighting each other.[34]

The atrocities of the war would leave lasting scars on the consciousness of the nation.

By the spring of 1947, Britain was reaching a point of exhaustion; it simply could not meet the increasingly high demands for money and supplies. The role of external patron was assumed by the United States. With the Greek case specifically in mind, Harry Truman set out in March 1947 a policy of global containment of Communist expansion, pledging US support to all free peoples under the threat of Communist take over: $400,000,000 in aid and military assistance was made available to Greece. United States advisers and military personnel under General James van Fleet came to Greece to train and supply the National Army and the security forces, which grew in time to over 250,000 men.[35]

The outcome was inevitable. But DAG mistakes hastened its fall. Nikos Zahariadis, who favoured a more conventional approach to war, ousted Markos. Shifting from guerrilla tactics to set piece battles proved a disaster. Outgunned and outmanned, the DAG found itself being pushed further northward and deeper into the mountains. The closure of the supply routes through Yugoslavia after Tito was expelled from Cominform only hastened the end. As the situation deteriorated, forced conscription of men and women and forced evacuation of children to the Communist bloc only eroded the DAG's popular base of support.

By the summer of 1949, the issue had been settled. In a futile last stand, the National Army routed the DAG at battles on the slopes Vitsi and Grammos in western Macedonia. The Civil War had come to an end. Greece would endure its legacy for decades to come.

After nearly ten years of fighting, the terrible decade had come to an end. All wars leave in their wake death, devastation and suffering, but because of their nature, civil wars tend to inflict even deeper, more lasting psychological wounds as well. Such was certainly the case in Greece. It would take years for the wounds of war to heal, and indeed, some scars remain to this day. What had the wars of resistance and civil strife accomplished? For one thing, the political conflict between Left and Right that had emerged in the inter-war period was settled, for the time being at least. The Right had won. Greece's destiny would henceforth lie with the western capitalist bloc. The monarchy was restored, but the constitutional question that had beset Greece since its founding refused to go away. Foreign dependency continued but with a changed orientation. The United States supplanted the former Great Powers of Europe as Greece's patron. Because of the influence that the United States exerted on Greece, some have gone so far as to label the early days of the Cold War as a period of *Amerikanikokratía*.[1] While this is an overstatement, it accurately conveys the sense that from the end of the Civil War onward, Greece's fortunes were tied to the western bloc.

In addition to that development, a number of other themes dominate the history of Greece from 1950 until 1967. We have already touched on one – the ongoing constitutional question. In the realm of politics, others included the rise of the Cyprus question as a major foreign policy concern. The period also witnessed an economic boom of sorts that left an indelible imprint on the country. The process of reconstruction and the uneven pace of economic development that it created inaugurated some far-reaching social, political, and economic changes that still shape the story of Greece to this day.

RECONSTRUCTION

The losses incurred during the Civil War were horrendous. At least 80,000 people had died; 20,000 more were detained in government prisons and concentration camps; approximately 5,000 others had been executed. The many years of fighting had made 700,000 people refugees in their own country. The Ministry of Welfare listed as indigent 1,617,132 men, women and children. Destitute, despondent, and directionless they looked to Athens for assistance. Another 80–100,000 had fled their homeland to be resettled in various parts of the Communist world; the largest such settlement was at Tashkent in Central Asia. Furthermore, the ravages of both the occupation and Civil War had crippled the economy of Greece. The countryside lay in ruins, the nation's industrial infrastructure was largely rubble, and the government was broke. The most pressing need, then, was the material reconstruction of the country, and massive amounts of United States aid were required to accomplish this task. Reinvigorating Greece was given a priority in the early days of the Cold War because of its strategic location. In a bipolar world, Greece's orientation was chosen for her.[2]

Related to the Marshall Plan for the reconstruction of Europe an American Mission of Aid to Greece (AMAG) was established on 22 May 1947. A few months before this event, Great Britain had informed the US State Department that as of 31 March it would cease providing monetary assistance to Greece and Turkey. The British Foreign Office made the case as to why the United States should agree to put on the mantle and provide the resources needed to restore stability to the region. This was the context for President Harry S. Truman's address to Congress in which he articulated what came to be called the Truman Doctrine. In that well-known speech, the American President laid out a foreign policy agenda aimed at containing the spread of Soviet communism. His Secretary of State, Dean Acheson, succinctly explained why Greece was so crucial, 'Like apples in a barrel infected by one rotten one, the corruption of Greece would affect Iran and all the East'.[3] Greece was seen as the first domino in the line, and should it be allowed to fall, it would topple the other fragile regimes in the Middle East and Africa. AMAG's function, then, was to prevent the 'corruption' of Greece by overseeing its military victory over the Communists and then by assisting in its economic and fiscal recovery.

Millions of American dollars poured into Greece. According to one estimate, between 1947 and 1950, $1,237,500,000 in foreign aid was sent to Greece. An additional $181,000,000 was allocated in fiscal year 1951–52 and $21,300,000 in the following year, by which time the Untied States government had already cancelled the reconstruction programme.[4] Even before the Mission had been established, various 'Greek experts' in the State Department and at the United States Embassy in Athens were expressing grave reservations about the ability of the Greek government to administer the aid effectively. Ambassador Paul Porter in particular was adamant in his view that without stringent United States control of the distribution and utilization of resources, the aid programme would fail. Consequently, the bilateral agreement that established AMAG gave the Mission officials 'very great powers in many vital fields normally regarded as internal matter[s]'.[5] United States officials could veto Greek governmental decisions and their approval was required before policies could be implemented. One newspaper reporter's description of AMAG chief Elliot Griswold as the most powerful man in Greece was not far off of the mark. At times AMAG came close to being a shadow government. Greece had become, for all intents and purposes, a client state to the United States.

Initially the bulk of foreign aid went into military expenditures, and so while other countries in Europe were using American dollars to rebuild the infrastructure of their industrial economies, Greece was forging a military apparatus whose sole function was to contain Communist expansion. It was widely recognized that if the Soviet Union and its Balkan allies launched an invasion of Greece, the Greek forces would be unable to stop them, regardless of the level of material support the United States provided them with. In reconstructing the Greek National army, then, the aim was to create a force capable of defeating the internal enemy of the government in Athens.[6] Though the issue was raised repeatedly, the Truman administration decided not to deploy United States troops in Greece. Instead, it established a military section within the framework of AMAG. American military advisors working in conjunction with their Greek counterparts devised the strategy that would eventually vanquish the Peoples' Democratic Army; thus began a long relationship between the United States and Greek armed forces. In addition, the American Mission played a direct role in altering the relationship between the Greek military and the civilian government. Motivated by the long and chequered history of the military's involvement in Greek politics, the military leadership was awarded control of the administration of the armed forces and the role of the civilian authorities in it greatly diminished. This institutional autonomy of the military would later have serious repercussions.[7] Expanded in size, equipped with United States supplies and arms, and directed by Greek and United States officers, the revamped National Army, as we saw in the last chapter, soon crushed their Communist foe.

With the cessation of the Civil War in 1949 the focus of aid spending shifted more toward civilian needs, and there were many of these. The drachma, for example, needed stabilization because of the horrendous bouts of hyperinflation during the war years that had rendered it valueless. Faith had to be restored in the monetary system.[8] The balance of trade had to be brought in line. One move in this direction was the decision to devalue the drachma in order to make Greek products more competitive in international markets. Other measures were taken to attract foreign capital to Greece. In addition to these financial reforms, the heart and soul of Greek agriculture and industry required reconstruction.

All of the major cities had suffered severe damage during the wars. The devastation of the countryside during the Axis occupation had been compounded by the policy implemented during the Civil War of forced relocation of peasants from their homes to temporary camps. These people had to be resettled and their villages rebuilt, in a process we will examine in more detail shortly. Greece quickly came to resemble a giant work site with building construction going on everywhere. Efforts were also made to establish a material infrastructure on which the modernization of the economy could be based. As a consequence, over 1,000 miles of new roads were built and scores of old ones refurbished; dams were built in order to produce hydroelectricity. These policies had a major impact, and the Greek economy grew. But as we shall see, it remained fragile. Moreover, economic assistance came at a price: foreign dependence in politics.

POLITICAL RESTORATION

The political situation in Greece during the late 1940s, not surprisingly, was tense. In 1947 the official Communist Party of Greece (KKE) as well as all other Communist parties was outlawed, and would remain legally banned for 27 years. And this was only a small minor element in the systematic repression of the Left. 'In the countryside, right-wing mobs lynched prominent leftists and the occupants of village prisons, while home guard units, anxious to claim the official bounty for the killing of "bandits", exhibited severed heads.'[9] Thousands more were rounded up and sent to concentration camps on remote islands. Tens of thousands were charged before military courts martial and many of them detained before ever facing any criminal charges. Others were confronted with bogus charges, some of which bordered on the absurd – as in the case of a man who was called on twice to testify in the cases of men who had been accused of having murdered him. Apparently his physical presence in the courtroom was insufficient grounds for the charges to be dropped. The arrests, detentions, and the deportations of Leftists, trade unionists and others who were less than forceful in support of the victors continued unabated, even after the Democratic Army was defeated. One of the few ways for former resistance fighters, their supporters, and their families to escape prison and all that went with it was to sign a declaration of repentance. To do so, however, was to shamefully buy one's safety by selling out the ideas and beliefs that so many comrades had fought and died for. Signing the declaration left a different kind of scar, but a scar nonetheless.[10] The wounds that these persecutions left could not easily be healed, especially when at the same time many of those who collaborated with the occupation forces not only eluded punishment but were in fact now occupying similar jobs under the post-Civil War governments. The schism in Greek society that had begun in the 1910s was destined to continue through much of the Cold War era.[11]

In addition, another hoary issue from the past re-emerged – the constitutional question. The issue *seemed* to have been solved with the plebiscite of September 1946 in which a two-thirds majority voted in favour of restoration. To be sure, the political atmosphere in which the election was held leads us to be suspicious of the vote. The position of the monarchy as an institution was placed on firmer ground with the accession of King Paul following the death of his brother George in 1947. Paul was not as tainted as his brother by association with the brutality and repression of the Metaxas years and by his conduct during the dark days of the occupation. The fact that his wife was a descendent of the old German royal family, however, did little to add to the couple's popularity. Though more palatable than his brother, popular support for the monarchy was thin and many among the political elite had serious reservations regarding the constitutional powers still vested in the King.

In March 1950, the first general election since 1946 was held. No less than 44 parties contested the 250 seats. Konstantine Tsaldaris and the Populists won 62 seats and so the balance of power was held by a number of centre-right parties: the Liberals, led by Sophokles Venizelos (son of Eleftherios), the National Progressive Centre Union under General Nicholaos Plastiras, and the modestly named George Papandreou Party. These three parties agreed to form a coalition government with Plastiras at the helm. The fragile alliance soon split, primarily over the issue of the degree of leniency to be shown to rank and file members of the Democratic Army. When the alliance collapsed in August, Venizelos was able to cobble together enough support to obtain the post of Prime Minister, but his 13-month long administration was relatively ineffective.

In the next general election of 1951 two new forces appeared on the scene. The Greek Rally with Field-Marshall Alexandros Papagos, still basking in the light of his successful stint as commander of the victorious National Army, stole the thunder from the Populists, garnering 114 seats to the Populists' two. The United Democratic Left, a front for the banned KKE, won 10 seats even though many of its candidates were in prison. The Liberals and the Centre Union won a combined 131. With no one faction gathering an overwhelming majority, yet another shaky centrist coalition was formed. At this point the sharp edge of United States dependency made itself felt. Utilizing the 'club', as Griswold once referred to American aid,[12] Ambassador John Peurifoy compelled politicians to amend the Greek constitution. He threatened to withdraw aid unless the Greeks changed the electoral system from proportional representation to simple majority, arguing that, with so many different political parities fielding candidates, unstable coalition governments would almost always be the result. Politicians grumbled, but made the change. The shift in electoral systems, however, tipped the balance in favour of the Greek Rally.

The election of 1952 swept the Right into power. The Greek Rally received 47 per cent of the vote and occupied 247 out of 300 parliamentary seats. This election was especially important for two reasons. First, it signified the emergence of a new political force, the Greek Rally, and it ushered in a period of political stability. Second, it represented a return to the old game practiced so often in the inter-war period of political parties altering the electoral laws while in office in ways aimed at ensuring electoral success. The former of these developments was a positive one because it established a stable political climate that was needed for reconstruction. The latter, however, reinvigorated a very dangerous practice, and one that, as we shall see, would come back to haunt parties of both the Left and the Right.[13]

Papagos' tenure as head of the Right did not last long, and it was a heretofore-unknown politician, Konstantine Karamanlis, who came to dominate Greek politics of the postwar era. Karamanlis was born in 1907 in Macedonia, the son of a schoolmaster turned tobacco merchant. A man of dynamism and drive, he rose quickly in local politics. He was elected as a Populist Party deputy in 1936, but his term was cut short when Metaxas seized power. Unlike some of his peers, he did not come out in open opposition to the dictatorship. Knowing that he was under surveillance, he chose the path of silent non-cooperation.

When fascist Italy invaded Greece in 1940, though he was 33 years old and so a member of one of the last age groups to be mobilized, he came forward voluntarily to join the armed forces but was rejected as being medically unfit. During the gloomy days of the Axis occupation he remained in Athens and tried to eke out a living as a lawyer, trying as best he could to keep a low profile. Toward the war's end, however, he joined a circle of politicians and intellectuals of various stripes that met surreptitiously to discuss the country's post-liberation future. As a group, they of course opposed the Axis powers but they distrusted EAM as well.

His feelings about the KKE were well known and as a consequence when the civil war broke out, the Communists detained him for time. He managed to escape and made his way to Egypt where he joined the government-in-exile. After the restoration of Greek civilian rule, Karamanlis's stock rose. He was well connected personally and he had solid conservative credentials. Moreover, his actions since the overthrow of the republic in 1935 made him a popular figure. He had abstained from having any dealings with the Metaxas dictatorship, had stayed in Greece and opposed the occupation – albeit in low-key fashion – and he was a committed anti-Communist. In the conservative government of 1952–55 he held the post of Minister of Public Works, a role in which he was very effective, though many bridled at his autocratic style of leadership. When Papagos died in 1955, much to the surprise of many on the political scene, King Paul chose Karamanlis to form a new government. The 48-year-old Macedonian reconstituted the Greek Rally as the National Radical Union and he developed a political machine that proceeded to hold on to power until 1963.[14]

ECONOMIC RECOVERY

The economy during the Karamanlis years continued to grow but not develop. Gross national product grew at a robust annual average rate of 7.3 per cent. The standard of living increased, and average per capita income went from $112 in 1951 to $500 in 1964. Industrial output rose dramatically. If we use the level of output from 1939 as our base and set it at 100, then the magnitude of the recovery becomes clear. Output during the 1940s fell to 54 and had risen to only 87 by 1949. It then began to climb, reaching 110 by 1951, 172 in 1954 and finally 325 by 1962. Prices remained stable, and in some years even fell, while wages rose only slightly.

Shipping was greatly increased, and Greek owned ships constituted the largest merchant marine in the world. By 1955, merchant shipping generated $28,000,000 in revenue and employed over 35,000 men. Construction continued at a rapid pace, and the building trade came to absorb ever-larger numbers of labourers. Faster, cheaper means of travel and a low cost of living started to attract tourists to visit Greece's splendid antiquities, as well as to experience the sun and sea. The tourist business would soon become a major industry in Greece.

In spite of these developments, there were signs of fragility in the economy. Agriculture was becoming more mechanized and efficient but on a per capita basis it remained the least profitable sector of the economy. The trade balance was still a serious problem. Greece imported far more than it exported. Also, there continued to be a 'capital crisis' in that most of the capital that fuelled the economy came from foreign loans and was distributed through state agencies. Indeed, by and large, the economy was still under state control, and restrictive legislation on, for example, trade unions, showed the negative side of government paternalism.

The state bureaucracy was the fastest growing employer in the nation. By 1963, 33 per cent of those not directly involved in agriculture were employed by the state. The bureaucracy was becoming bloated and inefficient, but politically entrenched. The service sector was the fastest growing element in the Greek economy. Nonetheless, for many Greeks, the 1950s saw a marked improvement in their standard of living, especially when contrasted with the sufferings of the previous years.[15]

SOCIETY IN THE 1950s AND 1960s

Domestically, the period 1950–67 witnessed some major changes in Greek society. There are three especially important ones that we need to discuss, and as will become clear during our discussion, all three are interrelated. The first area we need examine is the social and economic reconstruction of the Greek countryside. Developments in the countryside shaped in fundamental ways the other two major aspects of note – urbanization and emigration.

Unlike for our discussion of rural society during the nineteenth century, for the postwar era we have an abundance of sources. Foreign aid officers and government bureaucrats who had been sent out to assess the situation in the countryside have left us contemporary reports and *post hoc* memoirs. Most importantly, during the 1950s and 1960s, rural Greece emerged as a site for ethnographic studies by anthropologists. The village studies produced by them help us to examine in detail the impact that reconstruction had at the local level. In addition to these studies, the fieldwork for which was conducted then, there are also many more recent studies that examine peoples' memory of the period. Augmenting these anthropological works are the sociological studies that Greek and foreign scholars began to produce during the 1960s.

The richness and the diversity of the sources available for the postwar era, however, present some difficulties. When we tried to analyse rural society in the past, the paucity of materials meant that we had to draw broad generalizations from a slender base; for the modern period, the problem is how to draw generalizations from such a wide array of local studies.

First we need to appreciate just how devastated the Greek countryside was in the aftermath of the wars. According to one estimate by 1948, over 5,000 villages had been razed. Large swaths of the landscape lay uncultivated. Two-thirds of the rural population was suffering from malaria. The sheep, goat and cattle populations had been severely depleted. Approximately one-third of the country's forests had been destroyed.[16] All of these figures increased during the Civil War that followed the occupation. Because of the fighting and the forced evacuations, close to two million people were indigent refugees by 1947.

In addition to the physical devastation, the wars left deep psychological scars. William McNeill, for example, observed that

> when first I arrived in the village [of Nea Eleftherochori in 1947], no one was sure of his neighbour. Food was scant. Even an ordinary meal had become a furtive occasion. A knock at the door meant a scurry to put bread and cheese out of sight lest a stranger see what the family had to eat . . .. Cold darkness enveloped the village at night; fear was close at hand all the time. Hopelessness about the future daunted almost every spirit.[17]

Rekindling the spirit took longer than rebuilding the villages.

The Herculean task of reconstructing the countryside was begun in 1948, and by the winter of 1950 some form of shelter had been found for most of the refugees. Initially the focus was on repairing those salvageable houses in villages that were geographically distant from the fighting. Heads of families were provided with funds, some of which were in the form of a grant and the rest as a low interest loan, to rebuild their houses. By the end of 1953, over 175,000 new houses had been constructed. In addition to housing, AMAG and its associated agencies undertook a number of other rural initiatives.

If the agrarian economy was to recover, then, farming families had to be supplied with a great deal more than just houses. They also needed seeds, tools, fertilizer, livestock, and equipment. Agricultural advisers were dispatched to work with them to help improve the yields of wheat, rice, tobacco, and cotton. Lowland areas where mosquitoes bred were drained. Irrigation works were constructed in other areas. After the mission ceased to operate, Greek national agencies like the National Bank of Greece and the Agricultural Bank made low interest loans available to farmers for the purchase of tractors and combines, for the installation of irrigation systems, for the introduction of new crops or the expansion of the production of hitherto under-utilized crops (like citrus fruits and rice), and for the development of marketing co-operatives. Farming families in those parts of the country where arable lowlands were available, like, Boiotia, Thessaly, Macedonia, and some parts of the Peloponnesos, were able to modernize agricultural production through mechanization.

In mountainous and hilly regions of the country, such modernization was not possible. In broad terms, then, two very different rural landscapes developed – a potentially vibrant lowland sector and an antiquated upland sector where older patterns of life continued to predominate.[18] We see in operation the process of social change and the growing division in rural society reflected in the anthropological and sociological studies of the 1950s and early 1960s.

We can catch a glimpse of one part of this process in Ernestine Friedl's study of the village of Vasilika in Boiotia.[19] By the late 1950s, the households in this modestly sized farming village had recovered from the wars and were experiencing the changes initiated by reconstruction. Some had been able to purchase tractors and other machines. Combine harvesters, hired or rented from professional operators, were employed to do the grain harvesting, and gangs of hired labourers were called on to pick the other crops, like cotton. While subsistence was still an element of their production strategy, households were now producing cash crops in greater quantities than before the war. Elements of the old – small plots producing a variety of foodstuffs for domestic consumption produced with the same tools and technologies that had been used for centuries – were thus combined with the new. The construction of a paved highway nearby now more easily connected the small world of the village to the rest of the nation.

Much the same story appears in Irwin Sanders' accounts of the villages he visited located on Greece's best farmland.[20] We see the hand of change having an impact even on groups, like the shepherding *Sarakatsanoi*, whose way of life would seem to still be rooted the past. But as John Campbell's study of this group showed, their lifeways were also changing.[21] I am not, of course, arguing that Greek agriculture was totally modernized during the 1950s and 1960s. It was not, and there are aspects of it that are still troublesome to this day (see below, p. 215). Nonetheless, it was certainly the case that farming families in some areas were able to take advantage of the opportunities presented by the various initiatives at that time, and that as a consequence they witnessed an improvement in their material well being.[22] People in other regions of the country, however, were less fortunate.

Many aspects of modern, mechanized agriculture were simply inapplicable to upland, mountainous terrain, and since so much of the country falls into this category, the rural economy of hundreds of villages remained rooted in the traditional technologies and production strategies. In places like many of the Aegean islands, Epiros, Evrytania and central Greece, upland areas on Evvoia, and the mountainous districts of Peloponnesos, households continued to practice a type of agriculture very similar to one that existed in nineteenth century and which we discussed in Chapter 5.[23] Families worked small plots, often perched on terraces and scattered over a large area, on which they grew a variety of crops that were intended primarily to meet the household's subsistence needs. Some cash crops were also cultivated, but their production was ancillary. Each family would possess a few head of livestock, again aimed at meeting the family's needs.

As in the past, a variety of extra-household sources of income (gathering herbs, seasonal wage labour, making charcoal) were required for the household to make ends meet. This does not mean that the winds of change did not extend to the uplands. They did, and so elements, like the construction of roads, had an important impact on peoples' lives. The pace and magnitude of change, however, did not keep pace with peoples' expectations, especially those of the young, for a betterment of their way of life. And so, they began to abandon the countryside, leaving in their wake villages inhabited disproportionately by the elderly or by no one at all.

One of the most important consequences of the wars and the postwar recovery in the countryside was a very high level of mobility. Young Greeks were on the move. There was, however, more than one emigration stream. One flowed from the countryside to the cities, and especially Athens. Another reached out to the distant parts of the globe like Canada and Australia. And yet a third projected northward to the more industrialized areas of Europe. Let us focus first on the rural–urban migration inside of Greece. People flocked to Athens in numbers unheard of since the late nineteenth century (Table 9.1).

Table 9.1 Urbanization in Greece, 1941–1971: population distribution (percentage)

	Athens	Thessaloniki	Other cities	Rural	Total
1941	15.3	3.7	13.0	68.0	100
1951	18.6	4.0	14.3	63.1	100
1961	22.1	4.5	16.1	57.3	100
1971	29.0	6.4	17.4	47.2	100

Some of the movement toward the capital city began during the Civil War. People fleeing the unrest or forced out by government policies, settled as best they could in slums around the city. As one newspaper reporter observed at the time:

> ... in some of the left-wing areas of Piraeus, where one-room shacks cluster around mud swamps infested by sewerage from the town drains. Equal squalor can be found, often concealed behind the presentable façade, in

the heart of Athens. Close to Omonia Square a small shed without sanitation or furniture, except for broken planks covered in filthy rags used as a bed, was ... the home of an old woman, her consumptive son, his wife, and ailing children.[24]

The horrendous housing situation was one of the first problems to be addressed during the period of reconstruction. Athens came to resemble a huge construction site as young people in search of a better life flocked there by the thousand during the 1950s and early 1960s.

The growth rate *per annum* for Athens between 1951 and 1961 was 3 per cent; broken down into five-year segments, the rate rises to 4.13 per cent per year between 1951 and 1956 and 2.25 per cent between 1956 and 1961. A 1960 survey conducted by the Greek Statistical Service found that 56 per cent of the inhabitants of the Greater Athens area, approximately 1,300,000 people, were postwar migrants.[25] After the period of subsidized housing, families built accommodations out of cement and brick wherever they could. Many housing projects were illegal and hundreds of dwellings remained unfinished as people strived to save the money to foot the costs of financing them.[26] The reason why so many chose to relocate is clear.

According to Susan Sutton, 'The move from village to city enables individual migrants to leave low-cash-producing, low-power situations and enter ones with more possibilities for earning money and being close to the decision makers in Greek society'.[27] Parents increasingly wanted education for their sons so that they could obtain a job in the city; grooms sought brides whose dowry included an apartment in the city.[28] Chain migration linked families in the city with those who remained in the countryside.[29] Once one person had established himself, he then provided support for others to follow. Athens became populated by 'urban villagers' and neighbourhoods developed that replicated village life.[30]

In the countryside as well, there were rising expectations of material betterment. The Bishop of Messinia told sociologist Irwin Sanders:

People have now raised their standard of living well above their possibility to pay. They want running water in their homes, city clothes, and modern furniture. They don't necessarily go into debt to obtain these things, but they have stopped saving as they used to .... They all want a road right up to their village so automobiles can reach them; they all want electricity. The changes which would

have normally taken fifty years are now compressed into
ten.[31]

High expectations of a better life elsewhere, then, led to internal migration
and urbanization.

Their hopes of achieving those ambitions were much better in Athens than
anywhere else in the country. Athens, and to a lesser extent Thessaloniki,
experienced a rapid and quantitatively significant bout of industrial growth.
Industrial production grew in Greece at a rate of 10 per cent per year – the
highest growth rate in all of Europe. Foreign investment in industry fuelled the
development of capital-intensive industries. The result of these developments
was that the early 1960s for the first time in Greek history exports of

Fig. 9.1 *The American Express office in Athens (shown as it appeared in the 1950s)
has been a potent symbol of the tensions in Greece during the postwar era. To
some, it epitomized the benefits of the economic miracle of the 1950s. To
others, it represented the continuing foreign dependency of Greece and the
conquest of global capitalism, and so it has often been the target of protest.
(Photographer unknown.)*

manufactured goods exceeded agricultural exports. The prospect of jobs then was the magnet attracting rural dwellers to the city.[32]

The move to the city inaugurated a process of transition in the role of women and gender relations in Greek society. Women in very large numbers streamed into Athens; some were young and unmarried, others joined their spouses in the journey to the capital. Once established in the city, women took on wage labour outside of the household. A large percentage of working-class women worked as non-live-in domestic servants. Others took jobs in manufacturing, especially in the textile and food service industries. In increasing numbers, daughters went to work outside of the household as well. But the old ways of patriarchal control were not completely overthrown. Instead we see elements of the old and new combined.

Women and girls could work in only a relatively few occupations; all of them were traditional 'female' activities and in most cases they worked alongside other women, thus perpetuating the idea of gender segregation in public. Women's extra-household work, unlike men's, was seen as life-cycle dependent, meaning that a woman was supposed to work only until she married, at which time she was to revert to the more traditional lifestyle that centred on domestic duties. Married women were to stay at home and care for the children. In fact, women in the city contributed less to the household economy than did their rural sisters. What we see in the 1950s and 1960s in the city, then, is the beginning of a transition in gender as new aspects were introduced while old ones, rooted in the rural past, persisted.[33]

The dream of Greeks for an improvement in their lives led also to external migration. Two different migration streams developed in the postwar era. The first predominated during the 1950s and continued through the 1960s and it was characterized by the permanent migration of Greeks, often in families, to distant lands. Some who had relatives in the United States were able to move there, but the changes in United States immigration laws meant that many Greeks had to look elsewhere. The destination they chose was either Canada or Australia (see Table 9.2).[34] Some of the emigrants were Greeks from the diaspora, like those of Egypt who were compelled to leave after Nasser's revolution; others, like many of the Ionian Islanders, left when an earthquake destroyed their homes in 1954. Most, however, emigrated for the same reason that many of their compatriots moved to Athens.

The second migration stream of the postwar era consisted of Greeks who moved to some other region of Europe in search of work. These 'guest-workers' migrated on a temporary basis only; their goal was to work in one of the more industrialized countries to the north, save their earnings and then return to Greece. The countries of choice were Belgium, Italy, Sweden, and especially

Table 9.2 Post Civil War emigration

	1955–9	1960–4	1965–9	Total
Australia	32,484	57,451	59,371	149,306
USA	24,083	18,946	49,308	92,337
Canada	21,003	20,857	27,041	68,901
Total	77,570	97,254	135,720	310,544

the Federal Republic of Germany. Between 1960 and 1969, approximately 500,000 Greeks worked in West Germany as guest-workers. As in the past, the massive emigration of Greeks abroad was a mixed blessing. On the one hand, it provided a safety valve for draining off the pressures of a surplus rural population. And as in the past, the remittances sent home by emigrants or workers abroad helped to sustain the Greek economy. But it also impaired the development of a fully developed industrial economy by draining off surplus labour.[35]

By the mid-1960s, then, Greece looked rather different than it had in 1950. Athens had grown tremendously and came to exert an even greater influence over the country – politically, socially, economically and culturally – than it ever had before. Some areas of the countryside had experienced remarkable economic growth and social change, while others seemed to have been frozen into a timeless 'traditional' past. Finally, Greeks in greater numbers than ever before migrated abroad. Some extended the diaspora to even more distant reaches, like Australia, while others moved a much shorter distance to industrialized Europe. In so many ways, then, the age of reconstruction left an indelible mark on how Greek society would develop during the latter part of the twentieth century.

NATO AND CYPRUS

Turning away momentarily from domestic politics and social issues, in terms of foreign policy two issues dominated the immediate postwar era: the Cold War and Cyprus. Konstantine Karamanlis was firmly convinced that Greece's fortunes lay with the west and that Greece had to become 'European', thus, presumably, bringing to a close the long and tortured history of Greek identity.[36] The dictates of Cold War needs led to Greece's inclusion in the North Atlantic Treaty Organization (NATO). He also saw NATO membership as a means to better deal with the Cyprus situation. But Karamanlis wanted to go even further in solidifying Greece's position in the western bloc. He pushed for a relationship with the European Economic Community, and he won for

Greece 'associate' status beginning in 1962 and the promise of full member-ship in 1984. He also established close a relationship with Washington and at one point hosted a visit from Dwight D. Eisenhower. Greece was thus firmly ensconced in the western camp.

The other overriding issue of the day was Cyprus. The island housed the last significant population of unredeemed Greeks. Since the Treaty of Berlin in 1878 it had been controlled by Great Britain. The history of the British on Cyprus is a long and storied one. For centuries the Christian and Moslem communities had coexisted on the island. This is not to say there had not been bouts of unrest and tension.[37] There had, but it was only with the advent of modern nationalism – the Megali Idea on the Greek side and Atatürk's Turkish nationalism on the other – that intercommunal tensions really developed. But, most of the open unrest involved the Greek community, and their target was the British. In October 1931, for example, five days of vicious fighting between Greek Cypriots and government forces left many dead and thousands arrested. Severe restrictions on civil liberties were imposed as British rule took on an authoritarian edge.[38] Throughout the war years, British control of the island remained firm and forceful.

In the postwar climate of British decolonization, however, expectations in the Greek community were rising that Cyprus too might be set free from the grip of the British Colonial Office, and thus be able to join with Greece. There were two enormous issues that had to be dealt with before that could happen: would Britain agree to relinquishing the island in spite of its strategic importance and what would become of the Turkish population on the island.

For Britain, Cyprus had special significance. As Anthony Eden put it: 'No Cyprus, no certain facilities to protect our supply of oil. No oil, unemployment and hunger in Britain. It is as simple as that. We shall never relinquish Cyprus'.[39] Many other prominent members of the British government echoed this strident pronouncement.[40] The sizeable Turkish population on the island meant that Turkey also had a stake in the future disposition of the island, if Britain were to agree to any change in its status. But the rising tide of sentiment for unification of Cyprus and Greece would soon introduce violence in its wake.

On 1 April 1955, a series of bomb explosions rocked the island. Leaflets were circulated announcing, 'with God's help and the support of all the forces of Hellenism the struggle to throw off the British yoke had now begun'.[41] A terrorist organization called EOKA (National Organization of Cypriot Fighters) led by Colonel George Grivas, a former member of the *Khi* death squads during the 1940s, embarked on a campaign of violence aimed at disrupting British rule. The situation began to spiral out of control. In an attempt to stop the escalation of violence, the British government invited Greek and Turkish representatives to a conference in London. After some equivocation, the meeting began in August 1955. While the Tripartite Conference was in session, with the compliance of the Turkish government mobs of rioters attacked the Greek communities in Istanbul and Izmir (Smyrna). The talks broke down without resolution.

The Greek Cypriots under the leadership of Archbishop Makarios took their case to the United Nations. Violence continued on the island. Greek elections on 11 May 1958 returned Karamanlis' National Radical Union party to power with a sizeable majority. From a stronger position internally, Karamanlis pressed the case for Cypriot self-determination, obliquely suggesting to western representatives that failure to support the Greek case could lead his government to reassess its commitment to NATO and the west.[42]

After years of conflict and delicate negotiations, a settlement was finally reached in 1959. On 16 February 1959, the London–Zurich Agreement was finalized.[43] The island would be independent and ruled by a joint Helleno-Turkish government based on a complex formula according to each group's size. The Turkish minority had veto power. Britain got military bases. Greece and Turkey were able to station military advisers on the island. The three powers, Britain, Greece, and Turkey, jointly guaranteed the security of the island, and each had the right to intervene to defend it. The establishment of even temporary peace on Cyprus was a major accomplishment, but domestically in Greece, the solution arrived at was not a popular one.

THE SLIDE TO CHAOS

Seeking validation of his pro-Europe policies and the Cyprus treaty, Karamanlis went to the polls in 1961. His Radical Union Party obtained 51 per cent of the vote and held 176 seats. George Papandreou and his Centre Union Party, in association with some smaller centrist parties, gathered 34 per cent of the vote and won 100 seats. The United Democratic Left finished third with 15 per cent and 24 seats.[44]

The election was marred by widespread allegations of tampering and corruption. Pre-election fears of a fall in the vote on the Right brought out paramilitary groups and the security forces, which openly intimidated voters, especially in areas known for their left-wing sympathies. Papandreou found an issue to rally the people: he charged electoral fraud and demanded that the elections be declared void. When they were not, he announced his 'relentless struggle' to ensure free and fair elections in Greece.

Many people had grown weary of the stifling of the Left that had continued since the end of the war. Many leftists were still in prison; the security forces continued to wield great influence; advancement in the civil service and the military was directly linked to one's politics. In short, after a decade people were tired of the stifling of personal freedoms. As political violence increased, as exemplified by the assassination of the left wing deputy Dr Grigorios Lambrakis in 1963 by right wing thugs connected to the security forces, so did the sentiment for change.

Karamanlis felt the ground slipping out from under him both to the Left and to the Right. He clashed with King Paul and Queen Fredericka (the Greek nickname for her, 'Friki' – the horrible one – captures the public's opinion of her) on a number of issues, and in particular, on the relationship between the monarch and the military. In a speech in 1962 to the army of Macedonia, King Paul proclaimed, 'God has united us – I belong to you and you belong to me'.[45] Furthermore, Karamanlis also became convinced that the military was exerting an unacceptable amount of power for a democratic state. And indeed it was the case that the military had become a powerful institution within the state, with its own vested interests that often were at odds with those articulated by politicians on behalf of the nation.[46]

Once more the constitutional question regarding the role of the monarchy was rising to the surface of Greek political life, and as in the past, it inevitably drew the armed forces in as well. Finally in early 1963 Karamanlis found the situation unacceptable. His relationship with King Paul was strained; open hostility better captures the nature of his relationship with Queen Fredericka, a very powerful figure in her own right, and Crown Prince Konstantine.[47] On 17 June 1963, Karamanlis tendered his resignation. Upon its acceptance, he went into self-imposed exile in Paris.

After 1963, a number of developments came together which led to the coup by the military in 1967. The first development was the decline in the economy. The economic bubble had burst. Inflation began to rise while wages remained stagnant. Unemployment and under-employment increased.[48] As people's expectations of material betterment evaporated, some responded by migrating (452,300 left Greece during these four years alone), others turned to labour unions and went on strike more frequently and in greater numbers than ever before, and still others looked for political alternatives at the ballot box. Street protests and workers' strikes often led to clashes with the state's security forces.[49]

Another development centred on Cyprus. The 1959 treaty was proving unworkable and fighting broke out on the island. At one point, Turkey threatened to invade the island to 'protect' the Turkish Cypriots. Only the forceful intervention of United States President Lyndon B. Johnson prevented it. A number of American-brokered peace plans were proposed, but all failed. The Cyprus conflict convinced many in the military of the need to step-up war readiness.

Third, King Paul died and was succeeded by his young, untried son, Konstantine in March 1964. Just one month before this the Centre Union had won a resounding victory, garnering 52.7 per cent of the popular vote, which translated into 171 seats in a Parliament of 300. The Right was out of power. The military had lost its royal patron. 'Public order', in the eyes of the Right at least, was deteriorating. And the likelihood of war with Turkey seemed high.

The Papandreou government enacted a number of far-reaching social and political reforms, prominent among which was the releasing of most political prisoners. To deal with the economic crises, George Papandreou appointed his son Andreas, the former Chairman of the Economics Department at the University of California at Berkeley, as minister to the Prime Minister and then as the alternate minister of coordination. Many in the CU resented this move. In particular rising stars in the party, like Konstantine Mitsotakis, the future conservative party leader, felt slighted by the appointment. The younger Papandreou held far more radical views and he soon became involved with a group of left-leaning military officers known as *Aspida*. The Right viewed these developments suspiciously. In the army in particular, cabals formed as once again military men set themselves up as the 'protectors' of the nation. When Geroge Papandreou confronted the King with the demand that he be allowed to hold the portfolio of defence as well as being Prime Minister and the King refused, the constitutional question came to the forefront. In this case, it was over who controlled the military, King or Prime Minister?[50]

In disgust Papandreou resigned on 15 July 1965. A series of caretaker governments came and went in the succeeding months. The ship of state was adrift and chaos dominated the political scene. Konstantine finally called for elections in May of 1967, and an overwhelming Centre Union victory seemed certain. Fearful of the consequences, especially a likely purge of the military of hard-line right-wingers, a group of junior officers acted. On the morning of 21 April 1967, operation Prometheus was put into action and the government of Greece fell into the hands of the junta of the Colonels.[51]

10 Dictatorship, Democratic Restoration and the Era of PASOK

1967–1989

The period from 1967 when the banal but brutal regime of the Colonels stole Greek democracy until the fall of the Socialist government in 1989 was one of the momentous epochs in Greek history. Socially, economically, and culturally the Greece of 1967 would bear only a passing resemblance to the Greece of 1989. Politically, many of the key issues that had shaped the history and development of the nation – the constitutional question, Greece's place in the world, etc. – would either be resolved or moved closer to resolution. In this chapter, then, we shall trace the development of Greek society over these two important decades.

THE JUNTA

The leaders of the self-styled 'Glorious Revolution' were Colonels Giorgos Papadopoulos, Nikolaos Makarezos and Brigadier General Stilianos Pattakos. Their regime came to be called the junta or simply the Colonels. The leading members of the junta were mostly officers from lower-class backgrounds who had achieved career advancement through the armed forces. Many of them had previously served or were actively serving in the intelligence services, and some of them had received training in the United States. Moreover, most of them had been active in the right wing machinations of the parastate for some time. Papadopoulos, for example, had been the leader of the National Union of Young Officers, a group noted for its 'fervent nationalism and anti-communism [and its] contempt for parliamentary democracy'.[1] A number of groups within the military were conspiring with King Konstantine to overthrow or temporarily suspend democracy. The primary one that we know about involved General Giorgios Spandidakis and other high-ranking officers. The Colonels were part of that group. But fearful of losing their posts because of their involvement in right wing conspiracies, a worry that was exacerbated when the generals kept postponing the date of the coup, the Colonels struck first.[2]

In the early hours of 21 April 1967, tanks rolled through the streets of Athens. Some of them entered Sintagma Square and trained their weapons on the Parliament. Others shut down the main arteries into and out of the city. The key communications facilities were commandeered, giving the coup leaders control of the airwaves. Within a matter of hours, all of the major political figures had been detained or placed under house arrest 'for their own protection'. The CIA-trained Hellenic Raiding Force seized the headquarters of the Greek armed forces.

The people of Athens awoke that morning to news broadcasts announcing the takeover. 'The revolution, carried out bloodlessly, marches forward to fulfillment of its manifest destiny! Greeks, pure and of a superb race, let the flowers of regeneration bloom out of the debris of the regime of falsehood.'[3] The Colonels' claims that they staged the coup in order to forestall a Communist takeover are simply not credible. No such threat existed. They were able to succeed because of the vacuum of leadership which existed in political life at the time and because they were able to strike quickly and effectively. By seizing all of the major defence and communications facilities, they presented an unsuspecting nation with a fait accompli.

As Thanos Veremis scathingly notes, 'The Colonels came to power with no clear policies, no coherent ideology of their own, and no consistent views on the shape of the regime or the nature of its future options'.[4] Initially the junta's main problem was legitimacy and so it tried to rule through the King and the existing political system. They could find, however, very few politicians who would cooperate with them and immediately began to arrest prominent centrist and left wing politicians and anyone else who showed any signs of resisting the takeover. Within a matter of days, 10,000 people were arrested, including all of the major politicians. Prime Minister Kanellopoulos, George Papandreou, and Andreas Papandreou, for example, were arrested in night-time raids during the coup.[5] Finding a paucity of notable politicians who would work with them, the junta looked to the King to prevent the regime from becoming an international pariah. In the days immediately after 21 April, Konstantine had been approached by a number of military officers who urged him to oppose the junta by force. But his equivocation gave the coup leaders time to remove those officers from their posts and the opportunity to nip the dictatorship in the bud was lost.

After that unfortunate development, Konstantine cautiously agreed to cooperate. The pretence of parliamentary democracy was maintained and Konstantine Kollias, former Prosecutor to the Supreme Court, became Prime Minister. But power lay with the Colonels who were given ministerial appointments in the Kollias government. Once sworn into office the new administration suspended the relevant articles of the constitution that protected civil liberties, until all of the radical elements had been purged from society. Based upon the principle of 'guided democracy,' in May 1968 the junta appointed a Constitutional Commission to draft a new constitution; displeased by the document drafted by this group, the Colonels cobbled together their own version which was ratified in a rigged plebiscite in November 1968. These moves, plus the increasing use of violence and torture to quell all opposition, were too much for the young king to tolerate, and by summer he was openly disavowing the regime. As he told United States President Lyndon B. Johnson at a meeting in September, 'This is not my government!'[6]

While abroad, he contacted many of the leading politicians, like Konstantine Karamanlis, who either were already in exile or who had fled when the Colonels came to power, seeking their support. Emboldened by the responses he received from leaders abroad, when he returned to Athens in the autumn, the King organized a counter-coup. Calling on some pro-monarchy generals to mobilize a few small forces with which to seize key facilities, the King planned on making a broadcast urging the Greek people to rise up and join him. The counter-coup of December 1967 was poorly planned and even more poorly executed. It failed miserably. Konstantine fled into exile. In absentia, he was deposed and, after a period of time during which a regency was imposed, the monarchy was eventually abolished in 1974. How ironic it was that the slide toward the final demise of royal rule was commenced not by bourgeois republicans or Communist cadres but by forces of the Right – the monarchy's previous bastion of support.

With the King removed and the monarchy abolished, Papadopoulos rose to the top of the regime and remained there until November 1973. The junta's aims and policies were a curious mix of populist reforms and paternalistic authoritarianism backed up by propaganda and terror. The over-arching, proclaimed intent of the Colonels was to purge Greek society of the moral sickness that had developed since the war. The symptoms of this disease were the supposed spread of Communism and the failure of liberal democracy to achieve the union of Cyprus with Greece. The Colonels sought to create a new 'Helleno-Christian' state and this goal shaped their domestic agenda.[7]

Some of their more ludicrous policies were the banning of miniskirts and the imposition of mandatory hair length for men. Most of their domestic initiatives were aimed at removing anyone whose loyalty to the regime was suspect and at forcibly indoctrinating society with their peculiar brand of messianic nationalism. The civil service was revamped and anyone who did not pass the loyalty litmus test was removed. The judiciary and the legal profession likewise were stripped of independent thinkers.

Special emphasis was placed on reforming the education system. In addition to removing teachers and professors who did not toe the party line, the entire curriculum and the textbooks used in classes were revamped to reflect the Colonels' politically correct view of Greece's past. While recognizing the importance of controlling the flow of information and propaganda, 'the junta's media "philosophy" was so simple as to defy analysis'.[8] Their sloganeering was simplistic and provided Greeks with a source of satire and jokes. Though they were by and large ineffectual in getting out their own message, the dictators were more efficient in silencing, with their usual brutality, the opposition press.[9]

The Colonels inherited a fairly sound economy and that, more than anything that they actually did, accounted for the continuing growth of the Greek economy from 1967 to 1972. The junta endeavoured to attract foreign capital and industry to Greece, and it tried to wean back the major Greek ship-owners by offering them very generous concessions. This worked to some extent, though the benefits to the Greek economy of these policies were negligible. The Colonels borrowed heavily to finance their economic programme, and that fiscal irresponsibility would leave a lasting mark. One result at the time was inflation. But because they had muzzled the trade unions and other workers' associations through brutal repression, they were able to keep wages stable. More than anything else it was remittances from emigrants abroad and tourism that kept the fragile economy growing under the inept control of the military regime.[10] The only major economic 'achievement' of the junta was to exaggerate even further the maldistribution of wealth in Greek society.

Like so much else about it, the junta's foreign policy reflects a curious mixture of ideologies and intentions. Shortly after seizing power the regime found itself a pariah among European states. A group of northern Europe states filed complaints with the Council of Europe over the widespread use of torture and the rampant trampling of individual civil liberties by the dictatorship. The Colonels resigned membership in the Council only days before their regime was to be kicked out of the organization. Many European nations remained steadfast in withholding their recognition of what they considered to be a rogue regime.

Greece's relationship with NATO, however, was complicated, even though many of the same countries that belonged to the Council of Europe, were in NATO. The primary reason was the United States which was the first country to accord official recognition to the Colonel's government (Turkey and Great Britain did shortly thereafter). Even so, President Lyndon Johnson openly expressed his disquiet with the regime. It was under his successor, Richard Nixon, that relationships between the two countries became more cordial.

Partly this was due to personal factors, in particular the friendship between Vice President Spiro Agnew and a number of prominent members of the powerful Greek–American business community, which supported the dictatorship. Partly it was due to geostrategical factors. The Mediterranean had become a hot spot in the late 1960s. The seizure of power by Muammar al Qadhafi in Libya and the election of Dom Mintoff in Malta had deprived NATO of some key naval bases. At the same time, the continuing Arab–Israeli conflict and the increased Soviet naval presence in the region called for NATO and the United States to expand their forces in the region. More than ever in the Cold War era that meant that the west needed Greece. And so, though at times relations became testy, the junta maintained Greece's position in NATO and developed a working relationship with the Republican Nixon administration. But because it was outcast from so much of Europe, the Colonels reached out to some unexpected places, like many of the Balkan members of the eastern bloc, Albania and Rumania in particular, and some of the new states in what came to be called the Third World.[11]

The regime of the Colonels never developed a broad base of popular support and remained in power largely through terror, intimidation and coercion. They constructed a formidable secret police apparatus, which undertook the systematic persecution of, at first, leftists and then anyone suspected of opposing the regime. Torture and other human rights violations were legion and widely reported by international organizations like Amnesty International.[12] Indeed the brutality of the regime surpassed even the banality of its domestic policies.

The campaign of terror at home was effective, and so it was abroad that resistance movements to the Colonels formed. This is not to say that there were not resistance movements inside of Greece. As during the dark days of Nazi occupation, leftist parties provided a popular front within Greece. While they proved more effective than other movements because of greater expertise at clandestine activities, their radical political agenda drove off many moderates and anti-junta centrists, thus preventing the formation of a united opposition. But resistance activities did take place. A group called Democratic Defence formed very shortly after the coup, and they succeeded on a number of occasions in embarrassing the regime. Even after some of its leaders were arrested and sent into internal exile to one of the Aegean islands, the group continued to resist.[13] On one occasion, for example, an assassination attempt was made on the life of Papadopoulos, and just barely failed in its mission.

Nonetheless, the wholesale use of terror, repression, and exile effectively hamstrung all concerted attempts at open resistance at home. Strict censorship of the press and other media also made it very difficult for opposition to be expressed in public. Instead Greeks found clever ways to couch their opposition to the dictatorship by, for example, revitalizing traditional protest songs that had been incorporated into the national discourse and thus providing a veiled cover to the songs' real intent. Art and literature were also employed as poignant weapons of the weak to challenge the police state.[14]

Also very active at the time were various groups that formed abroad in London, Paris, New York, and elsewhere. Prominent among the overseas anti-junta groups was the Panhellenic Liberation Movement (PAK) led by Andreas Papandreou. It and organizations like it were instrumental in keeping the issue of the junta and its actions before the eyes of the international community. But it was the junta's own ineptitude and lack of legitimacy that led eventually to its downfall.

Three developments more than all of the others brought down the Colonels. The first was the student movement, the second was the global economic crisis of the early 1970s that plunged the Greek economy into turmoil, and the third was Cyprus. In January 1973, university students began to challenge the authority of the dictators. At the Law School and Medical School in Athens, at universities in Thessaloniki and Ioannina, students held protests, boycotted classes and in other ways disrupted the higher education system. On one occasion, Papadopoulos himself called for meetings with both academics and students, and made clear to them that he would never allow 'Communists' to bring down the universities. Large-scale student demonstrations that openly defied the junta's ban on public assemblies began in October 1973. When the students occupied the Polytechnic University in Athens in November and began to broadcast on clandestine radios calling for the people of Athens to rise up against the tyranny, the junta had to respond. They did so brutally by calling in the army. The streets of Athens ran with blood as tanks crushed the gathering on the night of 17 November 1973.[15]

The Polytechnic incident showed the bankruptcy of the regime and it demonstrated that resistance was not futile. Papadopoulos was toppled from power by a coup from his own right wing. Dimitirios Ioannides, former head of the secret police, replaced him and the junta lurched even further to the right. With this change in power, the issue of Cyprus once more took centre stage. During the first six years of the junta, the relationship between the Greek leadership and Archbishop Makarios, the President of Cyprus, had become severely strained. The Cypriot leader repeatedly called for a gradual, diplomatic solution to the island's bitter troubles. And so he was no supporter of the junta's hard line on unification. Moreover, the island had become, with his tacit support, a haven for opponents of the dictatorship at the same time that its President was pushing for the recall of the Greek National Guard. At least one assassination attempt was made upon Makarios and many others were plotted, and the junta was complicit in all of them.

Believing that a major nationalist cause would rally the people behind him Ioannides order yet another assassination attempt on Makarios. It failed, but it provided Turkey with a pretext to intervene. On 20 July 1974 (five days after the failed assassination attempt), Turkey invaded Cyprus. Turkish forces swept across the northern part of island.[16] Ioannides called immediately for a full mobilization of the Greek military: nothing happened. The regime had lost whatever base of support it had previously enjoyed.

The Colonels had to go. Military leaders, some of whom had escaped the earlier purges and others who in fact owed their positions to the Colonels, made it clear that they would no longer support the regime, and that they were prepared to use force if necessary to expedite their removal. At home and abroad, politicians from the pre-junta parties met and debated the country's future. Two men, one in Paris and one in London, anxiously awaited the results of the various deliberations.

King Konstantine and Konstantine Karamanlis had been two of the leading figures in exile who had presented the Greek case to the wider world, though they had done so in very different ways. The two had met in June and decided to cooperate when the time came. The King's position, however, was tenuous since the constitution of 1968, which, as we saw earlier, had been ratified by an, albeit suspect, popular referendum,[17] and had severely curtailed the powers of the monarchy. The hastily convened committee of military commanders and politicians in Athens decided that only Konstantinos Karamanlis possessed the ability and the level of popular support needed to dismantle the dictatorship and to restore democracy to Greece. On 24 July, the phone rang in his Paris apartment and Karamanlis received the call to return to his homeland and to save it from chaos. The other Konstantine sat in his London suite, waiting by a phone that did not ring. The restoration of democratic rule would proceed without a king.[18]

KARAMANLIS AND THE RESTORATION OF DEMOCRACY

Konstantine Karamanlis faced the formidable task of clearing the wreckage left by the seven years of military rule. There were two major domestic missions: the restoration of a full range of political parties and re-establishing the military as a positive force. Having been sworn into the office of Prime Minister, Karamanlis formed a council of ministers drawn from the leading politicians of the old centrist parties in order to establish a Government of

National Unity. Shortly thereafter, the council issued the 'Constitutional Act of August 1st.' This act restored the Constitution of 1952 until such time as a new constitution could be drafted and ratified. The Act, however, stipulated one important change to the old charter: it left the issue of the monarchy in limbo until a popular referendum could be held. The 1952 Constitution, following the model of the 1864 charter, created a 'crowned democracy' that invested sovereign power in the people. The Act restored democracy, but not the crown.[19] The immediate political goals of the Government of National Unity were the drafting of a new constitution and a legitimate referendum on the monarchy, but crafting a new role for the military remained a controversial and imperative objective as well. In the late summer of 1974, the army still presented a clear and present danger to the restoration of democracy. As Karamanlis's Minister of Defence, Evangelos Averoff, noted, the government was still the 'prisoner of the army'. On 11 August, Karamanlis had a showdown with military leaders at the Greek Pentagon and issued an ultimatum: 'Either me or the tanks'.[20] He carried the day, but the future was still in doubt.

In this uncertain climate, Karamanlis scheduled elections for November. But even before that he legalized the KKE, a symbolic step toward finally ending the tensions that had simmered under the surface of Greek politics since the Metaxas regime.[21] Karamanlis's newly formed party, New Democracy (*Nea Demokratia*, ND), swept into power with 54 per cent of the vote and 220 seats in Parliament. Surprisingly, the Panhellenic Socialist Movement (*Panhellinion Socialistiko Kinima*, PASOK), which Andreas Papandreou founded on the basis of his anti junta resistance group, the Panhellenic Liberation Movement, received nearly 14 per cent of the popular vote with a platform opposing western alliances and the monarchy. The Centre Union, the only major pre-coup party to appear on the 1974 ballot, gained 21 per cent of the vote – but it was soon to be a spent force. The United Left Party (*Enomeni Aristera*), a coalition of the pro-Moscow and anti-Moscow Communist factions that had separated in 1968, received 9 per cent of the vote. Now other political questions loomed; most important of these were the fate of the monarchy and the disposition of the junta and its followers.[22]

Karamanlis staged yet another referendum on the monarchy (the sixth since 1920), in an effort to settle finally the rancorous debate that had poisoned Greek politics throughout the twentieth century. In December 1974, a majority of 70 per cent of Greek voters opted to abolish the monarchy. Not coincidentally, this margin was nearly identical to the figure attained in the only other legitimate vote on the monarchy, that of 1924, which had established the inter-war republic. The Third Greek Republic thus came into existence. King Konstantine remained in exile, still hoping that some day the call beckoning him to his homeland would come.

Punishing the junta and reforming the military and the civil service were more delicate operations. Karamanlis wanted to avoid a repetition of the military retributions of the 1920s and to preserve relations between the civilian government and the military. Nonetheless, the leadership had to be made accountable. Accordingly, the three top leaders of the junta, Papadopoulos, Makarezos, and Pattakos, were charged with a bevy of crimes, including high treason, murder, conspiracy to commit murder, and obstruction of justice. Ioannides was charged with many of the same offences. Over the course of two years, all were tried and convicted. During the proceedings, the Colonels made abundantly clear the contempt they had for had for democratic society. Each received death sentences that were later commuted. None of the more than 100 civilian ministers who had served the junta was convicted of a criminal offence. Many people serving in the military and the police were tried and convicted of criminal offences, and universities were purged of junta sympathizers.

On 8 June 1975 the Revisionary Parliament completed the new constitution that established Greece as a republic with a political structure modelled on that of France. The constitution vested great power in the president, who is obligated to choose as prime minister the leader of the party gaining the most seats in parliamentary elections. Until the constitution was amended in 1986, the president could veto legislation, dissolve parliament, and call for a direct vote of no confidence in parliament. The sharp escalation of executive authority was controversial, but Karamanlis declared strong presidential powers necessary to deal with extraordinary episodes of Greece's political conflict. The five-year administration of Konstantinos Tsatsos, the first president under the new constitution, passed without his using the considerable powers that had been given to his office. The legislative branch consisted of a 300-person assembly elected by direct, universal, and secret ballot. The constitution also protected fundamental civil liberties such as freedom of assembly, speech, and association and it ensured the freedom of the press. The Orthodox Church was recognized as the 'established' rather than the 'state' church of Greece, thus allowing for the free practice of other religions. Nonetheless, the question of the rights of religious and other minorities still presents this largely homogenous culture with problems. By and large, however, the 1975 Constitution, still in force with some modifications today, established the framework of a modern liberal polity.[23]

Cyprus continued to dominate Greek foreign policy in the mid-1970s. From the Greek standpoint, the unresolved status of the island was chiefly the doing of the United States, and a substantial anti-western backlash coloured Greek foreign policy during that period. Since the invasion of 1974, Turkish troops have remained on the island. Although a ceasefire was negotiated in Geneva in August, talks broke off almost immediately, and the Turkish army began to expand its zone of occupation to a line that included 37 per cent of Cypriot territory. Karamanlis, however, was intent on avoiding armed conflict, for which Greece was unprepared, and talks resumed shortly thereafter. In many ways, then, the new administration had at its disposal a relatively limited range of options.[24] In 1975 a Turkish Federated State of Cyprus was declared in the northern part of the island, and negotiations continued intermittently for another two years. A 1977 agreement divided the island provisionally, but no lasting, workable solution was achieved. In 2001 the fate of Cyprus remains a pressing issue that continues to impair relations between Greece and Turkey.[25]

The Greek public reacted to the Turkish presence on Cyprus with resentment toward NATO and the United States. In the view of many Greeks, the benefits of membership in a west European security organization were meaningless if the alliance could not stop a NATO ally from invading a country such as Cyprus. In protest Karamanlis withdrew Greece from military structures of NATO, a status that remained until 1980. Greece held the United States and its foreign policy establishment particularly responsible for the Cyprus invasions because of its failure to prevent Turkish action or to compel Turkey's withdrawal after the fact. In 1975 the United States Central Intelligence Agency was still widely held responsible for aiding the junta's accession and supporting its regime. This hostility was partly a backlash against the dependent relationship of postwar Greece to the United States, partly the result of resentment for United States support of the junta.[26]

In blaming the United States for events in Cyprus, Greece also overestimated its leverage over Turkey. Tension increased in 1976 when the United States, having partially repealed its arms embargo, exchanged $1 billion in military equipment for military installations in Turkey. Greek protests resulted in a similar agreement with Greece, worth $700 million, and the establishment of a seven-to-ten ratio that became the standard formula for United States aid apportionment between the two countries.

In the late 1970s, two new issues exacerbated animosities between Greece and Turkey. The first involved the control of the northern Aegean. Each side claimed (and still claims) large areas of the region on the basis of offshore territorial rights. Because the boundaries between mainland Turkey and the Greek islands in the Aegean are so close, the six-mile offshore limits often overlap. Control of the continental shelf became much more critical with the discovery of oil in the region. On three occasions since the late 1970s, Greece and Turkey have nearly gone to war over this issue. Other sources of irritation were the question of air control over the Aegean, Greece's attempts to extend its six-mile limit to the 12-mile limit used elsewhere, and the two countries' treatment of their respective Greek and Turkish minorities. The end of the Cold War greatly diminished the incentive for cooperation against Communist neighbours, emboldening both countries to take more independent stands over regional issues.[27]

The period of domination by the ND included concerted attempts at national reconciliation. Economically, Karamanlis pushed for closer integration with Europe, a policy rewarded in 1981 with full membership in the EC. The ND government practiced statist capitalism, meaning that the state had an intrusive and direct role in determining economic policy at the same time that it tried to foster a free-market system. The primacy of the state in economic affairs was evident in all areas, from prices and wages to labour law. In post-junta Greece, the debate has centred on the degree, rather than the existence, of government intervention in the economy.[28]

Karamanlis called an election in 1977, a year earlier than required by the constitution. A particular goal of this strategy was to obtain validation of his government's foreign policy initiatives. The major surprise of the 1977 election results was the rise of Andreas Papandreou and PASOK. ND's share of the vote fell to 42 per cent (171 seats) while PASOK's share rose to 25 per cent (93 seats). The Centre Union dropped into a distant third place (12 per cent and 16 seats), barely ahead of the KKE (10 per cent, 11 seats). PASOK's success came largely at the expense of the declining Centre Union, which split into factions shortly thereafter. ND's losses had multiple causes. Some ND supporters moved to a new far-right party, and the political equilibrium that Karamanlis had achieved since 1974 removed some of the urgency with which Greeks had supported him in the previous election. ND lacked a clear ideology; instead, the charisma of its leader was its chief rallying point.[29]

At the same time, PASOK's message had increasing resonance with the people.

> During the period between 1974 and 1981 PASOK managed to establish itself as an entirely new party with a new political identity and novel ideas. It did this by exploiting, and at the same time transcending, the old divisions of Greek politics, namely those between conservatives and liberals, communists and anti-communists, and by advancing a new cleavage between the right-wing and the anti-right-wing forces.[30]

Thus, in his rhetoric, Papandreou crafted a skilful mix of nationalism ('Greece for the Greeks') and socialism ('PASOK in government, the people in power'). PASOK promised a 'third road' to socialism and a middle way in foreign policy, restoring national pride by breaking the bonds of foreign dependency and reorienting Greece with the non-aligned countries. PASOK's structure also gave it a base of grass roots support that other parties lacked. Besides its strong central committee, PASOK had local party offices and cadres in towns and villages across Greece. This system proved very effective in organizing support and validating the claim that the party was not based, like the others, on networks of patronage. And, perhaps most importantly, PASOK's slogan of 'change' (*allayi*) struck a chord with the Greek people's search for a new way forward after 40 years of conservative rule.

THE RISE AND FALL OF PAPANDREOU AND PASOK

By the elections of 1981, electoral momentum had shifted away from an uninspired ND to the promise of change offered by a newly moderate PASOK.

Fig. 10.1 This photograph of a PASOK rally on 3 October 1981 captures the emergence of this new party on to the political scene. Unlike older political parties, PASOK cast itself as a populist movement based on widespread grassroots support. The massive rallies, like the one captured here, aptly demonstrate this phenomenon. (Courtesy of the PASOK; photo available on the party's official website: http://www.pasok.gr.)

For the next eight years, Papandreou applied his programmes to society and the economy, with mixed results. In 1980 Karamanlis elevated himself to the presidency, leaving the lacklustre Giorgios Rallis as the incumbent Prime Minister in the next year's elections. In the elections of October 1981, PASOK and Papandreou swept into power with 48 per cent of the popular vote and 172 seats in Parliament. The ND, which could not match Papandreou's charisma or the novelty of PASOK's programme, finished a distant second with 36 per cent of the vote and 115 seats, and the KKE came in third with 11 per cent and 13 seats.

Between the 1977 and 1981 elections, PASOK and its leader had continued the move away from an initial image as a Marxism-based, class-oriented party, in order to reassure centrist voters. The 'privileged' class against which Papandreou ran in 1981 had shrunk considerably to a small number of Greece's wealthiest citizens. The societal results of the 'change' were left deliberately vague. The election result meant that, for the first time in Greek history, an explicitly left wing party held the reins of government. The transformation from authoritarian rule to democracy was finally complete.

As it exercised power for the next eight years, PASOK did oversee considerable change in some areas. The new government brought in a sweeping domestic reform programme under Papandreou's 'Contract with the People'. Many initial reforms were long-overdue and cost little. New laws legalized civil marriage, abolished (in theory) the dowry system, eased the process for obtaining a divorce, and decriminalized adultery.[31] Another law enhanced the legal status of women by dissolving the long-held notion that family and not the individual constituted the central unit in society, and that women, as the legally subordinate partners in marriage, were subsumed under the legal control of their husbands. In marriage, and in a number of other areas, the PASOK government passed legislation that endowed women with rights as autonomous individuals. Taken together these legal reforms represented a revolution in women's rights.[32]

The university system was overhauled, giving more power to staff and students.[33] In 1983, a comprehensive National Health Service was introduced. Under the control of the newly established Ministry of Health, Welfare and Social Security, the service made modern medical procedures available in rural areas for the first time. It also ensured equality of health care delivery across the country. It established nationally supervised training programmes for nurses. The programme dramatically changed the quality and level of health care for the average person but was expensive. By 1985, Greece spent five per cent of gross domestic product on the health service.[34]

Some of PASOK's initiatives met with considerably less success, especially its attempts to reform the civil service and to manage the economy. The pervasive blanket of smog over Athens, instead of being banished as promised, became thicker during the early 1980s. Endeavours to deal with this and other serious environmental issues have at times exposed the administrative incapacity of the central state.[35] Papandreou vowed to slay one of the great shibboleths of modern Greece: the bureaucracy and civil service. The only thing greater than the size and inefficiency of the civil service was the low esteem in which the vast majority of the population held it. 'Professionaliza- tion' and administrative streamlining were the cries of the day. In spite of a promising beginning, PASOK succumbed to the temptation that had ensnared so many governments before it of stocking the bureaucracy with the party faithful. 'These two goals, the professionalization of the bureaucracy and its transformation from a conservative bastion into a socialist battering ram, were inherently contradictory.'[36] In the end, the Socialists' reform programme met with mixed results.

Lastly, after PASOK reforms initially gave trade unions greater freedom of action and improved labour relations, circumstances soon caused Papandreou's labour policy to reaffirm state control over labour-union activity. The selective socialization of key means of production, which was to emphasize worker participation and improve productivity, led instead to increased state patronage for inept companies and continued state control of unions.[37] Papandreou also attempted to further national reconciliation by officially recognizing the role of the resistance during World War II, by granting rights of residence in Greece to those who had fled to Communist countries after the Civil War, and by ending all public ceremonies that celebrated the victories of the National Army over the Democratic Army of Greece. Only Greek refugees were allowed to return, however, excluding a large number of Macedonian Slav members of the DAG (see pages 178–9).

The greatest challenge to PASOK in the 1980s was managing the economy, and by almost any measure, they did not do it well. To be fair, PASOK inherited an economy that was already showing signs of weakness. Greece had never fully recovered from the 1972 oil crisis, and throughout the 1970s the economy grew at a very slow rate of only 1.8 per cent of gross domestic product. Wages had increased dramatically after the restoration of democratic rule and the inflation rate stood at 24.5 per cent when PASOK came to power.[38] The main problem facing Papandreou, then, was how to pay for PASOK's ambitious social programmes while keeping Greece militarily strong in such a bleak economic environment. In keeping with his campaign promise, Papandreou initially raised middle and low incomes, instituted price controls, and introduced tax incentives on investments, giving the state an even larger role than it had had under the ND regime. But by 1985, the annual inflation rate had risen to 25 per cent, which led to devaluation of the drachma in what was presented as an austerity plan. The budget deficit still grew, eventually reaching 10 per cent of the gross national product. The public debt that spiralled out of control in the late 1980s continues to be a serious deterrent to economic growth in Greece into the 1990s.[39]

In foreign policy, PASOK proved far more moderate in power than it had been as an opposition party.[40] Part of the PASOK platform on 1981 had called for a radical departure from anything that had come before regarding Greece's foreign relations. As we have seen throughout this book, foreign dependency has been a recurrent feature in the history of modern Greece. PASOK called for a break with the past: '... our opponents pretentiously ask us whether we are with the West or the East, and our reply is: We are for peace and support only Greece's interests'.[41] Although Papandreou's strident anti-American rhetoric caused friction with the administration of United States President Ronald Reagan, PASOK was willing to compromise on specific issues such as continuation of United States bases in Greece, after vigorous negotiations.[42] Despite his theoretical non-alignment and conciliation of *bêtes noires* of the west such as Muammar al Qadhafi of Libya, Saddam Hussein of Iraq, and Yasser Arafat of the Palestine Liberation Organization, Papandreou balanced Greece's international position by keeping Greece in NATO. With regard to membership in the European Community, here again the strident hard line of opposition was ameliorated once PASOK came into power. Certainly during Papandreou's second term of office from 1985 to 1989, Greece became fully integrated into the organization that it had once denigrated as an evil entity.[43]

In its policy toward Turkey, the PASOK government stood firm. In 1982 Papandreou became the first Greek Prime Minister to visit Cyprus, signalling strong support for the Greek population of the divided island. In 1984 he mobilized the Greek military for war when Turkish batteries opened fire on a Greek destroyer. And in 1987, he once again brought Greece to the brink of war when Turkey threatened to send an oil exploration vessel into Greek territorial waters. In 1988 a thaw resulted from a meeting between Papandreou and Turkey's President Turgut Özal in Davos, Switzerland, where new avenues of bilateral communication and consultation were arranged. Soon thereafter, however, the 'spirit of Davos' was strained again by disputes over the treatment of minorities, air space, and access to Aegean oil.[44]

Papandreou's fortunes began to turn during the summer of 1988. In August he underwent major heart surgery, but he refused to yield the reins of power. The opposition mocked his technique as 'government by fax'. A further complication was the announcement that Papandreou intended to divorce his

American wife of 37 years – herself a very popular figure in Greece – in order to marry a 34 year old airline stewardess who had gained influence in Papandreou's entourage. The family rift caused by this announcement damaged the cohesion within PASOK because Papandreou's sons occupied key positions in the party.

But it was a financial scandal that rocked the political world of Greece most violently. In November 1988, a shortfall of $132 million was discovered in the Bank of Crete some months after bank chairman Giorgios Koskotas, a Greek–American millionaire entrepreneur under investigation for large-scale financial crime, had fled the country. In the months that followed, alleged connections between Koskotas and the PASOK government, and even with Papandreou himself, brought the resignations of several ministers and demands for a vote of no confidence in the government. Papandreou, whose second four-year term was to expire within months, held on to power.

As he awaited PASOK's inevitable losses in the elections of June 1989, Papandreou adjusted the electoral system to make it more proportional and to hinder formation of a majority by a rival party. The strategy succeeded in part. Under the leadership of Papandreou's old rival Konstantinos Mitsotakis, ND won 44 per cent of the vote, but it fell six seats short of a majority. A short-lived conservative–communist coalition government was formed. In a matter of months, a second election also failed to produce a clear victor that could form an effective government. Finally, in April 1990, ND won a narrow majority of seats and formed the government. Papandreou and the Socialists were finally out of power after almost 10 years. With their fall, a very important chapter in the history of modern Greece had come to a close.

GREEK SOCIETY DURING THE ERA OF RESTORATION AND SOCIALISM

I want now to return to the arena of social history and examine the momentous developments that took place in Greek society during the period from the fall of the junta to the collapse of the Berlin wall. We can pick up the threads of analysis where we left off in the last chapter and explore the following areas: urbanization and the changes in urban lifeways, the continuing impact of migration on Greek society, and finally, the way that society and economy developed in the Greek countryside.

By the time of the census of 1991 Athens had become a megalopolis. In a country of approximately 10.2 million people, 3.1 million (or 31 per cent) of them lived in the greater Athens area. The rate of population growth of Athens and its suburbs had slowed considerably from the heyday of the 1960s, but it was still a not inconsequential 27 per cent during the 1970s and 21 per cent in the 1980s. The massive transference of population from the countryside to Athens had abated and the city's growth in the post-junta era was driven by a combination of in-migration from the countryside, the return of Greeks who had migrated abroad, and natural demographic growth among the city's population. In addition to the continued expansion of Athens, most of the other cities and large towns of Greece also expanded. As Table 10.1 demonstrates, by 1991 almost two-thirds of the entire population lived in urban areas. Only 50 years ago, the situation was the reverse, as the majority of the population resided in villages.

Table 10.1 Percentage of population in Greece from 1940 to 1991 based on category of settlement.
Urban: >10,000
Semi-urban: 10,000–5,000
Rural: <5,000

	Urban	Semi-urban	Rural
1940	33	15	52
1951	38	15	47
1961	43	13	44
1971	53	12	35
1981	58	12	30
1991	62	18	20

Attracting newcomers to the city between 1974 and 1989 was the prospect of work in the building trades and the service industries, or even higher paying jobs in manufacturing. These prospects were not as bright, however, as they had been during the halcyon days of the 1950s and 1960s. As second- or third-generation working class urbanites grew in number, they competed for the same types of work that attracted outsiders. Athens and Thessaloniki were still the locations for a significant portion of Greek industry. But, drawn by the prospect of higher profits, lower competition, and reduced labour costs, by the mid-1980s, the locus of dynamic growth in manufacturing had shifted away from the major cities to the smaller towns and the countryside.[45] This not only put a brake on urban migration but it also had an impact on lifeways in the countryside, as we shall see shortly. Another pattern of population movement was emerging, however. Increasingly those coming to the city were professionals or people, especially students, seeking professional training.

In addition to changing in size, during the 1970s and 1980s the character and quality of life in the city also underwent radical changes. 'The early sixties [sic.] were an 'idyllic' period for Athens.'[46] In spite of the very rapid in-migration of rural folk, Athens did not experience many of the social problems that so commonly accompany urbanization. Crime and violence, poverty and destitution, unemployment, class conflict, and other such social ills did not manifest themselves in Athens during the 1950s and 1960s. This was partly due to the pattern of migration, whereby large numbers of women and children were also part of the migrating population, and partly to the economic boom conditions.[47] It appears that many of the maladies associated with the modern city only appeared in Athens in the post-junta era.

From 1975 onward, the crime rate in Athens, and the rest of Greece, increased dramatically. Moreover, the types of crimes committed also shifted to a pattern more like urban areas elsewhere and less like the one found in rural areas. Evasion of market regulations and other laws pertaining to the economy, motor vehicle violations, and public offences (vagrancy, brawling, etc.) accounted for a large percentage of Athens' crime. Charges for drug possession increased considerably as well. Violence and homicide did occur, but only in very modest numbers.

One of the biggest changes in criminal activity involved who committed crimes. During the 1970s and especially during the 1980s Athenian women and juveniles were charged with criminal offences in numbers unheard of before this time. In the post-junta period then Greece experienced a modernization of crime, and thus the pattern of criminal activity in Athens came to resemble more closely that of other major cities around the world.[48]

Another social development in Athens was the increasing segregation of neighbourhoods according to class.[49] The 'urban village' phenomenon faded over time as second and third generation urbanites established neighbourhoods that centred more on a class than a regional identity. There was also a change in women's roles in the city. The process that had begun during the 1960s developed further during the post-junta era, and especially after the social reforms, discussed earlier. Women's participation in the workplace expanded greatly, and many women remained in the workforce even after marriage. More than ever, class also shaped women's life experiences. More women received higher education, including university degrees, than ever before, and this opened the door to careers that had previously been closed to women. In addition, the women's movement developed in Greece and drew its strength especially from educated urban women. New forms of inter-gender sociability developed between unmarried men and women, and married women demonstrated a greater autonomy of action, including over their reproductive behaviour, than ever before. In short, Greek society came increasingly to resemble other European societies with regard to social structural complexity, gender relations, and education.[50]

Greek rural society also continued to develop and change. The dimorphism of agricultural systems we discussed in Chapter 9 continued through the late 1970s and 1980s. When Greece became a full member of the European Community in 1981, the agrarian sector became subject to the EC's Common Agricultural Policy (CAP). CAP's aim was to solve the chronic agricultural problems of the community by supplying price-trading support and by providing capital to member states to address structural deficiencies; the latter in the Greek case were deemed to be the persistent problem of minifundia and the under-developed marketing system. Greek agriculture received additional EC support after the implementation of the Integrated Mediterranean Programmes. The aims of the IMPs were 'to improve incomes and the employment situation, by helping agriculture to modernize and by creating opportunities for jobs or sources of income on the non-farm sector, both for those who remain[ed] in agriculture and who those who desert[ed] it'.[51] The results of those programmes were that large amounts of capital in the form of investments and subsidies flowed into the countryside. It was, however, primarily in those regions that had already modernized to some extent that they had their greatest impact. Producers of commercial and cash crops such as tobacco, fruits and vegetables (especially, citrus fruits, tomatoes and the like), cotton and rice received the lion's share of the subsidies (over 79 per cent of the total input).[52] Only one part of rural society was effectively assisted by these programmes. Nonetheless, that sector did well.

Two other dynamics, however, marked the development of the Greek countryside. During the 1980s, rural manufacturing started to take off. Entrepreneurs, often returning Greek migrants, found it more profitable to establish industrial plants in the countryside or in small towns rather than in the major cities (see above, p. 213). Using capital saved from years of working abroad in conjunction with finances obtained through the IMPs, Greek merchants established textile mills and food processing plants.[53] We have already seen that there was a long tradition of pluriactivity among Greek farming families, and so the establishment of industrial concerns neatly tapped into a long held economic strategy among agricultural families. Men could supplement the income of their farm by working part-time in industry, and female members of the household could add to the family's total income by working full or part-time. Interestingly, young women dominated the labour force, especially of the textile mills, and the opening up of the labour market to women altered gender roles in much the same way that women's work had in industrializing Athens during the 1950s and 1960s.

Another important development in the countryside has been the advent of tourism. Villages and small towns adjacent to the major archeological sites or along coastal zones were transformed by the great increase in tourism. In 1987, for example, the receipts from tourism accounted for nearly 5 per cent of Greece's gross national product as over six and a half million foreign tourists came to visit a land that itself had a population of just over 10 million. In addition, during the 1980s internal tourism took off, as urban Greeks left the cities during the hot summer months to visit the village from which their grandparents or great-grandparents had come or simply to play tourist in their own land. By adding on a room or converting one to a guest bedroom, house-holds could take in boarders. 'Rooms to let' signs appeared along village streets like flowers in springtime. Providing food, snacks, ice cream and soft drinks became very lucrative.

The influx of revenue from tourism had a profound impact on rural society. It gave families a non-agricultural income that could, in many cases, surpass the income earned off the land. As a number of recent anthropological studies have shown, it dramatically changed gender roles and class relations. Because many of the activities related to servicing tourists fell into the categories of 'women's work', it was women who controlled this new source of revenue.[54] The combination of rural industries and tourism changed the face of the countryside significantly. Those areas that in the past had dwelt in a delicate balance between natural resources, agriculture, and population could now develop and perhaps even flourish with the aid of the new sources of income. The engine that had driven so many Greeks abroad for so long had at last been turned off.

In fact, it started to operate in reverse. During the post-junta era Greece witnessed the return by the thousand of those who had migrated abroad as guest-workers in foreign lands. These returning migrants brought with them expertise, capital, and dreams. Some settled in Athens or Thessaloniki, but many returned to their natal villages, where as we just saw, they played a key role in the development of both rural industry and tourism.[55] It seems to me that a clear measure of the positive development of Greek society from 1974 to 1990 was the fact that not only were Greeks returning from abroad, but that the country was now attracting immigrants seeking a better life. Village girls no longer served the Athenian bourgeoisie as maids; Filipino girls did. Seasonally migrant labour gangs still traversed the Greek countryside, but they were no longer poor men and women from the mountain villages, instead they were Roma or Albanians. Vendors hawking their wares on the streets of Athens were now migrants from Africa or the Middle East. While this in-migration of foreigners is one measure of Greece's successful development over the last 30 years, their intrusion into a society that has for much of its recent history been characterized by a remarkable degree of homogeneity raises a variety of new problems that Greeks will have to address. But at this point, discussion of them belongs to sociologists and analysts of public policy and not historians.

EPILOGUE

I have concluded this study of the development of modern Greek society in 1989. But of course, that does not mean that the story of Greece has ended. Greece during the 1990s underwent some very important developments, but there is logic to stopping this story at the end of the 1980s. Some of the themes that have run through this book reached the end of one phase in the late 1980s before starting another.

The constitutional question had, for example, at long last come to end. The termination of PASOK's reign and the transferral of power back to a coalition government that included the Communist party and then to the conservatives showed that the democratic institutions established at the end of the junta had taken root. Ballots, not tanks, would determine the fate of elections, indicating that clearly democracy in Greece is here to stay. The resurgence of PASOK under new leadership and the move by both parties toward the centre suggest that the sectarian divisions that beset Greece for much of the twentieth century have been put to rest. Certainly there remain extremist groups on both the Left and the Right, but that fact that neither enjoys any legitimacy with the public at large is the important point.

With the collapse of the Soviet bloc and the end of the Cold War, the foreign policy framework that shaped so much of Greece's history over the last 50 years was removed. At the same time, Greece's relationship with the European Community became even closer. Few would doubt in the year 2001 that Greece is part of Europe. But some issues from the past refuse to go easily into that good night of history. The furore over the name of the former Yugoslav republic of Macedonia, or the continuing conflict between the hierarchy of the Orthodox Church and the PASOK government of Kostas Simitis over the removal of religious affiliation from the national identity card, indicate that the long standing issues regarding Greek identity and the related insecurities over national territory that it generates still remain close to the surface.

At the same time a degree of interaction has developed between Greece and the global Greek diaspora unlike ever before. For much of the century, Greeks abroad looked on the homeland as a self-made man might look back to the humble abode of his parents. One now detects a greater patience among

Greeks in Greece with the often meddlesome and occasionally arrogant attitude that Greeks of the diaspora sometimes evinced in the past. In other words, it seems to me that both Greeks in the nation-state and Greeks abroad have come to a degree of mutual understanding. Greece's uneasy relations with Turkey and the ongoing struggles over Cyprus persist, and no easy solution appears in sight.

In sum, as we enter the twenty-first century, I find that many, but by no means all, of the issues and problems that shaped the nation's development for the previous 180 years have came to an end of sorts in 1989. How they have developed since, however, are still topics for political commentators, sociologists, and economists. As to their place in history, only time will tell.

Notes

Preface
[1] K.R. Legg and J.M. Roberts, *Modern Greece: A Civilization on the Periphery*, Boulder, 1997, p. 9.
[2] R. Clogg, 'Captive to History: Will Greece Ever Stop Relying on its Past?', *Odyssey*, July/August, 1996, p.74.

Chapter 1
[1] H. Inalcik, 'The Meaning of Legacy: The Ottoman Case', in L.C. Brown, ed., *Imperial Legacy: The Ottoman Imprint on the Balkans and the Middle East*, New York, 1996, pp. 17–29; M. Todorova, 'The Ottoman Legacy in the Balkans', in L.C. Brown, ed., *Imperial Legacy: The Ottoman Imprint on the Balkans and the Middle East*, New York, 1996, pp. 45–77.
[2] A.A. Mandrikas, *Krifo Scholeio: Mithos i Pragmatikotita*, Athens, 1992; A. Angelou, *To Krifo Scholeio: Chroniko enos Mithou*, Athens, 1997.
[3] R. Clogg, 'The Greek *Millet* in the Ottoman Empire', in R. Clogg, ed., *Anatolica: Studies in the Greek East in the 18th and 19th Centuries*, Brookfield, 1996, p. 185.
[4] V. Roudometof, 'From Rum Millet to Greek Nation: Enlightenment, Secularization, and National Identity in Ottoman Balkan Society, 1453–1821', *Journal of Modern Greek Studies*, 16, 1998, pp. 11–48.
[5] F. Adanir, 'The Ottoman Peasantries c.1360–c.1860', in T. Scott, ed., *The Peasantries of Europe from the Fourteenth to the Eighteenth Centuries*, New York, 1998, pp. 298–304; B. McGowan, *Economic Life in Ottoman Europe. Taxation, Trade and the Struggle for Land, 1600–1800*, Cambridge, 1981, pp. 65–81; V. Kremmydas, *Singiria kai Emborio stin Proepanastatiki Peloponniso 1793–1821*, Athens, 1980.
[6] S.D. Petmezas, 'Patterns of Protoindustrialization in the Ottoman Empire: The Case of Eastern Thessaly, ca. 1750–1860', *Journal of European Economic History*, 19, 1990, pp. 575–603; H.A. Forbes, 'The Agrarian Economy of the Ermionodha Around 1700: An Ethnohistorical Reconstruction', in S.B. Sutton, ed., *Contingent Countryside: Settlement, Economy, and Land Use in the Southern Argolid Since 1700*, Stanford, 2000, pp. 41–70; J.L. Davis, 'Contributions to a Mediterranean Rural Archaeology: Historical Case Studies from the Ottoman Cyclades', *Journal of Mediterranean Archaeology*, 4, 1991, pp. 131–215; Y. Triantafyllidou, 'L'industrie du Savon en Crete au Xviiie Siècle: Aspects Economiques et Sociaux', *Etudes Balkaniques*, 4, 1975, pp. 75–87.
[7] T. Stoianovich, 'The Conquering Balkan Orthodox Merchant', in T. Stoianovich, *Between East and West: The Balkan and Mediterranean Worlds. Volume 2. Economies and Societies: Traders, Towns and Households*, New Rochelle, 1992, pp. 1–78.
[8] E. Frangakis-Syrett, *The Commerce of Smyrna in the Eighteenth Century (1700–1820)*,

Athens, 1992; J.M. Wagstaff, 'The Role of the Eastern Mediterranean (Levant) for the Early Modern European World Economy 1500–1800', in H.-J. Nitz, ed., *The Early Modern World-System in Geographical Perspective*, Stuttgart, 1993, pp. 327–42.

Chapter 2

[1]   R. van Boeschoten, 'Myth and History in Greek Folk Songs Related to the War of Independence', *Journal of the Hellenic Diaspora*, 13, 1986, pp. 125–41.

[2]   P.M. Kitromilides, *I Yalliki Epanastasis kai i Notioanatoliki Evropi*, Athens, 1990, pp. 111–38.

[3]   S. Gourgouris, *Dream Nation: Enlightenment, Colonization, and the Institution of Modern Greece*, Stanford, 1996, p. 53.

[4]   R. Clogg, 'Korais and the Movement for Greek Independence', *History Today*, 33, 1983, pp. 10–14; S.G. Chaconas, *Adamantios Korais: a Study in Greek Nationalism*, New York, 1968; E.G. Vallianatos, *From Graikos to Hellene: Adamantios Koraes and the Greek Revolution*, Athens, 1987.

[5]   C.M. Woodhouse, *Rhigas Velestinlis, the Proto-Martyr of the Greek Revolution*, Limni, Evvia, 1997.

[6]   My discussion of Rigas's writings is based on the collection of works edited by Vranousis (L.I. Vranousis, ed., *Rigas – erevna, synagogi kai meleti*, Athens, 1953).

[7]   T. Vournas, *Elleniki Nomarchia: Hellenike Nomarchia, iti, Logos peri eleutherias, syntetheis te kai typois, ekdotheis idiois analomasi pros opheleian ton Ellenon*, Athens, 1982.

[8]   S.K. Pavlowitch, *A History of the Balkans 1804–1945*, New York, 1999, pp. 27–31.

[9]   J.D. Post, *The Last Great Subsistence Crisis in the Western World*, Baltimore, 1977, p.5.

[10]   E. Frangakis-Syrett, *The Commerce of Smyrna in the Eighteenth Century (1700–1820)*, Athens, 1992, pp. 27–30; V. Kremmydas, *Singiria kai Emborio stin Proepanastatike Peloponniso 1793–1821*, Athens, 1980, pp. 56–70.

[11]   G. Frangos, 'The *Philiki Etairia*: A Premature Coalition', in R. Clogg, ed., *The Struggle for Greek Independence: Essays to Mark the 150th Anniversary of the Greek War of Independence*, Basingstoke, 1973, pp. 87–103.

[12]   K.E. Fleming, *The Muslim Bonaparte: Diplomacy and Orientalism in Ali Pasha's Greece*, Princeton, 1999, on the historiographical lacuna concerning Ali, see, pp. 18–25.

[13]   This was an administrative unit placed under the control of an official appointed by the Porte; his primary duties were to oversee the collection of taxes and the maintenance of order.

[14]   D. Skiotis, 'From Bandit to Pasha: First Steps in the Rise to Power of Ali of Tepelen, 1750–1784', *International Journal of Middle East Studies*, 2, 1971, pp. 232–4; for the policy of appointing bandits to be police in the empire, see, K. Barkey, *Bandits and Bureaucrats: The Ottoman Route to State Centralization*, Ithaca, NY, 1994.

[15]   T.W. Gallant, 'Brigandage, Piracy, Capitalism, and State-formation: Transnational Crime from a Historical World Systems Perspective', in J. Heyman and A. Smart, eds, *States and Illegal Networks*, London, 1999, pp. 25–61.

[16]   D.N. Skiotis, 'The Greek Revolution: Ali Pasha's Last Gamble', in N.P. Diamandouros, J.P. Anton, J.A. Petropulos, and P. Topping, eds, *Hellenism and the First Greek War of Liberation (1821–1830): Continuity and Change*, Thessaloniki, 1976, pp. 97–110.

[17]   B. Jelavich, 'The Balkan Nations and the Greek War of Independence', in Diamandouros, *Hellenism and the First Greek War*, pp. 157–70.

[18] P.P. Argenti, *The Massacres of Chios, Described in Contemporary Diplomatic Reports*, London, 1932.

[19] W.M.M. Leake, *An Historical Outline of the Greek Revolution: With a Few Remarks on the Present State of Affairs in That Country*, London, 1826, pp. 34–7.

[20] Douglas Dakin, *The Greek Struggle for Independence 1821–1833*, Berkeley, 1973, p. 78.

[21] Quoted in D. Dakin, *The Unification of Greece, 1770–1923*, London, 1972, p. 59.

[22] T. Kolokotrones, *Apomnemoneumata*, Athens, 1981, p. 198.

[23] I. Makryiannes, *The Memoirs of General Makriyannis, 1797–1864*, London, 1966; repeatedly in his account of the war, Markiyannis comments on the difficulty of getting the peasants to join in the fighting, see, for example, pp. 48, 52, and 57.

[24] J.S. Koliopoulos, 'Military Entrepreneurship in Central Greece during the Greek War on National Liberation (1821–1830)', *Journal of Modern Greek Studies*, 2, 1984, pp. 163–87; A.E. Vakalopoulos, *Ta Ellenika Strateumata tou 1821: Organosi, Igesia, Taktiki, Ethi, Psychologia*, Thessaloniki, 1991.

[25] J.A. Petropulos, 'Forms of Collaboration with the Enemy during the Greek War of Liberation', in Diamandouros, *Hellenism and the First Greek War*, pp. 131–46.

[26] M. Glencross, 'Greece Restored: Greece and the Greek War of Independence in French Romantic Historiography 1821–1830', *Journal of European Studies*, 27, 1997, pp. 33–49.

[27] S. Schwartzberg, 'The Lion and the Phoenix. 1. British-Policy toward the Greek Question, 1831–1832', *Middle Eastern Studies*, 24, 1988, pp. 139–77.

[28] Dakin, *Greek Struggle*, p. 203.

[29] V. Sheremet, 'The Greek Revolution of 1821: A New Look at Old Problems', *Modern Greek Studies Yearbook*, 8, 1992, p. 46.

[30] C.M. Woodhouse, *Capodistria: The Founder of Greek Independence*, Oxford, 1973, pp. 354–6.

[31] T. Veremis, *Kapodistrias and the French: the Formation of a Regular Greek Army*, New York, 1979.

[32] D. Loules, 'The Assassination of I. Capodistrias and Russia', *Mnemon*, 10, 1985, pp. 77–95; C. Loukos, *I Antipolitevsi kata tou Kyverniti I. Kapodistria, 1828–1831*, Athens, 1988.

Chapter 3

[1] G. Finlay, *History of the Greek Revolution and the Reign of King Otho*, London, 1971 (1877), Volume V, p. 108.

[2] J.A. Petropoulos, *Politics and Statecraft in the Kingdom of Greece 1833–1843*, Princeton, 1968, p. 158.

[3] I.A. Petropoulos and A. Koumarianou, *I Themeliosi tou Ellinikou Kratous: Othoniki Periodos 1833–1843*, Athens, 1982, pp. 90–92.

[4] M. Economopoulou, *Parties and Politics in Greece (1844–1855)*, Athens, 1984, p. 39 for the quote, and pp. 33–42 for a discussion of the parties. See also, Petropulos, *Politics*, pp. 134–44 and G. Hering, *Die Politischen Parteien in Griechenland 1821–1936*, München, 1992, vol. 1, pp. 151–74.

[5] G. Cochrane, *Wanderings in Greece*, London, 1837, vol. 2, pp. 32–3.

[6] W.W. McGrew, *Land and Revolution in Modern Greece, 1800–1881. The Transition in the Tenure and Exploitation of Land From Ottoman Rule to Independence*, Kent, 1985, p. 19.

[7]   T.W. Gallant, *Risk and Survival in Ancient Greece: Reconstructing the Rural Domestic Economy*, Stanford, 1991, pp. 82–6.

[8]   McGrew, *Land and Revolution*, p. 165.

[9]   Gallant, *Risk and Survival*, pp. 101–12.

[10]   P. Kallígas, *Thanos Vlekas*, Athens, 1989 (1855), p. 17.

[11]   J.A. Petropulos, 'The Greek Economy during the First Decade of Othonian Rule', *Deltion tis Istorikis kai Ethnografikis Etairias tis Ellados*, 24, 1981, pp. 195–6.

[12]   V.A. Kardasi, *Syros: Stavrodromi tis Anatolikis Mesoyiou (1832–1857)*, Athens, 1987, pp. 23–63.

[13]   N. Bakounakis, *Patra: Mia Elliniki Protevousa ston 19o Aiona*, Athens, 1992, pp. 140–49; the economic expansion of Patras continued at even greater pace during the second period of Otto's rule: C. Papathanassopoulos, 'The Creation Of New Maritime Centres In Greece With The Emergence Of Steam, 1850–1870', *International Journal of Maritime History*, 5, 1993, pp. 193–202.

[14]   J. Mavrogordato, *Modern Greece: A Chronicle and a Survey, 1800–1931*, London, 1931, p. 39.

[15]   Cited in J.S. Koliopoulos, *Brigands With a Cause: Brigandage and Irredentism in Modern Greece, 1821–1912*, Oxford, 1987, p. 85.

[16]   K. Aroni-Tsihli, *Agrotikis Ekseyersis Stin Palia Ellada 1833–1881*, Athens, 1989, pp. 51–195, discusses just some of the over 30 recorded episodes of rural unrest during the first decade of Otto's regime.

[17]   E. About, *Greece and the Greeks of the Present Day*, London, 1857, p. 30.

[18]   'The Bankruptcy of Greece,' *Blackwood's Magazine*, September 1843. The article predicting the revolution was written well before the actual uprising took place.

[19]   I. Dimakis, *I Politiaki Metavoli Tou 1843 kai to Zitima ton Avtohthono kai Eterohthonon*, Athens, 1991, examines the issue in detail, but see especially, pp. 180–203.

[20]   Finlay, *History of the Greek Revolution*, vol. vii, p. 197.

[21]   P.E. Petrakis, 'The Borrowing Requirements of the Greek Public Sector, 1844–1869', *Journal of the Hellenic Diaspora*, 12, 1985, pp. 35–46.

[22]   Economopoulou, *Parties*, p. 152.

[23]   S.A. Brekis, *To 1848 Stin Hellada*, Athens, 1984.

[24]   D. Whitten Jr., 'The Don Pacifico Affair', *Historian*, 48, 1986, pp. 255–67; D. Hannell, 'Lord Palmerston and the 'Don Pacifico Affair' of 1850: The Ionian Connection', *European History Quarterly*, 19, 1989, pp. 495–507.

[25]   Economopoulou, *Parties*, p. 232 ; T.D. Sakellaropoulos, I *Kriseis stin Ellada 1830–1857: Oikonomikes, Koinonikes kai Politikes Opseis*, Athens, 1994.

[26]   J. Van der Kiste, *Kings of the Hellenes: The Greek Kings, 1863–1919*, London, 1994, 14–26.

[27]   C. Tsoucalas, 'On the Problem of Political Clientelism in Greece in the Nineteenth Century', *Journal of the Hellenic Diaspora*, 5, 1978, pp. 5–17.

[28]   K. Gardikas, *Politics and Parties in Greece, 1875–1885: Toward a Two Party System*, University of London, 1988, p. 21; D. Michalopoulos, *Vie Politique en Grece pendant Les Années 1862–1869*, Athens, 1981, pp. 129–49.

[29]   Michalopoulos, *Vie Politique*, pp. 81–7.

[30]   Gardikas, *Politics*, pp. 363–74.

[31]   A good introduction to the mechanics of the new system as demonstrated through a wonderful case study, can be found in K. Gardikas Alexander, 'Centre and Periphery

in the 1874 Greek Elections: Competition for Political Control in Gortynia', *Balkan Studies*, 36, 1995, pp. 11–30, especially pp. 26–9.

[32] A.N. Damianakos, *Charilaos Trikoupes and the Modernization of Greece, 1874–1894*, New York University, 1977, pp. 96–107.

[33] Most of the discussion of Trikoupis's social reforms, particularly those that dealt with problems caused by urbanization, takes places in Chapter 5.

[34] P.E. Petrakis and H. Panorios, 'Economic Fluctuations in Greece, 1844–1913', *Journal of Economic History*, 21, 1992, pp. 31–47.

[35] McGrew, *Land and Revolution*, pp. 207–14.

[36] P. P. Pizanias, *Oikonomiki Istoria tis Ellinikis Stafidas 1851–1921*, Athens, 1988 and 'I agrotiki paragogi ston elliniko 19ou ainoa: scheseis kai isodimata', *Ta Istorika*, 3, 1983, pp. 149–68.

[37] V. Kardassis, 'Greek Steam Liner Companies, 1858–1914', *International Journal of Maritime History*, 9, 1997, pp. 107–27; M. Sinarelli, *Dromi kai Limania stin Ellada 1830–1890*, Athens, 1989.

[38] C. Agriantoni, *Oi Aparhes tis Ekbiomehanisis stin Ellada ton 19o Aiona*, Athens, 1986.

[39] K. Tsoukalas, *Eksartisi kai Anaparayoyi. O Kinonikos Rolos ton Ekpaideftikon Mihanismon Stin Ellada (1830–1922)*, Athens, 1987, pp. 392–423; S. Ziogou-Karastergiou, *I Mesi Ekpaidevsi ton Koritsion stin Ellada (1830–1893)*, Athens, 1986, pp. 182–5.

[40] Tsoukalas, *Eksartisi kai Anaparayoyi*, pp. 197–207.

[41] S.B. Thomadakis, 'Monetary Arrangements and Economic Power in Nineteenth-century Greece: the National Bank in the Period of Convertibility (1841–77)', *Journal of the Hellenic Diaspora*, 12, 1985, pp. 48–54.

[42] S. Lazaretou, 'Monetary and Fiscal Policies in Greece: 1833–1914', *Journal of European Economic History*, 22, 1993, pp. 285–312; Petrakis, 'Borrowing,' 45–6.

[43] T. Tsiovaridou, 'La repercussion en Grèce a la Fin du XIXe siècle de la Crise du Raisin Sec', *Balkan Studies*, 21, 1980, pp. 127–45.

Chapter 4

[1] Ioannis Kolettis, address to National Assembly, 1844, cited in G. Augustinos, *Consciousness and History: Nationalist Critics of Greek Society, 1897–1914*, New York, 1977, p. 14.

[2] G.J. Andreopoulos, 'State and Irredentism: Some Reflexions on the Case of Greece', *Historical Journal*, 24, 1981, pp. 949–59.

[3] T.W. Gallant, 'Brigandage, Piracy, Capitalism, and State-formation: Transnational Crime from a Historical World Systems Perspective', in J. Heyman and A. Smart, eds, *States and Illegal Networks*, London, 1999, pp. 42, 47.

[4] J.S. Koliopoulos, *Brigands With a Cause: Brigandage and Irredentism in Modern Greece, 1821–1912*, Oxford, 1987, pp. 82–134.

[5] J.V. Kofas, *Financial Relations of Greece and the Great Powers, 1832–1862*, New York, 1981, pp. 38–41.

[6] D. Dakin, *The Unification of Greece, 1770–1923*, London, 1972, pp. 71–5; Koliopoulos, *Brigands*, pp. 116–19.

[7] J.V. Kofas, *International and Domestic Politics in Greece During the Crimean War*, New York, 1980, pp. 129–33.

[8] T.D. Sfikas, 'National Movements and Nation Building in the Balkans, 1804–1922:

Historic Origins, Contemporary Misunderstandings', in T.D. Sfikas and C. Williams, eds, *Ethnicity and Nationalism in East Central Europe and the Balkans*, Aldershot, 1999, pp. 13–44; V.N. Todorov, *Greek Federalism During the Nineteenth Century: Ideas and Projects*, New York, 1995, 59–82.

[9] *London Times*, 19 March 1878. The newspaper reporter, a man named Ogle, was murdered by Turkish irregulars ten days after this story was published.

[10] L. Sergeant, *Greece in the Nineteenth Century: A Record of Hellenic Emancipation and Progress: 1821–1897*, London, 1897, p. 41.

[11] E. Kofos, *Greece and the Eastern Crisis 1875–1878*, Thessaloniki, 1975.

[12] E.E. Marcoglou, *The American Interest in the Cretan Revolution, 1866–1869*, Athens, 1971, pp. 39–54, 115–31.

[13] W. Miller, 'Finlay's "History of the Insurrection in Crete" ', *Annual of the British School at Athens*, 27, 1925, p. 108.

[14] Z. Purvanova, 'Changes in the Political Status of the Island of Crete 1894–1899' *Etudes Balkaniques*, 25, 1989, pp. 64–84.

[15] I.D. Michailidis, 'The War of Statistics: Traditional Recipes for the Preparation of the Macedonian Salad', *East European Quarterly*, 32, 1998, pp. 9–22.

[16] D. Dakin, *The Greek Struggle in Macedonia 1897–1913*, Thessaloniki, 1993, p. 2.

[17] R.S. Peckham, 'Map Mania: Nationalism and the Politics of Place in Greece, 1870–1922', *Political Geography*, 19, 2000, p. 79.

[18] G. Agelopoulos, 'Perceptions, Constructions, and Definitions of Greek National identity in Late Nineteenth-early Twentieth Century Macedonia', *Balkan Studies*, 36, 1995, pp. 247–63; G. Agelopoulos, 'From Bulgarievo to Nea Krasia, from "Two Settlements" to "One Village": Community Formation, Collective Identities and the Role of the Individual', in P.A. Mackridge and E. Yannakakis, eds, *Ourselves and Others : the Development of a Greek Macedonian Identity Since 1912*, Washington, 1997, pp. 133–52; J.K. Cowan, 'Idioms of Belonging: Polyglot Articulations of Local Identity in a Greek Macedonian Town', in Mackridge *Ourselves and Others*, pp. 153–74; A.N. Karakasidou, *Fields of Wheat, Hills of Blood: Passages to Nationhood in Greek Macedonia, 1870–1990*, Chicago, 1997, pp. 77–99; V. Roudometof, 'Culture, Identity, and the Macedonian Question', in V. Roudometof, ed., *The Macedonian Question*, New York, 2000, pp. 1–24.

[19] B.C. Gounaris, 'Social Gatherings and Macedonian Lobbying: Symbols of Irredentism and Living Legends in Early Twentieth-century Athens', in P. Carabott, ed., *Greek Society in the Making, 1863–1913: Realities, Symbols and Visions*, Brookfield, 1997, pp. 99–113; G. Margaritis, 'The Nation and the Individual: Social Aspects of Life and Death in Greece (1896–1911)', in Carabott, *Greek Society in the Making*, pp. 87–98.

[20] R. Just, 'Ethnicity and the Village: The "Them" and "Us" in Rural Greece', in J. Burke and S. Gauntlett, eds, *Neohellenism*, Melbourne, Australia, 1992, p. 114; see also his essay, 'The Triumph of the Ethnos', in E. Tonkin, M. McDonald, and M. Chapman, eds, *History and Ethnicity*, New York, 1989, pp. 71–8

[21] This dualism in Greek identity has been much discussed, but still the best introduction to the topic is the work of anthropologist Michael Herzfeld; see, especially his: *Ours Once More: Folklore, Ideology and the Making of Modern Greece*, Austin, 1982, *Anthropology Through the Looking Glass: Critical Ethnography in the Margins of Europe*, Cambridge, 1987, and 'Hellenism and Occidentalism: The Permutations of Performance in Greek Bourgeois Identity', in J.G. Carrier, ed., *Occidentalism: Images of the West*, Oxford, 1995, pp. 218–33.

[22] V. Roudometof, 'Invented Traditions, Symbolic Boundaries, and National Identity in Southeastern Europe: Greece and Serbia in Comparative Historical Perspective (1830–1880)', *East European Quarterly*, 32, 1999, p. 429.

[23] T. Veremis, 'From the National State to the Stateless Nation 1821–1910', *European History Quarterly*, 19, 1989, p. 136.

[24] K. Aroni-Tsihli, *Agrotikis Ekseyersis stin Palia Ellada 1833–1881*, Athens, 1989; Roudometof, 'Invented Traditions,' pp. 433–35.

[25] *Athen*, 11 November 1861. Cited in E. Skopetea, *To 'Protypo Vasileio' kai i Megali Idea (1830–1880)*, Athens, 1988, p. 291.

[26] My discussion of the 1871 jubilee is based on an unpublished manuscript by Dr Alexander Kitroeff entitled 'Balkan Nationalism Transformed: Greece's "Great Idea" 1821–1909.' I thank Dr Kitroeff for allowing me to read and to cite his work, and I very much look forward to its publication. The Patriarch's body had been recovered and sent to Odessa, where it was buried. In 1871, it was disinterred and shipped to Athens.

[27] Y. Hamilakis and E. Yalouri, 'Antiquities as Symbolic Capital in Modern Greek Society', *Antiquity*, 70, 1996, pp. 117–30; I. Morris, 'Archaeologies of Greece', in I. Morris, ed., *Classical Greece: Ancient Histories and Modern Archaeologies*, Cambridge, 1994, pp. 8–40; A. Kokkou, *I Merimna Gia Tis Archaiotetes Stin Ellada Kai Ta Prota Mouseia*, Athens, 1977.

[28] Augustinos, *Consciousness*, p. 16; C. Hatzidimitriou, 'From Paparrigopoulos to Vacalopoulos – Modern Greek History on the Ottoman Period', in L. Macrakis and P.-N. Diamandouros, eds, *New Trends in Modern Greek Histiography*, New Haven, 1982, pp. 13–24.

[29] E. Bastea, *The Creation of Modern Athens: Planning the Myth*, New York, 1999, pp. 1–5; A. Yerolympos, 'A New City for a New State. City Planning and the Formation of National Identity in the Balkans (1820s–1920s)', *Planning Perspectives*, 8, 1993, pp. 233–57.

[30] C. Koulouri, 'Voluntary Associations and New Forms of Sociability: Greek Sports Clubs at the Turn of the Nineteenth Century', in Carabott, *Greek Society in the Making*, pp. 145–60.

[31] K. Georgousopoulos, 'Ellinikotita kai Theatro', in D.Y. Tsaousis, ed., *Ellinismos-Ellinikotita*, Athens, 1983, pp. 205–10; K. Georgousopoulos, 'I elliniki kinonia mesa apo to Theatro tou 19ou aiona', in D.Y. Tsaousis, ed., *Opsis tis ellinikis kinonias tou 19ou aiona*, Athens, 1984, pp. 123–48.

[32] K. Tsoucalas, *Eksartisi kai Anaparayoyi. O Kinonikos Rolos ton Ekpaideftikon Mihanismon stin Ellada (1830–1922)*, Athens, 1987.

[33] C. Koulouri, *Dimensions Idologiques De L'Historicité En Gréce, 1834–1914: Les Manuels Scolaires D'Histoire Et De Geographie*, Frankfurt am Main, 1991.

[34] K. Kalliataki Merticopoulou, 'Literacy and Unredeemed Peasants: Late Nineteenth-Century Rural Crete Faces Education', in Carabott, *Greek Society in the Making, 1863–1913*, pp. 115–30.

Chapter 5

[1] Reconstructing the demographic history of Greece with exactitude is a difficult task. Until the 1860 census, the population figures were estimates based on calculations from the birth and death statistics provided by the provincial administrations. In spite of the relative demerits of the data, it is still possible to paint a relatively accurate picture of

the situation. See, L.F. Kallivretakis, 'Geographie et Demographie historiques de la Grèce: Le Probleme des sources', *Histoire et Mesure*, 10, 1995, pp. 9–23 and M. Houliaraki, *Geografiki, Diikitiki Kai Plithismiaki Ekseliksis Tis Ellados, 1821–1971*, Athina, 1973, volume 1, and V.G. Valaoras, 'A Reconstruction of the Demographic History of Modern Greece', *Milbank Memorial Fund Quarterly*, 38, 1960, pp. 116–18 for discussions on the limitations of the nineteenth-century data.

[2] Valaoras, 'Reconstruction,' p. 132.

[3] M. Tomara-Sideri, 'Oikonomiki Dinamiki kai Dimografiki Metavasis', *Epitheorisi Kinonikon Erevnon*, 80, 1991, pp. 75–6 : she found that the birth rate of the Ionian island of Lefkas averaged 28.9/1000 over the period 1823–1862, while the average mortality rate was 23.8.

[4] I base my discussion in this section largely on the excellent studies by Violetta Hionidou and Roxane Caftanzoglou. V. Hionidou, 'The Demographic System of a Mediterranean Island: Mykonos, Greece 1859–1959', *International Journal of Population Geography*, 1, 1995, pp. 125–46, 'Nineteenth-century Urban Greek Households: the Case of Hermoupolis, 1861–1879', *Continuity and Change*, 14, 1999, pp. 403–28, and 'Nuptiality Patterns and Household Structure on the Greek Island of Mykonos, 1849–1959', *Journal of Family History*, 20, 1995, pp. 67–103; R. Caftanzoglou, 'The Household Formation Pattern of a Vlach Mountain Community of Greece: Syrrako 1898–1929', *Journal of Family History*, 19, 1994, pp. 79–98 and 'Shepherds, Innkeepers, and Census-takers: The 1905 Census in Two Villages in Epirus', *Continuity and Change*, 12, 1997, pp. 403–24.

[5] Valaoras, 'Reconstruction,' p. 132.

[6] J.K. Campbell and P. Sherrard, *Modern Greece*, New York, 1968, p. 334. The centrality of the household in modern Greek society has been widely noted in the ethnographic literature.

[7] This discussion is based on Caftanzoglou, 'Shepherds, Innkeepers, and Census-takers,' Hionidou, 'The Case of Hermoupolis,' and P. Loizos and E. Papataxiarchis, 'Gender and Kinship in Marriage and Alternative Contexts', in P. Loizos and E. Papataxiarchis, eds, *Contested Identities: Gender and Kinship in Modern Greece*, Princeton, 1991, pp. 3–25. The comparative literature on this topic is vast; for a good discussion of the Greek data within a Balkan context, see: M. Todorova, *Balkan Family Structure and the European Pattern: Demographic Developments in Ottoman Bulgaria*, Washington, 1993.

[8] T.J. Bent, 'Greek Peasant Life', *The Fortnightly Review*, August, 1886, pp. 214.

[9] M. Couroucli, *Les Oliviers Du Lignage*, Paris, 1985. A similar tendency has been found among sharecropping families in Italy: D.I. Kertzer, *Family Life in Central Italy, 1880–1910: Sharecropping, Wage Labor and Coresidence*, New Brunswick, 1984.

[10] The feudal system of the Ionian islands is discussed later in this chapter; see pp. 94–5.

[11] P. Loizos and E. Papataxiarchis, 'Gender and Kinship in Marriage and Alternative Contexts', in Loizos *Contested Identities*, pp. 10–11; M. Couroucli, 'Dote et societe en Grèce moderne', in G. Augustins and G. Ravis-Giordani, eds, *Femmes et patrimoine dans les sociétés rurales de l'Europe méditerranéenne*, Paris, 1987, pp. 327–48; P. Sant Cassia, with Constantina Bada, *The Making of the Modern Greek Family: Marriage and Exchange in Nineteenth-Century Athens*, Cambridge, 1992.

¹² M. Herzfeld, *The Poetics of Manhood: Contest and Identity in a Cretan Mountain Village*, Princeton, 1985, pp. 56–60; P.H. Stahl, *Household, Village, and Village Confederation in Southeastern Europe*, New York, 1986; E.P. Alexakis, *Ta Yeni kai Oi Oikogenia stin Paradosiaki Koinonia tis Manis*, Athens, 1980.

¹³ E. Papataxiarchis, 'La valeur du ménages. Classes sociales, stratégies matrimoniales, et loi ecclésiastiques a Lesbos au XIXe siècle', in S.J. Woolf, ed., *Espaces et familles dans l'Europe du Sud l'age moderne*, Paris, 1993, pp. 109–42; Loizos and Papataxiarchis, 'Gender and Kinship,' pp. 9–10 ; B. Vernier, 'Putting Kin and Kinship to Good Use: The Circulation of Goods, Labour and Names on Karpathos (Greece)', in H. Medick and D.W. Sabean, eds, *Interest and Emotion: Essays on the Study of Family and Kinship*, New York, 1986, pp. 28–76.

¹⁴ V. Panayiotopulos, *Plithismos kai Oikismos tis Peloponnisou, 13os–18os Aionos*, Athens, 1985, pp. 195–215.

¹⁵ R. Rodd, *The Customs and Lore of Modern Greece*, London, 1892, pp. 56–7.

¹⁶ There are some truly excellent examples of traditional mountain houses preserved in the Zagorochoria region of Epiros.

¹⁷ Some of the most prominent works involved in these debates are: N.P. Mouzelis, *Modern Greece: Facets of Underdevelopment*, London, 1978; W.W. McGrew, *Land and Revolution in Modern Greece, 1800–1881. The Transition in the Tenure and Exploitation of Land From Ottoman Rule to Independence*, Kent, 1985; S. Damianakos, 'The Ongoing Quest for a Model of Greek Agriculture', *Sociologia Ruralis*, 37, 1997, pp. 190–208; Y. Dertilis, 'Introduction: structuration sociale et spécifités historiques (XVIIIe–XXe siècle)', in Y. Dertilis, ed., *Banquiers, usuriers et paysans: Réseaux de crédit et stratégies du capital en grèce*, Paris, 1988, pp. 11–32; A. Franghiadis, 'Dowry, Capital Accumulation and Social Reproduction in 19th Century Greek Agriculture', in S. Woolf, ed., *The World of the Peasantry*, Florence, 1993, pp. 129–53; A. Franghiadis, 'Réforme agraire et développement de la propriété individuelle en Grèce au XIXe siècle. La distribution des domianes nationaux 1871–1887', in S.J. Woolf, ed., *Espaces et familles dans l'Europe du Sud l' age moderne*, Paris, 1993, pp. 53–75; T.W. Gallant, *Risk and Survival in Ancient Greece: Reconstructing the Rural Domestic Economy*, Stanford, 1991; T. Kalafatis, *Agrotiki Pisti kai Ikonomikos Metaschimatismos sti V. Peloponnesos (Aiyialeia teli 19ou Aiona)*, Athens, 1990; C. Kasimis and A.G. Papadopoulos, 'Farming and Capitalist Development in Greek Agriculture. A Critical Review of the Literature', *Sociologia Ruralis*, 37, 1997, pp. 209–27; D.K. Psychogios, *Proikes, Phoroi, Staphida kai Psomi Oikonomia kai Oikogeneia stin Agrotiki Ellada tou 19. Aiona*, Athens, 1987; S. Seferiades, 'Small Rural Ownership, Subsistence Agriculture, and Peasant Protest in Interwar Greece: the Agrarian Question Recast', *Journal of Modern Greek Studies*, 17, 1999, pp. 277–324.

¹⁸ Gallant, *Risk*, pp. 41–5; H.A. Forbes, 'Dowry and Inheritance: Their Relationship to Land Fragmentation and Risk Reduction on Methana', in S.B. Sutton, ed., *Contingent Countryside: Settlement, Economy, and Land Use in the Southern Argolid Since 1700*, Stanford, 2000, pp. 200–27; K.W. Adams, 'Mutable Boundaries: Subdivision and Consolidation in a Greek Village, 1936–1978', in S.B. Sutton, ed., *Contingent Countryside: Settlement, Economy, and Land Use in the Southern Argolid Since 1700*, Stanford, 2000, pp. 228–40.

¹⁹ One of the most serious problems that confronted small owners who tried to generate a cash income from the cultivation of currants was that they had to rely on middlemen merchants to sell their crops. As we discussed elsewhere, the currants were

earmarked for the international markets of northern Europe, and so peasant farms had to sell their crops to merchants who would then transship the currants to the ports of Patras or Nafplion for foreign export. It should occasion little surprise to learn that merchants sought to purchase the grapes for the lowest price possible or that it was the peasant proprietors who were forced to bear the burden of price fluctuations. The small farmers had no choice since the middlemen effectively monopolized the marketing system.

[20] McGrew, *Land and Revolution*, pp. 207–14.

[21] Y. Dertilis, 'Réseaux du crédit et stratégies du capital', in Dertilis, *Banquiers, usuriers et paysans*, pp. 33–81; L. Fontaine, 'La montagne et la ville: le crédit enchaîné', in Y. Dertilis, ed., *Banquiers, usuriers et paysans: Réseaux de crédit et stratégies du capital en grèce*, Paris, 1988, pp. 95–104.

[22] Kassimis and Papadopoulos, 'Family Farming', p. 220.

[23] T.W. Gallant, 'Currant Production and Social Relations in the Ionian Islands during the 18th & 19th Centuries: Some Preliminary Thoughts', in *Proceedings of the Ies Jornades sobre la Viticultura de la Conca Mediterrania*, Tarragona, 1986, pp. 515–32; M.E. Franks, 'Cadastral Kerkyra: The World System in Eighteenth Century Venetian Commodity Production', *Journal of the Hellenic Diaspora*, 24, 1998, pp. 41–68.

[24] Y.A. Petropoulos, *Notariakai Praksis Kefallenias tis Silloyis E. Blessa Ton Eton 1701–1856*, Athens, 1962, pp. 441–3.

[25] S. Sotiropulos, *Trikonta Eks' Imeron Aixmalosia kai Simviosis meta Liston*, Athens, 1866, pp. 3–6; see also the description of similar estates in Rennell Rodd, *The Customs and Lore of Modern Greece*, London, 1892, p. 52–3.

[26] Farms of this type in Boiotia and Thessaly produced as their main cash crops cotton or tobacco rather than currants.

[27] T. Kolokotronis, *Apomnimonefmata*, Athens, 1977 [original 1851], p. 144.

[28] S.B. Sutton, 'Settlement Patterns, Settlement Perceptions: Rethinking the Greek Village', in P.N. Kardulias, ed., *Beyond the Site: Regional Studies in the Aegean Area*, Lanham, 1994, pp. 313–35.

[29] M. Stamatoyannopoulou, 'Déplacement saisonnier et exploitation rurale en Grèce dans la deuxième moitié du XIXe siècle. La cas de Krathis', in S.J. Woolf, ed., *Espaces et familles dans l'Europe du Sud l' age moderne*, Paris, 1993, pp. 205–213.

[30] We discussed earlier in this chapter the example of the men of Aristi in Epiros who specialized as innkeepers and who resided on a temporary basis in cities throughout the Balkans.

[31] The development of folklore studies in Greece was tied to the Fallmerayer debate about the degree of continuity between ancient and modern Greece. Believing that the peasantry was the repository of customs and traditions that proved the continuity thesis, scholars went to visit villages with the aim of recording the evidence that proved the case. See, M. Herzfeld, *Ours Once More: Folklore, Ideology and the Making of Modern Greece*, Austin, 1982.

[32] There are numerous examples of Greeks playing tricks on foreign visitors through fabrications and misinformation. One of my personal favorites involves Theodore Bent who records how he was told by an old 'witch' on Gatharonisi about the time that her household's flocks had been bewitched by the dreaded *skatopoúlia*, literally the 'shitbirds' (Bent, "Peasant Life," p. 216). One suspects that there was probably a good deal of laughter heard when the Englishman continued his travels elsewhere in Greece

and went from village to village asking people if they too had had problems with the awful shitbirds.

[33] V. Kirkwall, *Four Years in the Ionian Islands: Their Political and Social Conditions*, London, 1864, pp. 57–60.

[34] C.K. Tuckerman, *The Greeks of To-Day*, London, 1872, p. 340.

[35] T.W. Gallant, 'Honor, Masculinity, and Ritual Knife-fighting in Nineteenth Century Greece', *American Historical Review*, 105, 2000, pp. 359–60.

[36] E. About, *Greece and the Greeks of the Present Day*, London, 1857, p. 144.

[37] H.M. Baird, *Modern Greece: A Narrative of a Residence and Travels in That Country*, New York, 1856, pp. 71–2.

[38] P.S. Allen, 'La gestation des conflits dans le Magne: de la féodalité à l'adjudication', *Droit et Cultures*, 20, 1990, pp. 83–99.

[39] About, *Greece and the Greeks*, p. 134.

[40] Gallant, 'Honor', p. 368.

[41] T.W. Gallant, 'Turning the Horns: Cultural Metaphors, Material Conditions, and the Peasant Language of Resistance in Ionian Islands (Greece) during the Nineteenth Century', *Comparative Studies in Society and History*, 36, 1994, pp. 702–19.

[42] T.W. Gallant, 'Greek Bandit Gangs: Lone Wolves or a Family Affair?', *Journal of Modern Greek Studies*, 6, 1988, pp. 279–81 discusses the importance of fictive kinship among bandit families.

[43] *Evridiki*, 21 November 1870, cited in Sant Cassia and Bada, *Making*, pp. 223–4.

[44] E. Friedl, 'The Position of Women: Appearance and Reality', in J. Dubisch, ed., *Gender and Power in Rural Greece*, Princeton, 1986, pp. 42–52; for a good overview of this topic, an excellent starting point are the following collections of essays: J. Dubisch, ed., *Gender and Power in Rural Greece*, Princeton, 1986 and P. Loizos and E. Papataxiarchis, eds., *Contested Identities: Gender and Kinship in Modern Greece*, Princeton, 1991.

[45] T.W. Gallant, ' "We're all Whores Here!" Women, Slander and the Criminal Justice System', in *Experiencing Dominion: Culture, Identity and Resistance in Britain's Greek Empire* (unpublished manuscript).

[46] E. About, *Greece and the Greeks*, p. 162.

[47] E. Bastea, *The Creation of Modern Athens: Planning the Myth*, New York, 1999, p. 9.

[48] Bastea, *Creation*, p. 131.

[49] T.W. Gallant, 'Murder in a Mediterranean City: Homicide Trends in Athens, 1850–1936', *Journal of the Hellenic Diaspora*, 24, 1998, pp. 1–27.

[50] *Avgi*, January 13, 1895, col. 3 para. 4. Cited in Gallant, 'Murder', p. 23.

[51] H.M. Baird, *Modern Greece: A Narrative of a Residence and Travels in That Country*, New York, 1856, pp. 74–5.

[52] E. Kalligas, *I Pronia yia to Paidí stin Ellada to 19ou Aiona*, Ioannina, 1990.

[53] T.W. Gallant, 'Crime, Violence, and Reform of the Criminal Justice System during the Era of Trikoupis', in K. Aroni-Tsihli and L. Triha, eds, *O Harilaos Trikoupis and I Epochi tou*, Athens, 2000, 401–10.

[54] H.P. Fairchild, *Greek Immigration to the United States*, New Haven, 1911, pp. 72–3; the internal quotes refer to material that Fairchild cited from a report by the US Consul to Greece, George Horton, 'Report on Industrial Conditions in 1908.'

[55] L. Leontidou, *Polis tis Siopis: Ergatikos Epikismos tis Athinas kai Piraia 1909–1940*, Athens, 1989, p. 117.

[56] Gallant, 'Murder', p. 25. As the police chief of Sparti told Henry Pratt Fairchild (1911,

p. 191): '... since emigration had been so large Sparta had changed from a very turbulent locality to one of the quietest places imaginable. In fact, he said that not only his own district, but Greece in general, seemed to be pretty well rid of her more vicious criminals.'

Chapter 6

[1] L. Macrakis, 'Eleftherios Venizelos in Crete, 1864–1910: The Main Problems', in L. Macrakis and P. N. Diamandouros, eds, *New Trends in Modern Greek Historiography*, New Haven, 1982, p. 85.

[2] G.I. Panagiotakis, *O Venizelos stin Epanastasi kai tin Politiki*, Herakleion, 1993, pp. 15–65.

[3] R.F. Holland, 'Nationalism, Ethnicity and the Concert of Europe: the Case of the High Commissionership of Prince George of Greece in Crete, 1898–1906', *Journal of Modern Greek Studies*, 17, 1999, pp. 253–76; D. Dakin, *The Unification of Greece, 1770–1923*, London, 1972, pp. 171–2; S.V. Papacosma, *The Military in Greek Politics: The 1909 Coup D'Etat*, Kent, 1977, pp. 32–4; Panagiotakis, *Venizelos*, pp.67–151.

[4] Papacosma, *The Military in Politics*, p. 16.

[5] G. Augustinos, *Consciousness and History: Nationalist Critics of Greek Society, 1897–1914*, New York, 1977.

[6] A. Liakos, 'Problems on the Formation of the Greek Working Class', *Etudes Balkaniques*, 24, 1988, pp. 43–54. L. Apostolakou, ' "All for One and One for All": Anarchists, Socialists and Demoticists in the Labour Centre of Volos (1908–1911)', in P. Carabott, ed., *Greek Society in the Making, 1863–1913: Realities, Symbols and Visions*, Brookfield, 1997, pp. 35–54; L. Apostolakou, ' "Greek" Workers or Communist "Others": the Contending Identities of Organized Labour in Greece, c.1914–36', *Journal of Contemporary History*, 32, 1997, pp. 409–25; C. Hadziiossif, 'Class Structure and Class Antagonism in Late Nineteenth-century Greece', in P. Carabott, ed., *Greek Society in the Making, 1863–1913: Realities, Symbols and Visions*, Brookfield, 1997, pp. 3–19.

[7] B.C. Gounaris, 'Social Gatherings and Macedonian Lobbying: Symbols of Irredentism and Living Legends in Early Twentieth-century Athens,' in Carabott, *Greek Society in the Making*, pp. 99–113.

[8] P. Carabott, 'Politics, Orthodoxy and the Language Question in Greece: The Gospel Riots of November 1901', *Journal of Mediterranean Studies*, 3, 1993, pp. 117–38.

[9] S. Seferiades, 'Small Rural Ownership, Subsistence Agriculture, and Peasant Protest in Interwar Greece: the Agrarian Question Recast', *Journal of Modern Greek Studies*, 17, 1999, pp. 283–5, 310.

[10] Papacosma, *The Military in Politics*, pp. 17–27; T. Veremis, *The Military in Greek Politics From Independence to Democracy*, New York, 1997, pp. 43–4.

[11] Dakin, *Unification*, p. 311.

[12] G.J. Andreopoulos, 'Liberalism and the Formation of the Nation-state', *Journal of Modern Greek Studies*, 7, 1989, pp. 193–225.

[13] Of course, passing laws was only one side of the equation. How those laws were implemented and enforced was another matter all together. Efi Avedla has shown the ways that the laws regarding women and children in the workplace produced deleterious consequences unintended by the lawmakers: E. Avdela, ' "To Protect the Most Weak and Needy": Women's Protective Labor Legislation in Greece', in U. Wikander, A. Kessler-Harris, and J. Lewis, eds, *Protecting Women: Comparative Essays*

on *Labor Legislation in Europe, the United States, and Australia, 1890–1920,* Urbana, 1995, pp. 290–317; and 'Contested Meanings: Protection and Resistance in Labour Inspectors' Reports in Twentieth-Century Greece', *Gender & History,* 9, 1997, pp. 310–32.

¹⁴ The best starting place for an assessment of the accomplishments and failures of the liberal regime is the following collection of essays: G.Th. Mavrogordatos and Ch. Hatsiosiff, eds, *Venizélismos kai Astikós Eksinkronismós,* Athens, 1988 and T. Veremis and G. Goulimi, eds, *Eleftherios Venizelso: Kinonía-Ikonomía-Politiki Stin Epohi Tou,* Athens, 1989.

¹⁵ D. Dakin, *The Greek Struggle in Macedonia 1897–1913,* Thessaloniki, 1993; G. Agelopoulos, 'Perceptions, Constructions, and Definitions of Greek National identity in Late Nineteenth-early Twentieth Century Macedonia', *Balkan Studies,* 36, 1995, p. 247; A.N. Karakasidou, *Fields of Wheat, Hills of Blood: Passages to Nationhood in Greek Macedonia, 1870–1990,* Chicago, 1997, pp. 108–37; D.M. Perry, *The Politics of Terror: The Macedonian Revolutionary Movements, 1893–1903,* Durham, 1988.

¹⁶ Dakin, *Unification,* pp. 195–200; J. Van der Kiste, *Kings of the Hellenes: The Greek Kings, 1863–1919,* London, 1994, pp. 73–5.

¹⁷ Konstantine in fact held the rank of Field Marshall in the German Imperial army. There was no personal love lost between the Danish-descended monarch and his overbearing brother-in-law. Nonetheless, the relationship put real pressure on the Greek king to act cautiously toward the Reich, and the French in particular were piqued by comments made by Konstantine at a banquet in Berlin that singled out Germany for its assistance during the Balkan Wars.

¹⁸ Cited in M.L. Smith, *Ionian Vision: Greece in Asia Minor 1919–1922,* London, 1998, 2nd ed., p. xiii.

¹⁹ Van der Kiste, *Kings,* p. 93; the church on Tinos where the miraculous icon is housed and is still visited by thousands of pilgrims each year: J. Dubisch, 'Pilgrimage and Popular Religion at a Greek Holy Shrine', in E. Badone, ed., *Religious Orthodoxy and Popular Faith in European Society,* Princeton, 1990, pp. 113–39 and J. Dubisch, *In a Different Place Pilgrimage, Gender, and Politics at a Greek Island Shrine,* Princeton, 1995.

²⁰ G.B. Leon, *Greece and the Great Powers, 1914–1917,* Thessaloniki, 1974.

²¹ My discussion in this and the following section relies primarily on: N. Petsales-Diomedes, *I Ellada ton Dyo Kyverneseon, 1916–17: Kathestotika, Diplomatika kai Ekonomika Provlemata tou Ethniko Dichasmou,* Athens, 1988; T. Veremis, 'The Greek Officer Corps in Greece, 1912–1936', *Byzantine and Modern Greek Studies,* II, 1976, pp. 113–33.

²² Dakin, *Unification,* p. 215.

²³ Y.G. Mourelos, 'British Policy Toward King Constantine's Dethronement and Greece's Entry into the War', in K. Svolopoulos, ed., *Greece and Great Britain During World War I,* Thessaloniki, 1985, pp. 134–5.

²⁴ Dakin, *Unification,* p. 216.

Chapter 7

¹ M. L. Smith, *Ionian Vision: Greece in Asia Minor 1919–1922,* London, 1998, 2nd ed., p. 67. The best discussion of the peace conference in English remains N. Petsales-Diomedes, *Greece at the Paris Peace Conference (1919),* Thessaloniki, 1978.

² Smith, *Ionian Vision,* p. xvi,

[3] M. Mazower, 'The Messiah and the Bourgeoisie: Venizelos and Politics in Greece, 1909–1922', *Historical Journal*, 35, 1992, cited on p. 904.

[4] M. Mazower, *Greece and the Inter-War Economic Crisis*, Oxford, 1991, p. 55.

[5] G.B. Leondaritis, *Greece and the First World War: From Neutrality to Intervention, 1917–1918*, New York, 1990; A. Liakos, *Ergasia kai Politiki stin Ellada tou Mespolemou. To Diethnes Grafio Ergasias kai i Anadisi ton Kinonikon Thesmon*, Athens, 1993; L. Apostolakou, ' "Greek" Workers or Communist "Others": the Contending Identities of Organized Labour in Greece, c.1914–36', *Journal of Contemporary History*, 32, 1997, pp. 409–25; K. Moskof, *Istoria tou Kinimatos tis Ergatikis Taksis*, Athina, 1988.

[6] G. Hering, *Die Politischen Parteien in Griechenland 1821–1936*, München, 1992, pp. 792–851; Smith, *Ionian Vision*, pp. 152–179.

[7] A.J. Toynbee, *The Western Question in Greece and Turkey*, New York, 1922, p. 252.

[8] Smith, *Ionian Vision*, p. 227.

[9] G. Horton, *The Blight of Asia an Account of the Systematic Extermination of Christian Populations by Mohammedans and of the Culpability of Certain Great powers; With a True Story of the Burning of Smyrna*, Indianapolis, 1926, p. 119.

[10] E. Hemingway, *Dateline Toronto: The Complete Toronto Star Dispatches, 1920–1924*, New York, 1985, p. 232.

[11] H. Morgenthau, *I Was Sent to Athens*, Garden City, 1929, pp. 48–9.

[12] D. Giannuli, 'American Philanthropy in Action: The American Red Cross in Greece, 1918–1923', *East European Politics and Societies*, 10, 1996, pp. 108–33.

[13] Mazower, *Greece and the Inter-War Economic Crisis*, pp.79–91.

[14] The best discussion of this process is in: A.N. Karakasidou, *Fields of Wheat, Hills of Blood : Passages to Nationhood in Greek Macedonia, 1870–1990*, Chicago, 1997, pp. 164–186. Her analysis has now been amply buttressed by the detailed work by Seferiades (S. Seferiades, 'Small Rural Ownership, Subsistence Agriculture, and Peasant Protest in Interwar Greece: the Agrarian Question Recast', *Journal of Modern Greek Studies*, 17, 1999, pp. 277–324).

[15] Mazower, *Greece and the Inter-War Economic Crisis*, pp. 91–100.

[16] Antonis Dalgas recorded the song in Athens around 1930. He was born in Constantinople in 1892 and migrated to Athens in the mid-1920s. One of the greatest Greek singers of the century, he died in Athens in 1945.

[17] R. Hirschon, *Heirs of the Catastrophe: The Social Life of Asia Minor Refugees in Piraeus*, Oxford, 1989, p. 31.

[18] The novel was first published in 1945. The passage reproduced here is taken from T. Doulis, *Disaster and Fiction: Modern Greek Fiction and the Impact of the Asia Minor Disaster of 1922*, Berkeley, 1977, pp. 64–5.

[19] A. Rihos, *I V' Elliniki Dimokratias 1924–1935, Kinonikes Diastasis tis Politikis Skinis*, Athens, 1988, p. 175.

[20] G. Theotokas, *Argos*, Athens, 1951, p. 101.

[21] The quote is from the polemical tract D*iati Eimathe Vasilofrones [Why We Are Royalists]*, published in Athens in 1935 by Xenophon Hatzisarandos and cited in G.Th. Mavrogordatos, *Stillborn Republic: Social Coalitions and Party Strategies in Greece, 1922–1936*, Berkeley, 1983, p. 62.

[22] Mavrogordatos, *Stillborn Republic*, pp. 111–81.

[23] S.E. Aschenbrenner, *Live in a Changing Greek Village: Karpofora and Its Reluctant Farmers*, Dubuque, 1986, pp. 90–91.

24 Mavrogordatos, *Stillborn Republic*, pp. 210–11.

25 D.H. Close, *The Origins of the Greek Civil War*, New York, 1995, pp. 24–7.

26 J.S. Koliopoulos, *Greece and the British Connection 1935–1941*, Oxford, 1977, p. 43.

27 P.J. Vatikiotis, *Popular Autocracy in Greece, 1936–41: a Political Biography of General Ioannis Metaxas*, London, 1998, 185–95.

28 D.H. Close, 'The Police in the Fourth-of-August Regime', *Journal of the Hellenic Diaspora*, 13, 1986, pp. 91–106; M.E. Kenna, 'The Social Organization of Exile: The Everday Life of Political Exiles in the Cyclades in the 1930s', *Journal of Modern Greek Studies*, 9, 1991, pp. 63–81.

29 M. Pelt, *Tobacco, Arms and Politics: Greece and Germany From World Crisis to World War 1929–41*, Denmark, 1998, pp. 185–93.

Chapter 8

1 D.H. Close, *The Origins of the Greek Civil War*, New York, 1995, p. 54.

2 Close, *Origins*, p. 55.

3 M. Pelt, *Tobacco, Arms and Politics: Greece and Germany From World Crisis to World War 1929–41*, Denmark, 1998, pp. 250–51.

4 P.J. Vatikiotis, *Popular Autocracy in Greece, 1936–41 a Political Biography of General Ioannis Metaxas*, London, Portland, 1998, p. 214. The official cause of death was septicemia brought on by a streptococcus infection. Metaxas had in fact been ill with various ailments for some time, among them was a serious kidney infection that may have finally claimed his life.

5 The passage was taken from the journal of Lieutant-Colonel R.P. Weller and was quoted in I.McD.G. Stewart, *The Struggle for Crete*, New York, 1991, pp. 18–19.

6 H.-J. Hoppe, 'Germany, Bulgaria, Greece: Their Relations and Bulgarian Policy in Occupied Greece', *Journal of the Hellenic Diaspora*, 11, 1984, pp. 41–54.

7 J.S. Koliopoulos, *Plundered Loyalties: World War II and Civil War in Greek West Macedonia*, New York, 1999, p. 54.

8 E. Averoff-Tossizza, *The Call of the Earth*, New Rochelle, 1981, p. 195. Though the passage cited here is fictional, it is supported by historical accounts of the activities of the Vlach legionnaires; see Koliopoulos, *Plundered Loyalties*, pp. 81–90.

9 Cited in M. Mazower, *Inside Hitler's Greece: The Experience of Occupation, 1941–1944*, New Haven, 1993, p. 32.

10 Mazower, *Inside Hitler's Greece*, pp. 23–72; J.L. Hondros, *Occupation and Resistance: The Greek Agony 1941–1944*, New York, 1978, pp. 61–76; S.B. Thomadakis, 'Black Markets, Inflation and Force in the Economy of Occupied Greece,' in J.O. Iatrides, ed., *Greece in the 1940s: A Nation in Crisis*, Hanover, 1981, pp. 61–80.

11 A. Avgoustidis, 'EEAM: The Workers' Resistance', *Journal of the Hellenic Diaspora*, 11, 1984, pp. 55–68.

12 J.O. Iatrides, 'Greece at the Crossroads, 1944–1950', in J.O. Iatrides and L. Wrigley, eds, *Greece at the Crossroads: The Civil War and Its Legacy*, University Park, 1995, p. 20.

13 H. Fleischer, 'The National Liberation Front (EAM), 1941–1947: A Reassessment', in Iatrides, *Greece at the Crossroads*, pp. 48–89; H. Vlavianos, *Greece, 1941–1949: From Resistance to Civil War: The Strategy of the Greek Communist Party*, New York, 1992; L.S. Stavrianos, 'The Greek National Liberation Front (EAM). A Study in Resistance Organization and Administration', *Journal of Modern History*, 24:1, 1952, pp. 42–55.

[14] Quoted in D. Eudes, *The Kapitanios: Partisans and Civil War in Greece 1943–1949*, London, 1975, p. 6.

[15] Close, *Origins*, p. 100.

[16] O.L. Smith, ' "The First Round" – Civil War during the Occupation', in D.H. Close, ed., *The Greek Civil War, 1943–1950: Studies of Polarization*, New York, 1993, pp. 60–61.

[17] The passage was taken from an affidavit sworn to by a soldier who had taken part in the massacre. Quoted in M. Mazower, 'Military Violence and National Socialist Values: The Wehrmacht in Greece, 1941–1944', *Past & Present*, 134, 1992, pp. 129–30.

[18] A. Gerolymatos, 'The Security Battalions and the Civil War', *Journal of the Hellenic Diaspora*, 12, 1985, pp. 17–28; J.L. Hondros, 'Greece and the German Occupation', in Close, *The Greek Civil War*, pp. 50–51; Mazower, *Inside Hitler's Greece*, pp. 324–5.

[19] A. Kitroeff, *War-Time Jews the Case of Athens*, Athens, 1995 and his article, 'Documents: The Jews in Greece, 1941–1944 – Eyewitness Accounts', *Journal of the Hellenic Diaspora*, 12, 1985, pp. 5–32; Mazower, *Inside Hitler's Greece*, pp. 235–61.

[20] P. Papastratis, *British Policy Towards Greece During the Second World War 1941–1944*, Cambridge, 1984, pp. 148–60.

[21] C.M. Woodhouse, *Apple of Discord: A Survey of Recent Greek Politics in the International Setting*, Reston, 1948 [rpt. 1985], p. 47.

[22] J. Hart, *New Voices in the Nation: Women and the Greek Resistance, 1941–1964*, Ithaca, 1996, p. 104.

[23] Papastratis, *British Policy*, pp. 198–200; P.J. Stavrakis, *Moscow and Greek Communism, 1944–1949*, Ithaca, NY, 1989, pp. 15–35.

[24] Close, *Origins*, p.108.

[25] Close, *Origins*, p. 118.

[26] L. Baerentzen and D.H. Close, 'The British Defeat of EAM, 1944–5', in Close, *The Greek Civil War*, pp. 79.

[27] O.L. Smith, 'Communist Perceptions, Strategies, and Tactics, 1945–1949', in Iatrides, *Greece at the Crossroads*, pp. 90–121; O.L. Smith, ' "The First Round" – Civil War During the Occupation', in D.H. Close, ed., *The Greek Civil War, 1943–1950: Studies of Polarization*, New York, 1993, pp. 58–71.

[28] G. Chandler, *The Divided Land: An Anglo–Greek Tragedy*, London, 1959 [revised 1994], p. 31.

[29] L. Baerentzen, 'The Demonstration in Syntagma Square on Sunday 3rd December 1944', *Scandinavian Studies in Modern Greek*, 2, 1978, pp. 3–52. This is not only the best account of the incident, but Baerentzen was also able to find a large number of photographs that vividly capture the moment of the shootings.

[30] Stavrakis, *Moscow and Greek Communism*, pp. 37–8.

[31] Close, *Origins*, pp. 137–45; H. Richter, 'The Varkiza Agreement and the Origins of the Civil War', in J.O. Iatrides, ed., *Greece in the 1940s: A Nation in Crisis*, Hanover, 1981, pp. 167–80.

[32] N.C. Alivisatos, 'The "Emergency Regime" and Civil Liberties, 1946–1949', in Iatrides, *Greece in the 1940s*, pp. 220–28.

[33] C. Chiclet, 'The Greek Civil War 1946–1949', in M. Sarafis and M. Eve, eds, *Background to Contemporary Greece*, New York, 1990, p. 209.

[34] A. Collard, 'The Experience of Civil War in the Mountain Villages of Central Greece', in M. Sarafis and M. Eve, eds, *Background to Contemporary Greece*, New York, 1990, pp. 223–254, this quote is taken from p. 236 and the previous one from p. 238.

[35] L.S. Wittner, *American Intervention in Greece 1943–1949*, New York, 1982; H. Jones, *'A New Kind of War': America's Global Strategy and the Truman Doctrine in Greece*, Oxford, 1989.

Chapter 9

[1] This term, or one that carries a similar sense, has been employed by a number of scholars: J.V. Kofas, 'The Greek Economy', in M. Sarafis and M. Eve, eds, *Background to Contemporary Greece*, New York, 1990, p. 54; see also his J.V. Kofas, *Intervention and Underdevelopment: Greece During the Cold War*, College Park, 1989; A.A. Fatouros, 'Building Formal Structures of Penetration: The United States in Greece, 1947–1948', in J.O. Iatrides, ed., *Greece in the 1940s: A Nation in Crisis*, Hanover, 1981, pp. 239–58; P. Murtagh, *The Rape of Greece: the King, the Colonels and the Resistance*, London, New York, 1994, pp. 16–21.

[2] The figures cited here were compiled from: Kofas, 'Greek Economy', pp. 81, 87; W.H. McNeill, *Greece: American Aid in Action, 1947–1956*, New York, 1957; B. Sweet-Escott, *Greece. A Political and Economic Survey 1939–1953*, London, 1954.

[3] Cited in L.S. Wittner, *American Intervention in Greece 1943–1949*, New York, 1982, p. 71: Acheson's comments were made in a meeting with a Congressional delegation before Truman's address to the full Congress, in which the Secretary of State was trying to explain why Greece was so important. A recent reassessment suggests that Dean Acheson was in fact the primary driving force for the US decision to intervene in Greece: R. Frazier, 'Acheson and the Formulation of the Truman Doctrine', *Journal of Modern Greek Studies*, 17, 1999, pp. 229–52.

[4] Kofas, 'Greek Economy', p. 87.

[5] This quote comes from a memorandum by Dwight Griswold, the official chosen to head AMAG, and was taken from: Fatouros, 'Building Structures', p. 249.

[6] Y.P. Roubatis, *Tangled Webs: The US in Greece 1947–1967*, New York, 1987, p. 77, reproduces a National Security Council Memorandum that makes this point explicitly.

[7] N.K. Alivizatos, 'The Greek Army in the Late Forties: Towards an Institutional Autonomy', *Journal of the Hellenic Diaspora*, 5, 1978, pp. 37–45; M.M. Amen, 'American Institutional Penetration into Greek Military and Political Policy-Making Structures: June 1947–October 1949', *Journal of the Hellenic Diaspora*, 5, 1978, pp. 89–113.

[8] G. Stathakis, 'US Economic Policies in Post Civil-War Greece, 1949–1953: Stabilization and Monetary Reform', *Journal of European Economic History*, 24, 1995, pp. 375–405.

[9] Wittner, *American Intervention*, p. 137.

[10] J. Hart, 'Tales from the Walled City: Aesthetics of Political Prison Culture in Post-war Greece', *Comparative Studies in Society and History*, 41, 1999, pp. 484–5.

[11] C. Tsoucalas, 'The Ideological Impact of the Civil War', in Iatrides, *Greece in the 1940s*, pp. 319–41.

[12] Quoted in Wittner, *American Intervention*, p. 103.

[13] R. Clogg, *Parties and Elections in Greece: The Search for Legitimacy*, London, 1988, pp. 17–32; K.R. Legg, *Politics in Modern Greece*, Stanford, 1969, pp. 74–5, 147–8; K. Tsoukalas, *Kratos, Kinonia, Ergasia Stin Metapolemiki Ellada*, Athens, 1987, pp. 27–8.

[14] C.M. Woodhouse, *Karamanlis: The Restorer of Greek Democracy*, Oxford, 1982.

[15] G. Augustinos, 'Development Through the Market in Greece: The State, Entrepreneurs

and Society', in G. Augustinos, ed., *Diverse Paths to Modernity in Southeastern Europe: Essays in National Development*, Westport, 1991, pp. 89–134.

[16] Sweet-Escott, *Greece*, pp. 94, 98, 143.

[17] W.H. McNeill, *The Metamorphosis of Greece Since World War II*, Oxford, 1978, pp. 143–4.

[18] S. Damianakos, 'The Ongoing Quest for a Model of Greek Agriculture', *Sociologia Ruralis*, 37, 1997, pp. 190–208; C. Kasimis and A.G. Papadopoulos, 'Farming and Capitalist Development in Greek Agriculture. A Critical Review of the Literature', *Sociologia Ruralis*, 37, 1997, pp. 209–27; C. Kasimis and A.G. Papadopoulos, 'The heterogeneity of Greek family farming: Emerging policy principles', *Sociologia Ruralis*, 34, 1994, pp. 206–28.

[19] E. Friedl, *Vasilika: A Village in Modern Greece*, New York, 1962.

[20] I. Sanders, *Rainbow in the Rock. The People of Rural Greece*, Cambridge, 1962, pp. 59–69.

[21] J.K. Campbell, *Honour, Family and Patronage. A Study of Institutional and Moral Values in a Greek Mountain Community*, Oxford, 1964.

[22] Though the introduction of new technologies clearly improved overall incomes for farming households, it may also have had deleterious implications for some sectors of society. Maria Stratigaki, for example, has argued that modernization and mechanization of agriculture have diminished women's roles in rural society. M. Stratigaki, 'Agricultural Modernization and Gender Division of Labor – the Case of Herakleion, Greece', *Sociologia Ruralis*, 28, 1988, pp. 248–62.

[23] J. du Boulay, *Portrait of a Greek Mountain Village*, Oxford, 1974, pp. 27–38; A.A. Pepelasis and K. Thompson, 'Agriculture in a Restrictive Environment: the Case of Greece', *Economic Geography*, 36, 1960, pp. 145–57; P. Halstead and G. Jones, 'Agrarian Ecology in the Greek Islands: Time Stress, Sale, and Risk', *Journal of Hellenic Studies*, 109, 1989, pp. 41–55; M.H. Clarke, 'The Changing Household Economy on Methana, 1880–1996', in S.B. Sutton, eds, *Contingent Countryside: Settlement, Economy, and Land Use in the Southern Argolid Since 1700*, Stanford, 2000, pp. 183–9; S.E. Aschenbrenner, *Live in a Changing Greek Village: Karpofora and Its Reluctant Farmers*, Dubuque, 1986, pp. H.A. Forbes, *Strategies and Soils: Technology, Production and Environment In the Peninsula of Methana, Greece*, University of Pennsylvania, 1982; S. Damianakos, ed., *Procedures of Community Transition in Agricultural Greece*, Athens, 1987.

[24] The news report by Nancy Crawshaw appeared in the *Manchester Guardian* in April 1953 and was reproduced in Sweet-Escott, *Greece*, p. 132.

[25] J.J. Baxevanis, 'Population, Internal Migration and Urbanization in Greece', *Balkan Studies*, 6, 1965, pp. 83–98; B. Kayser, P.-Y. Pechoux, and M. Sivignon, *Exode Rural et Attraction Urbaine en Grèce*, Athens, 1971.

[26] L. Leontidou, *The Mediterranean City in Transition: Social Change and Urban Development*, Cambridge, 1989, pp. 127–55; C.V. Patton and C.M. Sophoulis, 'Unauthorized Suburban Housing Production in Greece', *Urban Geography*, 10, 1989, pp. 139–56.

[27] S.B. Sutton, 'Rural-Urban Migration in Greece', in M. Kenny and D.I. Kertzer, eds, *Urban Life in Mediterranean Europe: Anthropological Perspectives*, Urbana, 1983, p. 243.

[28] Friedl, *Vasilika*, pp. 52, 55; P.S. Allen, 'Female Inheritance, Housing and Urbanization in Greece', *Anthropology*, 10, 1986, pp. 1–18.

[29] M. Kenna, 'Institutional and Transformational Migration and the Politics of Community: Greek Internal Migrants and their Migrants' Association in Athens', *Archive of European Sociology*, 24, 1983, pp. 263–87.

[30] J. Andromedas, 'The Enduring Urban Ties of Modern Greek Folk Subculture', in J.G. Peristiany, ed., *Contributions to Mediterranean Sociology*, Paris, 1963, pp. 269–73; J. Dubisch, 'The City as Resource: Migration from a Greek Island Village', *Urban Anthropology*, 6, 1977, pp. 65–81.

[31] Sanders, *Rainbow in the Rock*, p. 296; for an extended treatment of this topic see J.A. Costa, 'The History of Migration and Political Economy in Rural Greece: A Case Study', *Journal of Modern Greek Studies*, 6, 1988, pp. 159–86.

[32] Leontidou, *The Mediterranean City*, pp. 105–9; H. Louri, 'Urban-growth and Productivity: The Case of Greece', *Urban Studies*, 25, 1988, pp. 433–8; W.O. Candilis, *The Economy of Greece, 1944–1966: Efforts for Stability and Development*, New York, 1968; A.F. Freris, *The Greek Economy in the Twentieth Century*, New York, 1986, pp. 128–54.

[33] S.B. Sutton, 'Family and Work: New Patterns for Village Women in Athens', *Journal of Modern Greek Studies*, 4, 1986, pp. 33–50; H. Symeonidou-Alatopoulou, 'Female Labour Force Participation in Greece', *Epitheorisi Koinonikon Erevnon*, 1980, pp. 104–20. I. Lambire-Demake, *Women Factory Workers in a Greek Rural Town*, Athens, 1961; I. Lambiri, *Social Change in a Greek Country Town: the Impact of Factory Work on the Position of Women*, Athens, 1965; R. Hirschon, 'Under One Roof: Marriage, Dowry, and Family Relations in Piraeus', in M. Kenny and D.I. Kertzer, eds, *Urban Life in Mediterranean Europe: Anthropological Perspectives*, Urbana, 1983, pp. 299–323; J. Cavounides, 'Capitalist Development and Women's Work in Greece', *Journal of Modern Greek Studies*, 1, 1983, pp. 321–38.

[34] P.D. Chimbos, 'The Greeks in Canada: an Historical and Sociological Perspective', in R. Clogg, ed., *The Greek Diaspora in the Twentieth Century*, New York, 1999, pp. 87–102; N. Doumanis, 'The Greeks in Australia', in Clogg, *The Greek Diaspora*, pp. 58–86; G. Bottomley, *After the Odyssey: A Study of Greeks in Australia*, St. Lucia, 1979.

[35] K. Unger, 'Greek Emigration To and Return From West Germany', *Ekistics*, 48, 1981, pp. 369–74; X.E. Zolotas, *International Labor Migration and Economic Development, With Special Reference to Greece*, Athens, 1966.

[36] C.M. Woodhouse, *Karamanlis: The Restorer of Greek Democracy*, Oxford, 1982, p. 103.

[37] P.S. Cassia, 'Religion, Politics and Ethnicity in Cyprus during the Turkokratia (1571–1878)', *Archives of European Sociology*, 27, 1986, pp. 3–28; P.S. Cassia, 'Banditry, Myth, and Terror in Cyprus and Other Mediterranean Societies', *Comparative Studies in Society and History*, 35, 1993, pp. 773–96.

[38] S. Panteli, *A New History of Cyprus*, London, 1984, pp. 138–55; for developments during the 1940s, pp. 156–236.

[39] Cited in H. Richter, 'The Greek-Turkish Conflict', in: M. Sarafis and M. Eve, eds, *Background to Contemporary Greece*, New York, 1990, pp. 316–59.

[40] N. Crawshaw, *The Cyprus Revolt: An Account of the Struggle for Union With Greece*, London, 1978, pp. 77–83.

[41] Crawshaw, *The Cyprus Revolt*, p. 114.

[42] Woodhouse, *Karamanlis*, p. 77.

[43] C.W. McCaskill, 'Cyprus Twenty-five Years Later: An American Diplomat Looks Back', *Journal of Modern Greek Studies*, 9, 1991, pp. 28–30; Crawshaw, *The Cyprus Revolt*, pp. 340–51; E. Averoff-Tossizza, *Lost Opportunities: The Cyprus Question, 1950–1963*, New Rochelle, 1986, pp. 331–62; E.D.A. Vlanton, 'The 1959 Cyprus Agreement: Oracle of Disaster', *Journal of the Hellenic Diaspora*, 11, 1984, pp. 5–8.

⁴⁴ Clogg, *Politics*, pp. 43–8.

⁴⁵ Woodhouse, *Karamanlis*, p. 141.

⁴⁶ N. Antonakis, 'Military Expenditure and Economic Growth in Greece, 1960–90', *Journal of Peace Research*, 34, 1997, pp. 89–101; V.K. Kapetanyannis, *Socio-Political Conflicts and Military Interventions: The Case of Greece, 1950–1967*, University of London, 1986.

⁴⁷ Woodhouse, *Karamanlis*, p. 148.

⁴⁸ Freris, *The Greek Economy*, pp. 163–5.

⁴⁹ T.W. Gallant, 'Collective Action and Atomistic Actors: Labor Unions, Strikes, and Crime in Greece in the Post-war Era', in T. Stavrou and D. Constas, eds, *Greece Toward the 21st Century*, Baltimore, 1995, pp. 160–63.

⁵⁰ Y.P. Roubatis, *Tangled Webs: The US in Greece 1947–1967*, New York, 1987, pp. 185–99.

⁵¹ P. Murtagh, *The Rape of Greece*, pp. 70–105; Clogg, *Parties*, pp. 48–53.

Chapter 10

¹ T. Veremis, *The Military in Greek Politics From Independence to Democracy*, New York, 1997, p. 153; for a detailed list of the group's membership see R. McDonald, 'The Colonel's Dictatorship 1967–1974', in M. Sarafis and M. Eve, eds, *Background to Contemporary Greece*, New York, 1990, pp. 216–2.

² P. Murtagh, *The Rape of Greece: the King, the Colonels and the Resistance*, London, New York, 1994, pp. 106–8.

³ Murtagh, *Rape*, p. 118.

⁴ Veremis, *Military*, p. 159.

⁵ The story of Andreas Papandreou's arrest is movingly told in *Nightmare in Athens*, London, 1970, written by his then wife Margaret.

⁶ Quoted in C.M. Woodhouse, *The Rise and Fall of the Greek Colonels*, London, 1982, p. 35

⁷ Woodhouse, *The Greek Colonels*, pp. 49–73.

⁸ D.K. Katsoudas, 'The Media', in K. Featherstone and D.K. Katsoudas, eds, *Political Change in Greece: Before the Colonels and After*, New York, 1987, p. 195.

⁹ R. McDonald, *Pillar and Tinderbox: The Greek Press and the Dictatorship*, London, 1982.

¹⁰ A.F. Freris, *The Greek Economy in the Twentieth Century*, New York, 1986, pp. 161–3; N. Bermeo, 'Classification and Consolidation: Some Lessons from the Greek Dictatorship', *Political Science Quarterly*, Fall, 1995, pp. 437–8; T. Giannitsis, 'Transformation and Problems of Greek Industry: The Experience of the Period 1974–1985', in S. Vryonis Jr, ed., *Greece on the Road to Democracy: From the Junta to PASOK 1974–1986*, New Rochelle, 1991, pp. 217–18; T.W. Gallant, 'Collective Action and Atomistic Actors: Labor Unions, Strikes, and Crime in Greece in the Post-war Era', in T. Stavrou and D. Constas, eds, *Greece Toward the 21st Century*, Baltimore, 1995, pp. 154–5; G. Yannopoulos, 'Workers and Peasants under the Military Dictatorship', in R. Clogg and G. Yannopoulos, eds, *Greece Under Military Rule*, New York, 1972, pp. 109–26.

¹¹ McDonald, 'The Colonels', pp. 279–80; Murtagh, *Rape*, 201–8; S.W. Rousseas, *The Death of Democracy: Greece and the American Conscience*, New York, 1967, pp. 99–114; V. Coufoudakis, 'Greek Foreign Police, 1945–1985', in K. Featherstone and D.K. Katsoudas, eds, *Political Change in Greece: Before the Colonels and After*, New York, 1987, pp. 233–4; L. Stern, *The Wrong Horse: The Politics of Intervention and the Failure of American Diplomacy*, New York, 1977.

[12] Amnesty International, *The First Torturers' Trial 1975*, London, 1977; J. Becket, *Barbarism in Greece*, New York, 1970; P. Korovessis, *The Method*, London, 1970, contains chilling accounts of the brutal torture carried out by the junta's secret police.

[13] G. Mylonas, *Escape From Amorgos*, New York, 1974.

[14] M. Theodorakis, *Journals of Resistance*, London, 1973; K. Van Dyck, *Kassandra and the Censors: Greek Poetry Since 1967*, Ithaca, NY, 1998; S.E. Constantinidis, 'Existential Protest in Greek Drama during the Junta', *Journal of Modern Greek Studies*, 3, 2, 1985, pp. 137–44.

[15] Woodhouse, *The Colonels*, pp.126–41; K. Andrews, *Greece in the Dark 1967–1974*, Amsterdam, 1980.

[16] K.C. Makrides, *The Rise and Fall of the Cyprus Republic*, Yale University Press, pp. 122–177; P. Loizos, *The Heart Grown Bitter*, Cambridge, 1987.

[17] According to the 'official' tally, 92 per cent of the people voted in favor of the new constitution. R. McDonald, 'The Colonel's Dictatorship 1967–1974', in M. Sarafis and M. Eve, eds., *Background to Contemporary Greece*, New York, 1990, p. 275.

[18] Murtagh, *Rape*, pp. 254–5; C.M. Woodhouse, *Karamanlis: The Restorer of Greek Democracy*, Oxford, 1982, pp. 208–9; Woodhouse, *The Colonels*, pp. 166–7.

[19] D.K. Katsoudas, 'The Constitutional Framework', in Featherstone, *Political Change in Greece*, pp. 19–21.

[20] Woodhouse, *Karamanlis*, pp. 214–16. This celebrated phrase became proverbial, though it appears that Karamanlis never used those exact words. The gist of his harangue, however, was much the same.

[21] D. Kitsikis, 'Greek Communism and the Karamanlis Government', *Problems of Communism*, 26, 1977, pp. 42–56.

[22] R. Clogg, *Parties and Elections in Greece: The Search for Legitimacy*, London, 1988, pp. 60–61; D.K. Katsoudas, 'The Conservative Movement and New Democracy: From Past to Present', in Featherstone, *Political Change in Greece*, pp. 85–111; New Democracy: In or Out of Social Democracy?', in S. Vryonis Jr, ed., *Greece on the Road to Democracy: From the Junta to PASOK 1974–1986*, New Rochelle, 1991, pp. 1–14.

[23] Katsoudas, 'The Constitutional Framework', pp. 21–7; A. Pollis, 'The State, the Law and Human-Rights in Modern Greece', *Human Rights Quarterly*, 9, 1987, pp. 587–614; A. Pollis, 'Greek National Identity: Religious Minorities, Rights and European Norms', *Journal of Modern Greek Studies*, 10, 1992, pp. 171–96; A. Pollis, 'Eastern Orthodoxy and Human Rights', *Human Rights Quarterly*, 15, 1993, pp. 339–56.

[24] V. Coufoudakis, 'Greece and the Problem of Cyprus 1974–1986', in Vryonis, *Greece on the Road to Democracy*, pp. 125–132.

[25] T. Bahcheli, T.A. Couloumbis, and P. Carley, *Greek-Turkish Relations and U.S. Foreign Policy: Cyprus, the Aegean, and Regional Stability*, Washington, 1997; M. Stearns, *Entangled Allies: U.S. Policy Toward Greece, Turkey and Cyprus*, New York, 1992.

[26] B. O'Malley, *The Cyprus Conspiracy: America, Espionage, and the Turkish Invasion*, London, 1999.

[27] H. Richter, 'The Greek-Turkish Conflict', in M. Sarafis and M. Eve, eds, *Background to Contemporary Greece*, New York, 1990, pp. 316–59.

[28] S. Verney, 'To Be or Not to Be within the European Community: The Party Debate and Democratic Consolidation in Greece', in G. Pridham, ed., *Securing Democracy: Political Parties and Regime Consolidation in Southern Europe*, London, 1990, pp. 203–23.

[29] Clogg, *Parties*, pp. 70–81.

30   C. Lyrintzis, 'PASOK in Power: From Change to Disenchantment', in R. Clogg, ed., *Greece, 1981–89: The Populist Decade*, London, 1993, p. 29, also pp. 33–6; a number of works have appeared that analyse the 'short march' of PASOK to power. A useful summary can be found in D. Kioukas, 'Political Ideology in Post-dictatorial Greece: The Experience of Socialist Dominance', *Journal of Modern Greek Studies*, 11, 1993, pp. 51–75. A more detailed list is contained in the bibliography.

31   T. Papademetriou, *Marriage and Marital Property Under the New Greek Family Law*, Washington, 1985.

32   A. Pollis, 'Gender and Social Change in Greece: The Role of Women', in T.C. Kariotis, ed., *The Greek Socialist Experiment: Papandreou's Greece, 1981–1989*, New York, 1992, pp. 249–304; E. Stamiris, 'The Women's Movement in Greece', *New Left Review*, 158, 1986, pp. 98–112.

33   G.H. Grant, 'University Reform in Greece: 1982 and After', *Journal of Modern Greek Studies*, 4, 1, 1986, pp. 17–32.

34   G. Tsalikis, 'Evaluation of the Socialist Health Policy in Greece', *International Journal of Health Services*, 18, 1988, pp. 543–61; G. Mathiankakes, 'Socio-ecological Changes and Basic Health Care in Post War Greek Society', *Sunchronkia Themata*, 29, 1986, pp. 72–80.

35   D. Close, 'Environmental Crisis in Greece and Recent Challenges to Centralized State Authority', *Journal of Modern Greek Studies*, 17, 1999, pp. 325–52.

36   D.A. Sotiropoulos, *Populism and Bureaucracy: the Case of Greece Under PASOK, 1981–1989*, Notre Dame, Ind., 1996, pp. 79–80; M. Samatas, 'Debureaucratization Failure in Post-Dictatorial Greece: A Sociopolitical Approach', *Journal of Modern Greek Studies*, 11, 1993, pp. 187–218.

37   A. Papaionannou, 'The Greek Labor Movement and Industrial Relations in the 1980s', *Comparative Labor Law Journal*, 11, 1990, pp. 295–316; Gallant, 'Collective Action', pp. 156–9.

38   R. McDonald, 'Prospects for the Greek Economy', *Hellenic Foundation for Defense and Foreign Policy (ELIAMEP)*, 1991, p. 237; N.G. Pirounakis, *The Greek Economy: Past, Present and Future*, London, 1997, pp. 37–42.

39   Pirounakis, *The Greek Economy*, pp. 250–71 for a summary of his very detailed statistical studies of various aspects of the economy; K. Vergopoulos, 'The Political Economy of Greece during the Eighties', in Kariotis, *The Greek Socialist Experiment*, pp. 179–202.

40   T.A. Couloumbis, 'PASOK's Foreign Policy, 1981–89: Continuity or Change', in R. Clogg, ed., *Greece, 1981–89: The Populist Decade*, London, 1993, pp. 128–30.

41   Speech by Andreas Papandreou on 19 October 1983, cited in, J.O. Iatrides, 'Papandreou's Foreign Policy', in Kariotis, *The Greek Socialist Experiment*, p. 128.

42   J.O. Iatrides, 'Beneath the Sound and the Fury: US Relations with the PASOK Government', in Clogg, *Greece, 1981–89*, pp. 154–66.

43   S. Verney, 'Greece and the European Community', in Featherstone, *Political Change in Greece*, pp. 253–70; S. Verney, 'From the "Special Relationship" to Europeanism: PASOK and the European Community, 1981–89', in Clogg, *Greece, 1981–89*, pp. 131–52.

44   V. Coufoudakis, 'PASOK on Greco-Turkish Relations and Cyprus, 1981–1989: Ideology, Pragmatism, Deadlock', in Kariotis, *The Greek Socialist Experiment*, pp. 161–78.

45   H. Louri, 'Entry in Greek Manufacturing Industry: Athens vs the Rest of Greece', *Urban Studies*, 32, 1995, pp. 1127–34.

[46] G. Prevelakis, 'Center-Periphery and the Urban Crisis of Athens', *Ekistics*, 340/341, 1990, p. 36.

[47] P.S. Allen, 'Positive Aspects of Greek Urbanization: The Case of Athens by 1980', *Ekistics*, 318/319, 1986, pp. 187–94.

[48] Gallant, 'Collective Action', pp. 165–85; P.D. Chimbos, 'A Study of Patterns in Criminal Homicides in Greece', *International Journal of Comparative Sociology*, 34, 1993, pp. 260–71.

[49] T. Maloutas, 'Social Segregation in Athens', *Antipode*, 25, 1993, pp. 223–39.

[50] C. Marouli, 'Women Resisting (In) The City: Struggles, Gender, Class and Space in Athens', *International Journal of Urban and Regional Research*, 19, 1995, pp. 534–49; C. Meghir, Y. Ioannides and C. Pissarides, 'Female Participation and Male Unemployment in Greece: Evidence from the Labour Force Survey', *European Economic Review*, 33, 1989, pp. 395–407; Z. Tzannatos, 'Women's Wages and Equal Pay in Greece', *Journal of Modern Greek Studies*, 7, 1989, pp. 155–70; J.K. Cowan, 'Going Out for Coffee? Contesting the Grounds of Gendered Pleasures in Everyday Sociability', in P. Loizos and E. Papataxiarchis, eds, *Contested Identities: Gender and Kinship in Modern Greece*, Princeton, 1991, pp. 180–202.

[51] G. Lazaridis, 'Aspects of Greek and Cretan Rural Development: The Implications of the Implementation of the Common Agricultural Policy and of the Integrated Mediterranean Programmes for Agricultural Development', *Journal of Mediterranean Studies*, 5, 1995, p. 114; see also V. Tsapsaris-Manitea, 'Crisis in Greek Agriculture: Diagnosis and an Alternative Strategy', *Capital & Class*, 27, 1986, pp. 107–30 and T. Lianos and D. Parliarou, 'Land-tenure in Greek Agriculture', *Land Economics*, 63, 1987, pp. 237–47.

[52] Freris, *Greek Economy*, p. 208; T. Lianos and G. Rizopoulos, 'Estimation of Social-welfare Weights in Agricultural policy – the Case of Greek Cotton', *Journal of Agricultural Economics*, 39, 1988, pp. 61–8.

[53] C. Simmons, 'Entrepreneurial Strategies in Southern Europe: Rural Workers in the Garment Industry of Greece', *Journal of Economic Issues*, 30, 1996, pp. 121–43; C.P. Simmons and C. Kalantaridis, 'Flexible Specialization in the Southern European Periphery: The Growth of Garment Manufacturing in Peonia County, Greece', *Comparative Studies in Society and History*, 36, 1994, pp. 621–48.

[54] V. Galani-Moutafi, 'From Agriculture to Tourism: Property, Labor, Gender, and Kinship in a Greek Island Village (Part One)', *Journal of Modern Greek Studies*, 11, 1993, pp. 241–70; 'From Agriculture to Tourism: Property, Labor, Gender, and Kinship in a Greek Island Village (Part Two)', *Journal of Modern Greek Studies*, 12, 1994, pp. 113–32; M.E. Kenna, 'Return Migrants and Tourism Development: An Example from the Cyclades', *Journal of Modern Greek Studies*, 11, 1993, pp. 75–96.

[55] M. Dikaiou, 'Present Realities and Future Prospects among Greek Returners', *International Migration*, 32, 1994, pp. 29–47; E. Emke-Poulopoulou, *Problem of Migration-Repatriation*, Athens, 1986. E. Petras and M. Kousis, 'Returning Migrant Characteristics and Labor-market Demand in Greece', *International Migration Review*, 22, 1988, pp. 586–608.

Suggestions for Further Reading

The lists of suggestions for further reading appended below are aimed primarily at an English-speaking audience. I have, therefore, kept to a minimum the number of works written in Greek. As I made clear repeatedly by the numerous works by Greek scholars written in Greek referred to in the notes, a great deal of excellent work is coming out of Greece. For those interested in following up on materials in Greek, I have provided citations to some published bibliographies.

General Works
J.K. Campbell and P. Sherrard, *Modern Greece*, New York, 1968.
M.J. Clogg and R. Clogg, compilers, *Greece*, Santa Barbara, 1980.
R. Clogg, *A Concise History of Greece*, Cambridge, 1992.
S.E. Constantinidis, ed., *Greece in Modern Times: an Annotated Bibliography of Works Published in English in Twenty-Two Academic Disciplines During the Twentieth Century*, Lanham, 2000.
Y.B. Dertilis and K. Kostis, eds, *Themata Neoellinikis Istorias (18os-20os Aionas)*, Athens, 1991.
B. Jelavich, *History of the Balkans, 1. Eighteenth and Nineteenth Centuries*, Cambridge, 1983.
K.R. Legg and J.M. Roberts, *Modern Greece: A Civilization on the Periphery*, Boulder, 1997.
S.K. Pavlowitch, *A History of the Balkans 1804–1945*, New York, 1999.
M. Sarafis and M. Eve, eds, *Background to Contemporary Greece*, New York, 1990.
T. Stoianovich, *Balkan Worlds: The First and the Last Europe*, Armonk, 1994.
T. Veremis and M. Dragoumis, *Greece (Historical Dictionary)*, New York, 1998.
C.M. Woodhouse, *Modern Greece: A Short History*, London, 1985.

Chapter 1. The Ottoman Legacy
J.C. Alexander, *Brigandage and Public Order in the Morea, 1685–1806*, Athens, 1985.
H. Angelomatis-Tsougarakis, *The Eve of the Greek Revival: Travellers' Perceptions of Early Nineteenth-Century Greece*, New York, 1990.
O. Augustinos, *French Odysseys: Greece in French Travel Literature From the Renaissance to the Romantic Era*, Baltimore, 1994.
K. Barkey, *Bandits and Bureaucrats: The Ottoman Route to State Centralization*, Ithaca, 1994.
L.C. Brown, ed., *Imperial Legacy: The Ottoman Imprint on the Balkans and the Middle East*, New York, 1996.

A. Bryer and H. Lowry, eds, *Continuity and Change in Late Byzantine and Early Ottoman Society*, Washington, 1986.

R. Clogg, ed., *Anatolica: Studies in the Greek East in the 18th and 19th Centuries*, Brookfield, 1996.

S. Faroqhi, *Towns and Townsmen of Ottoman Anatolia. Trade, Craft and Food Production in an Urban Setting, 1520–1650*, Cambridge, 1984.

E. Frangakis-Syrett, *The Commerce of Smyrna in the Eighteenth Century (1700–1820)*, Athens, 1992.

C.A. Frazee, *Catholics and Sultans: the Church and the Ottoman Empire, 1453–1923*, New York, 1983.

M. Greene, *A Shared World: Christians and Muslims in the Early Modern Mediterranean*, Princeton, 2000.

H. Inalcik, *The Middle East and the Balkans Under the Ottoman Empire: Essays on Economy and Society*, Bloomington, 1993.

H. Inalcik and D. Quataert, eds, *An Economic and Social History of the Ottoman Empire, 1300–1914*, New York, 1994.

R.C. Jennings, *Christians and Muslins in Ottoman Cyprus and the Mediterranean World, 1571–1640*, New York, 1992.

O. Katsiardi-Hering, *Lismonimeni Orizontes Ellinon Emboron: to Paniyiri Stin Senigallia (18os-Arhes 19ou Aiona)*, Athens, 1989.

Y.M. Katsuli, M. Nikolinakou and V. Filia, *Ikonomiki Istoria tis Neoteris Elladas, apo to 1453 Mehri 1830*, Athens, 1986.

P.M. Kitromilides, *I Yalliki Epanastasis kai i Notioanatoliki Evropi*, Athens, 1990.

P.M. Kitromilides, *The Enlightenment as Social Criticism: Iosipos Moisiodax and Greek Culture in the Eighteenth Century*, Princeton, 1992.

B. McGowan, *Economic Life in Ottoman Europe. Taxation, Trade and the Struggle for Land, 1600–1800*, Cambridge, 1981.

R. Murphey, *Ottoman Warfare, 1500–1700*, London, 1999.

N.I. Pantazopoulos, *Church and Law in the Balkan Peninsula During the Ottoman Rule*, Thessaloniki, 1967.

S. Runciman, *The Great Church in Captivity*, Cambridge, 1985.

L.S. Stavrianos, *The Balkans Since 1453*, New York, 1958.

F.-M. Tsigakou, *The Rediscovery of Greece: Travellers and Painters of the Romantic Era*, New York, 1981.

A.E. Vacalopoulos, *The Greek Nation, 1453–1669. The Cultural and Economic Background of Modern Greek Society*, New Brunswick, 1976.

D.A. Zakythinos, *The Making of Modern Greece: From Byzantium to Independence*, Oxford, 1976.

Chapter 2. The Birth of the Modern Greek State

N.M. Athanassoglou-Kallmyer, *French Images From the Greek War of Independence (1821–1830)*, New Haven, 1989.

J. Braddock, *The Greek Phoenix*, New York, 1973.

R. Clogg, ed., *The Struggle for Greek Independence; Essays to Mark the 150th Anniversary of the Greek War of Independence*, Hamden, 1973.

D. Crane, *Lord Byron's Jackal: the Life of Edward John Trelawny*, London, 1998.

C.W. Crawley, *The Question of Greek Independence: A Study of British Policy in the Near East, 1821–1833*, New York, 1973.

D. Dakin, *British and American Philhellenes During the War of Greek Independence, 1821–1833*, Thessaloniki, 1955.

D. Dakin, *The Greek Struggle for Independence 1821–1833*, Berkeley, 1973.

P.N. Diamandouros, *Political Cleavage, Social Conflict and Cultural Cleavage in the Formation of the Modern Greek State, 1821–1828*, New York, 1972.

P.N. Diamandouros and others, eds, *Hellenism and the First Greek War of Liberation (1821–1830): Continuity and Change*, Thessaloniki, 1976.

G. Finlay, *History of the Greek Revolution, and the Reign of King Otho*, London, 1971.

K.E. Fleming, *The Muslim Bonaparte: Diplomacy and Orientalism in Ali Pasha's Greece*, Princeton, 1999.

S. Gourgouris, *Dream Nation: Enlightenment, Colonization, and the Institution of Modern Greece*, Stanford, 1996.

C.G. Hatzidimitriou, ed., *Founded on Freedom and Virtue: Documents Illustrating the Impact in the United States of the Greek War of Independence, 1821–1829*, New York, 1999.

D. Howarth, *The Greek Adventure: Lord Byron and Other Eccentrics in the War of Independence*, New York, 1976.

E.E. Koukkou, *Ioannis Kapodistrias, o Anthropos – o Diplomatis, 1800–1828*, Athens, 1997.

V. Kremmydas, *Singiria kai Emborio stin Proepanastatike Peloponniso 1793–1821*, Athens, 1980.

W. McGrew, *Land and Revolution in Modern Greece, 1800–1881. The Transition in the Tenure and Exploitation of Land From Ottoman Rule to Independence*, Kent, 1985.

L.P. Papanikolaou, *Kinoniki Istoria tis Ellinikis Epanastasis tou 19ou Aiona*, Athens, 1991.

T.C. Prousis, *Russian Society and the Greek Revolution*, DeKalb, 1994.

D.N. Skiotis, *Mountain Warriors and the Greek Revolution*, London, 1975.

W. St. Clair, *That Greece Might Still Be Free: The Philhellenes in the War of Independence*, Oxford, 1972.

T. Veremis, *The Military in Greek Politics From Independence to Democracy*, New York, 1997.

C.M. Woodhouse, *Capodistria: The Founder of Greek Independence*, Oxford, 1973.

C.M. Woodhouse, *The Greek War of Independence*, London, 1952.

C.M. Woodhouse, *The Philhellenes*, London, 1969.

C.M. Woodhouse, *Rhigas Velestinlis, the Proto-Martyr of the Greek Revolution*, Athens, 1997.

Chapter 3. Building the Modern State, 1833–1909

C. Agriantoni, *I Aparhes tis Ekbiomehanisis stin Ellada ton 19o Aiona*, Athens, 1986.

K. Aroni-Tsihli, *Agrotikes Ekseyersis stin Palia Ellada 1833–1881*, Athens, 1989.

K. Aroni-Tsihli and L. Triha, eds, *O Harilaos Trikoupis and I Epochi tou*, Athens, 2000.

R.A.H. Bickford-Smith, *Greece Under King George*, London, 1893.

D. Dakin, *The Unification of Greece, 1770–1923*, London, 1972.

A.N. Damianakos, *Charilaos Trikoupes and the Modernization of Greece, 1874–1894*, New York University, 1977.

I. Dimakis, *I Politiaki Metavoli tou 1843 kai to Zitima ton Avtohthono kai Eterohthonon*, Athens, 1991.

M. Economopoulou, *Parties and Politics in Greece (1844–1855)*, Athens, 1984.

C. Frazee, *The Orthodox Church and Independent Greece 1821–1852*, Cambridge, 1969.

K. Gardikas, *Politics and Parties in Greece, 1875–1885: Toward a Two Party System*, University of London, 1988.

D. Gondicas and C. Issawi, eds, *Ottoman Greeks in the Age of Nationalism: Politics, Economy, and Society on the Nineteenth Century*, Princeton, 1999.

B.C. Gounaris, *Steam Over Macedonia, 1870–1912: Socio-Economic Change and the Railway Factor*, New York, 1993.

K.-D. Grothusen and others, eds, *Eksinchronismos kai Biomihaniki Epanastasis sta Valkania ton 19o Aiona*, Athens, 1980.

G. Hering, *Die Politischen Parteien in Griechenland 1821–1936*, München, 1992.

R. Jenkins, *The Dilessi Murders*, London, 1999.

V.A. Kardasi, *Syros: Stavrodromi tis Antaloikis Mesoyiou (1832–1857)*, Athens, 1987.

J.V. Kofas, *Financial Relations of Greece and the Great Powers, 1832–1862*, New York, 1981.

J.V. Kofas, *International and Domestic Politics in Greece During the Crimean War*, New York, 1980.

E. Kofos, *Greece and the Eastern Crisis 1875–1878*, Thessaloniki, 1975.

J.S. Koliopoulos, *Brigands With a Cause: Brigandage and Irredentism in Modern Greece, 1821–1912*, Oxford, 1987.

N. Mouzelis, *Politics in the Semi-Periphery. Early Parliamentarianism and Late Industrialization in the Balkans and Latin America*, London, 1986.

J.A. Petropulos, *Politics and Statecraft in the Kingdom of Greece 1833–1843*, Princeton, 1968.

I.A. Petropoulos and A. Koumarianou, *I Themeliosi tou Ellinikou Kratous: Othoniki Periodos 1833–1843*, Athens, 1982.

T.D. Sakellaropoulos, *I Kriseis stin Ellada 1830–1857 : Oikonomikes, Koinonikes kai Politikes Opseis*, Athens, 1994.

T.G. Tatsios, *The Megali Idea and the Greek-Turkish War of 1897: the Impact of The Cretan Problem on Greek Irredentism 1866–1897*, New York, 1984.

K. Tsoukalas, *Eksartisi Kai Anaparayoyi. O Kinonikos Rolos Ton Ekpaideftikon Mihanismon Stin Ellada (1830–1922)*, Athens, 1987.

Chapter 4. Constructing the Modern Nation: Irredentism, Nationalism and Identity during the Nineteenth Century

G. Augustinos, *Consciousness and History: Nationalist Critics of Greek Society, 1897–1914*, New York, 1977.

E. Bastea, *The Creation of Modern Athens: Planning the Myth*, New York, 1999.

M. Blinkhorn and T. Veremis, *Modern Greece Nationalism & Nationality*, Athens, 1990.

J. Burke and S. Gauntlett, eds, *Neohellenism*, Canberra, Australia, 1992.

D. Dakin, *The Greek Struggle in Macedonia 1897–1913*, Thessaloniki, 1993.

L.M. Danforth, *The Macedonian Conflict: Ethnic Nationalism in a Transnational World*, Princeton, 1995.

M. Herzfeld, *Anthropology Through the Looking Glass: Critical Ethnography in the Margins of Europe*, Cambridge, 1987.

M. Herzfeld, *Ours Once More: Folklore, Ideology and the Making of Modern Greece,* Austin, 1982.

A.N. Karakasidou, *Fields of Wheat, Hills of Blood : Passages to Nationhood in Greek Macedonia, 1870–1990,* Chicago, 1997.

E. Kofos, *Greece and the Eastern Crisis 1875–1878,* Thessaloniki, 1975.

J.S. Koliopoulos, *Brigands With a Cause: Brigandage and Irredentism in Modern Greece, 1821–1912,* Oxford, 1987.

C. Koulouri, *Dimensions Idologiques De L'Historicité En Gréce, 1834–1914: Les Manuels Scolaires D'Histoire Et De Geographie,* Frankfurt am Main, 1991.

A. Leontis, *Topographies of Hellenism: Mapping the Homeland,* Ithaca, 1995.

D.M. Perry, *The Politics of Terror: The Macedonian Revolutionary Movements, 1893–1903,* Durham, 1988.

D. Ricks and P. Magdalino, eds, *Byzantium and the Modern Greek Identity,* Aldershot, 1998.

V. Roudometof, ed., *The Macedonian Question,* New York, 2000.

T.D. Sfikas and C. Williams, eds., *Ethnicity and Nationalism in East Central Europe and the Balkans,* Aldershot, 1999.

E. Skopetea, *To 'Protypo Vasileio' kai i Megali Idea (1830–1880),* Athens, 1988.

V.N. Todorov, *Greek Federalism During the Nineteenth Century: Ideas and Projects,* New York, 1995.

M. Todorova, *Imagining the Balkans,* New York, 1997.

D.Y. Tsaousis, ed., *Ellinismos-Ellinikotita,* Athens, 1983.

D.Y. Tsaousis, ed., *Opsis tis Ellinikis Kinonias tou 19ou Aiona,* Athens, 1984.

D. Tziovas, *The Nationism of the Demoticists and Its Impact on Their Literary Theory (1888–1930) an Analysis Based on Their Literary Criticism and Essays,* Amsterdam, 1986.

Chapter 5. Society and Economy in the Nineteenth and Early Twentieth Centuries

P. Carabott, ed., *Greek Society in the Making, 1863–1913 : Realities, Symbols, and Visions,* Brookfield, 1997.

M. Herzfeld, *Ours Once More: Folklore, Ideology and the Making of Modern Greece,* Austin, 1982.

M. Herzfeld, *The Poetics of Manhood: Contest and Identity in a Cretan Mountain Village,* Princeton, 1985.

A. Kitroeff, *Griegos En America,* Madrid, 1992.

L. Leontidou, *The Mediterranean City in Transition: Social Change and Urban Development,* Cambridge, 1989.

P. Loizos and E. Papataxiarchis, eds, *Contested Identities: Gender and Kinship in Modern Greece,* Princeton, 1991.

P.F. Martin, *Greece of the Twentieth Century,* London, 1913.

W. Miller, *Greek Life in Town and Country,* London, 1905.

N.P. Mouzelis, *Modern Greece: Facets of Underdevelopment,* London, 1978.

M. Palairet, *The Balkan Economies c. 1800–1914,* New York, 1997.

T. Saloutos, *The Greeks in the United States,* Cambridge, 1964.

P. Sant Cassia, with Constantina Bada, *The Making of the Modern Greek Family: Marriage and Exchange in Nineteenth-Century Athens,* Cambridge, 1992.

S.B. Sutton, ed., *Contingent Countryside: Settlement, Economy, and Land Use in the Southern Argolid Since 1700*, Stanford, 2000.

F.-M. Tsigakou, *The Rediscovery of Greece: Travellers and Painters of the Romantic Era*, New York, 1981.

C.K. Tuckerman, *The Greeks of To-Day*, London, 1872.

A.J.B. Wace and M.S. Thompson, *The Nomads of the Balkans*, London, 1972.

Chapter 6. From a Nation United to a Nation Divided

D. Alastos, *Venizelos*, Gulf Breeze, 1978.

G. Augustinos, *Consciousness and History: Nationalist Critics of Greek Society, 1897–1914*, New York, 1977.

D. Dutton, *The Politics of Diplomacy Britain and France in the Balkans in the First World War*, London, New York, 1998.

A.F. Freris, *The Greek Economy in the Twentieth Century*, New York, 1986.

H. Gardikas, *Greek Foreign Policy, 1911–1913*, University of London, 1988.

E. Gardikas-Katsiadaki, ed., *I Athina ton Valkanikon Polemon 1912–1913*, Athens, 1993.

E.C. Helmreich, *The Diplomacy of the Balkan Wars, 1912–1913*, New York, 1969.

V. Kondis, *Greece and Albania, 1908–1914*, Ann Arbor, 1975.

G.B. Leon, *Greece and the Great Powers, 1914–1917*, Thessaloniki, 1974.

G.B. Leon, *The Greek Socialist Movement and the First World War*, Boulder, 1976.

G.B. Leondaritis, *Greece and the First World War: From Neutrality to Intervention, 1917–1918*, New York, 1990.

G.Th. Mavrogordatos, *Stillborn Republic: Social Coalitions and Party Strategies in Greece, 1922–1936*, Berkeley, 1983.

G.Th. Mavrogordatos and Ch. Hatsiosiff, eds, *Venizelismos kai Astikos Eksinkronismos*, Athens, 1988.

A.S. Mitrakos, *France in Greece During World War I: A Study in the Politics of Power*, New York, 1982.

Y.G. Mourelos, *L'Intervention De La Grèce Dans La Grande Guerre 1916–1917*, Athens, 1983.

N.K. Moutsopoulos, *Thessaloniki 1900–1917*, Thessaloniki, 1980.

S.V. Papacosma, *The Military in Greek Politics: The 1909 Coup D'Etat*, Kent, 1977.

D.M. Perry, *The Politics of Terror: The Macedonian Revolutionary Movements, 1893–1903*, Durham, 1988.

N. Petsales-Diomedes, *I Hellada ton Dio Kivernision, 1916–17: Kathestotika, Diplomatika Kai Economika Provlimata tou Ethniko Dichasmou*, Athens, 1988.

E. Spyropoulos, *The Greek Military (1909–1941) and the Greek Mutinies in the Middle East (1941–1944)*, New York, 1993.

C. Svolopoulos and others, *Greece and Great Britain During World War I*, Thessaloniki, 1985.

E.L. Terzopoulos, *Greece: The Failure to Create a Bourgeois State, 1909–1932*, New School For Social Research, 1974.

A.J. Toynbee, *The Western Question in Greece and Turkey*, New York, 1922.

T. Veremis, *I Epembasis tou Stratou stin Elliniki Politiki 1916–1936*, Athens, 1983.

T. Veremis and G. Goulimi, eds, *Eleftherios Venizelos: Kinonia-Ikonomia-Politiki stin Epohi Tou*, Athens, 1989.

Chapter 7. The Inter-war Period, 1919–1940: A Time of Turmoil

I. Andrikopoulou, *I Dimokratia tou Mesopolemou, 1922–1936*, Athens, 1987.

L.P. Cassimatis, *American Influence in Greece, 1917–1927*, Kent, 1988.

H.C. Cliadakis, *Greece, 1935–1941: The Metaxas Regime and the Diplomatic Background to World War II*, New York, 1970.

D.H. Close, *The Character of the Metaxas Dictatorship: An International Perspective*, London, 1990.

M.H. Dobkin, *Smyrna 1922 the Destruction of a City*, Kent, 1988.

T. Doulis, *Disaster and Fiction: Modern Greek Fiction and the Impact of the Asia Minor Disaster of 1922*, Berkeley, 1977.

N. Doumanis, *Myth and Memory in the Mediterranean: Remembering Fascism's Empire*, New York, 1997.

C. Eddy, *Greece and the Greek Refugees*, London, 1931.

V. Gizeli, *Kinoniki Metaschismatismi kai Prolevsi tis Kininikis Katikias Stin Ellada (1920–1930)*, Athens, 1984.

R. Higham and T. Veremis, eds, *The Metaxas Dictatorship: Aspects of Greec 1936–1940*, Athens, 1993.

R. Hirschon, *Heirs of the Catastrophe: The Social Life of Asia Minor Refugees in Piraeus*, Oxford, 1989.

P.M. Kitromilides, ed., *Mikrasiatiki Katastrofi kai Elleniki Kinonia*, Athens, 1992.

D. Kitzikis, *I Ellas tis 4i Avgoustou kai i Megalis Dinamis*, Athens, 1990.

J.V. Kofas, *Authoritarianism in Greece: the Metaxas Regime*, New York, 1983.

J.S. Koliopoulos, *Greece and the British Connection 1935–1941*, Oxford, 1977.

K. Kostis, *I Trapezes kai i Krisi 1929–1932*, Athens, 1986.

S.P. Ladas, *The Exchange of Minorities, Bulgaria, Greece and Turkey*, New York, 1932.

L. Leontidou, *The Mediterranean City in Transition: Social Change and Urban Development*, Cambridge, 1989.

A. Liakos, *Ergasia kai Politiki stin Ellada tou Mespolemou. To Diethnes Grafio Ergasias kai i Anadisi ton Kinonikon Thesmon*, Athens, 1993.

S. Linardatos, *4i Avgoustou*, Athens, 1988.

S. Linardatos, *Pos Eftasame Stin 4iAvgoustou*, Athens, 1988.

D. Livieratos, *Kinoniki Agones Stin Ellada (1923–1927). Epanastatikes Eksangelies*, Athens, 1985.

D. Livieratos, *Kinoniki Agones Stin Ellada (1927–1931). Apo to Katafronia mia Kainouryia Avyi*, Athens, 1987.

G.Th. Mavrogordatos, *Stillborn Republic: Social Coalitions and Party Strategies in Greece, 1922–1936*, Berkeley, 1983.

M. Mazower, *Greece and the Inter-War Economic Crisis*, Oxford, 1991.

H. Morgenthau, *I Was Sent to Athens*, Garden City, NY, 1929.

Y.G. Mourelos, *Fictions Et Réalités La France, La Grèce Et La Stratégie Des Opérations Périphériques Dans Le Sud-Est Européen, 1939–1940*, Thessaloniki, 1990.

A.A. Pallis, *Greece's Anatolian Adventure and After: A Survey of the Diplomatic and Political Aspects of the Greek Expedition to Asia Minor (1915–1922)*, London, 1937.

M. Pelt, *Tobacco, Arms and Politics: Greece and Germany From World Crisis to World War 1929–41*, Denmark, 1998.

D. Pentzopoulos, *The Balkan Exchange of Minorities and Its Impact Upon Greece*, The Hague, 1962.

N. Petsales-Diomedes, *Greece at the Paris Peace Conference (1919)*, Thessaloniki, 1978.

A. Rihos, *I V' Elliniki Dimokratias 1924–1935, Kinonikes Diastasis tis Politikis Skinis*, Athens, 1988.

M.L. Smith, *Ionian Vision: Greece in Asia Minor 1919–1922*, London, 1973.

S.-S. Spiliotis, *Transterritorialität und Nationale Abgrenzung Konstitutionsprozesse der Griechischen Gesellschaft und Ansätze Ihrer Faschistoiden Transformation, 1922/24–1941*, München, 1998.

P.J. Vatikiotis, *Popular Autocracy in Greece, 1936–41 a Political Biography of General Ioannis Metaxas*, London, 1998.

Chapter 8. The Terrible Decade: Occupation and Civil War, 1940–1950

G.E. Alexander, *The Prelude to the Truman Doctrine: British Policy on Greece 1944–1947*, Oxford, 1982.

L. Baerentzen, J.O. Iatrides and O. Smith, eds, *Studies in the History of the Greek Civil War 1945–1949*, Copenhagen, 1987.

C. Chiclet, *Les Communistes Grecs Dans La Guerre*, Paris, 1987.

D.H. Close, ed., *The Greek Civil War, 1943–1950: Studies of Polarization*, New York, 1993.

D.H. Close, *The Origins of the Greek Civil War*, New York, 1995.

D. Eudes, *The Kapitanios: Partisans and Civil War in Greece 1943–1949*, London, 1975.

H. Flaiser and N. Svoronos, eds, *Ellada 1936–1944: Diktatoria-Katohi-Antistasi*, Athens, 1989.

H. Flaiser, *Stemma kai Svastika: I Ellada tis Katohis kai tis Andistatis. 1941–1944*, Athens, 1988.

A. Gerolymatos, *Guerilla Warfare and Espionage in Greece 1940–1944*, New York, 1993.

N. Hammond, *Venture into Greece: With the Guerrillas 1943–1944*, London, 1983.

J. Hart, *New Voices in the Nation: Women and the Greek Resistance, 1941–1964*, Ithaca, 1996.

J.L. Hondros, *Occupation and Resistance: The Greek Agony 1941–1944*, New York, 1978.

J.O. Iatrides, ed., *Greece in the 1940s: A Nation in Crisis*, Hanover, 1981.

J.O. Iatrides and L. Wrigley, eds, *Greece at the Crossroads: The Civil War and Its Legacy*, University Park, 1995.

H. Jones, *'A New Kind of War': America's Global Strategy and the Truman Doctrine in Greece*, Oxford, 1989.

A. Kitroeff, *War-Time Jews the Case of Athens*, Athens, 1995.

J.S. Koliopoulos, *Plundered Loyalties: World War II and Civil War in Greek West Macedonia*, New York, 1999.

V. Kondis, *Anglo-American Policy and the Greek Problem, 1945–1949*, Thessaloniki, 1986.

K. Matthews, *Memories of a Mountain War: Greece 1944–1949*, London, 1972.

M. Mazower, *Inside Hitler's Greece: The Experience of Occupation, 1941–1944*, New Haven, 1993.

E.C.W. Myers, *Greek Entanglement*, London, 1985.

A. Nachmani, *International Intervention in the Greek Civil War: The United Nations Special Committee on the Balkans, 1947–1952*, New York, 1990.

M. Palairet, *The Four Ends of the Greek Hyperinflation of 1941–1946*, London, 2000.

P. Papastratis, *British Policy Towards Greece During the Second World War 1941–1944*, Cambridge, 1984.

H. Richter, *British Intervention in Greece: From Varkiza to Civil War*, London, 1986.

M. Sarafis, ed., *Greece: From Resistance to Civil War*, Nottingham, 1980.

C.R. Shrader, *The Withered Vine: Logistics and the Communist Insurgency in Greece, 1945–1949*, Westport, 1999.

E. Spyropoulos, *The Greek Military (1909–1941) and the Greek Mutinies in the Middle East (1941–1944)*, New York, 1993.

P.J. Stavrakis, *Moscow and Greek Communism, 1944–1949*, Ithaca, 1989.

H. Vlavianos, *Greece, 1941–1949: From Resistance to Civil War: The Strategy of the Greek Communist Party*, New York, 1992.

C.M. Woodhouse, *Apple of Discord: A Survey of Recent Greek Politics in the International Setting*, Reston, 1948.

C.M. Woodhouse, *The Struggle for Greece 1941–1949*, London, 1976.

Chapter 9. Reconstruction and Retribution, 1950–1967

S.E. Aschenbrenner, *Life in a Changing Greek Village: Karpofora and Its Reluctant Farmers*, Dubuque, 1986.

G. Augustinos, ed., *Diverse Paths to Modernity in Southeastern Europe: Essays in National Development*, Westport, 1991.

J.J. Baxevanis, *Economy and Population Movements in the Peloponnesos of Greece*, Athens, 1972.

J.K. Campbell, *Honour, Family and Patronage. A Study of Institutional and Moral Values in a Greek Mountain Community*, Oxford, 1964.

J. Carey and A. Carey, *The Web of Modern Greek Politics*, New York, 1968.

R. Clogg, ed., *The Greek Diaspora in the Twentieth Century*, New York, 1999.

R. Clogg, *Parties and Elections in Greece: The Search for Legitimacy*, London, 1988.

T.A. Couloumbis, *Greek Political Reaction to American and NATO Influences*, New Haven, 1966.

J. du Boulay, *Portrait of a Greek Mountain Village*, Oxford, 1974.

K. Featherstone and D.K. Katsoudas, eds, *Political Change in Greece: Before and After the Colonels*, London, 1987.

E. Friedl, *Vasilika: A Village in Modern Greece*, New York, 1962.

D. Haralabis, *Stratos kai Politiki Eksousia: i Domi tis Exousias stin Metamfiliaki Ellada*, Athens, 1985.

G.A. Jouganatos, *The Development of the Greek Economy, 1950–1991: An Historical, Empirical, and Econometric Analysis*, Greenwood, 1992.

B. Kayser, P.-Y. Pechoux, and M. Sivignon, *Exode Rural Et Attraction Urbaine En Grèce*, Athens, 1971.

J.V. Kofas, *Intervention and Underdevelopment: Greece During the Cold War*, College Park, 1989.

K.R. Legg, *Politics in Modern Greece*, Stanford, 1969.

W.H. McNeill, *Greece: American Aid in Action, 1947–1956*, New York, 1957.

W.H. McNeill, *The Greek Dilemma: War and Aftermath*, London, 1947.

W.H. McNeill, *The Metamorphosis of Greece Since World War II*, Oxford, 1978.

C. Moustaka, *The Internal Migrant*, Athens, 1964.

M. Mazower, ed., *After the War Was Over: Reconstructing the Family, Nation and State in Greece, 1943–1960*, Princeton, 2000.

P. Murtagh, *The Rape of Greece: the King, the Colonels and the Resistance*, London, New York, 1994.

M. Pelt, *A Lopsided Triangle: The Reconstruction of Greece and the United States and West Germany, 1945–1967*, London, 2000.

Y.P. Roubatis, *Tangled Webs: The US in Greece 1947–1967*, New York, 1987.

E. Sandis, *Refugees and Economic Migrants in Greater Athens*, Athens, 1973.

B. Sweet-Escott, *Greece. A Political and Economic Survey 1939–1953*, London, 1954.

L.S. Wittner, *American Intervention in Greece 1943–1949*, New York, 1982.

C.M. Woodhouse, *Karamanlis: The Restorer of Greek Democracy*, Oxford, 1982.

S. Zinovieff, *The History of Emigration From Greece*, New York, 1996.

Cyprus

T. Bahcheli, T.A. Couloumbis, and P. Carley, *Greek-Turkish Relations and U.S. Foreign Policy: Cyprus, the Aegean, and Regional Stability*, Washington, 1997.

N. Crawshaw, *The Cyprus Revolt: An Account of the Struggle for Union With Greece*, London, 1978.

P.T. Hart, *Two NATO Allies at the Theshold of War: Cyprus, A Firsthand Account of Crisis Management, 1965–1968*, Durham, 1990.

C. Hitchens, *Cyprus*, London, 1984.

C.P. Ioannides, ed., *Cyprus: Domestic Dynamics, External Constraints*, New Rochelle, 1992.

C.P. Ioannides, *In Turkey's Image: The Transformation of Occupied Cyprus into a Turkish Province*, New Rochelle, 1991.

J.T.A. Koumoulides, ed., *Cyprus in Transition, 1960–1985*, London, 1986.

P. Loizos, *The Greek Gift: Politics in a Cypriote Village*, Oxford, 1975.

P. Loizos, *The Heart Grown Bitter*, Cambridge, 1987.

K.C. Makrides, *The Rise and Fall of the Cyprus Republic*, Yale University Press.

C. Mavratsas, "Approaches to Nationalism: Basic Theoretical Considerations in the Study of the Greek-Cypriot Case and Historical overview", *Journal of the Hellenic Diaspora*, 22, 1996, pp. 77–103.

C.V. Mavratsas, "The Ideological Contest Between Greek-Cypriot Nationalism and Cypriotism 1974—1995: Politics, Social Memory and Identity", *Ethnic and Racial Studies*, 20, 1997, pp. 717–38.

B. O'Malley, *The Cyprus Conspiracy: America, Espionage, and the Turkish Invasion*, London, 1999.

S. Panteli, *A New History of Cyprus*, London, 1984.

Y. Papadakis, "Greek Cypriot Narratives of History and Collective Identity: Nationalism as a Contested Process", *American Ethnologist*, 25, 1998, pp. 149–65.

J. Reddaway, *Burdened With Cyprus: The British Connection*, London, 1986.

M. Stearns, *Entangled Allies: U.S. Policy Toward Greece, Turkey and Cyprus*, New York, 1992.

I.D. Stefanidis, *Isle of Discord: Nationalism, Imperialism, and the Making of the Cyprus Problem*, New York, 1999.

Chapter 10. Dictatorship and Democratic Restoration and the Era of PASOK, 1967–1989

R. Clogg, ed., *Greece, 1981–89: The Populist Decade*, London, 1993.

R. Clogg, ed., *Greece in the 1980's*, London, 1983.

R. Clogg, *Parties and Elections in Greece: The Search for Legitimacy*, London, 1988.

R. Clogg and G. Yiannopoulos, eds, *Greece Under Military Rule*, London, 1972.

D. Constas and T.G. Stavrou, eds, *Greece Prepares for the Twenty-First Century*, Baltimore, 1995.

C.P. Danopoulos, *Warriors and Politicians in Modern Greece*, Chapel Hill, 1985.

M. Herzfeld, *A Place in History: Social and Monumental Time in a Cretan Town*, Princeton, 1991.

T.C. Kariotis, ed., *The Greek Socialist Experiment: Papandreou's Greece, 1981–1989*, New York, 1992.

G.A. Kourvetaris, *Studies on Modern Greek Society and Politics*, New York, 1999.

P. Loizos, *The Heart Grown Bitter*, Cambridge, 1987.

P. Loizos and E. Papataxiarchis, eds, *Contested Identities: Gender and Kinship in Modern Greece*, Princeton, 1991.

G.Th. Mavrogordatos, *The Rise of the Green Sun. The Greek Election of 1981*, London, 1983.

R. McDonald, *Pillar and Tinderbox: The Greek Press and the Dictatorship*, London, 1982.

A. Papandreou, *Democracy at Gunpoint: The Greek Front*, Harmondsworth, 1971.

M. Papandreou, *Nightmare in Athens*, London, 1970.

N.G. Pirounakis, *The Greek Economy: Past, Present and Future*, London, 1997.

N. Poulantzas, *The Crisis of Dictatorships: Portugal, Greece, Spain*, Atlantic Highlands, 1976.

H.J. Psomidae and S.B. Thomadakis, eds., *Greece, the New Europe, and the Changing International Order*, New York, 1993.

M. Spourdalakes, *The Rise of the Greek Socialist Party*, Boston, 1988.

L. Tsoukalis, *The European Community and Its Mediterranean Enlargement*, Boston, 1981.

Z. Tzannatos, ed., *Socialism in Greece: the First Four Years*, Brookfield, 1986.

K. Van Dyck, *Kassandra and the Censors Greek Poetry Since 1967*, Ithaca, 1998.

S. Vryonis Jr., ed., *Greece on the Road to Democracy: From the Junta to PASOK 1974–1986*, New Rochelle, 1991.

C.M. Woodhouse, *Karamanlis: The Restorer of Greek Democracy*, Oxford, 1982.

C.M. Woodhouse, *The Rise and Fall of the Greek Colonels*, London, 1982.

Index